PANZER WEDGE
VOLUME TWO

0 11557 01205 7

The Stackpole Military History Series

THE AMERICAN CIVIL WAR
Cavalry Raids of the Civil War
Ghost, Thunderbolt, and Wizard
In the Lion's Mouth
Pickett's Charge
Witness to Gettysburg

WORLD WAR I
Doughboy War

WORLD WAR II
After D-Day
Airborne Combat
Armor Battles of the Waffen-SS,
　1943–45
Armoured Guardsmen
Army of the West
Arnhem 1944
Australian Commandos
The B-24 in China
Backwater War
The Battle of France
The Battle of Sicily
Battle of the Bulge, Vol. 1
Battle of the Bulge, Vol. 2
Beyond the Beachhead
Beyond Stalingrad
The Black Bull
Blitzkrieg Unleashed
Blossoming Silk against the Rising Sun
Bodenplatte
The Brandenburger Commandos
The Brigade
Bringing the Thunder
The Canadian Army and the Normandy
　Campaign
Coast Watching in World War II
Colossal Cracks
Condor
A Dangerous Assignment
D-Day Bombers
D-Day Deception
D-Day to Berlin
Decision in the Ukraine
Destination Normandy
Dive Bomber!
A Drop Too Many
Eagles of the Third Reich
The Early Battles of Eighth Army
Eastern Front Combat
Europe in Flames
Exit Rommel
The Face of Courage
Fist from the Sky
Flying American Combat Aircraft of
　World War II
For Europe
Forging the Thunderbolt
For the Homeland
Fortress France

The German Defeat in the East,
　1944–45
German Order of Battle, Vol. 1
German Order of Battle, Vol. 2
German Order of Battle, Vol. 3
The Germans in Normandy
Germany's Panzer Arm in World War II
GI Ingenuity
Goodwood
The Great Ships
Grenadiers
Guns against the Reich
Hitler's Nemesis
Hold the Westwall
Infantry Aces
In the Fire of the Eastern Front
Iron Arm
Iron Knights
Japanese Army Fighter Aces
Japanese Naval Fighter Aces
JG 26 Luftwaffe Fighter Wing War Diary,
　Vol. 1
JG 26 Luftwaffe Fighter Wing War Diary,
　Vol. 2
Kampfgruppe Peiper at the Battle of
　the Bulge
The Key to the Bulge
Knight's Cross Panzers
Kursk
Luftwaffe Aces
Luftwaffe Fighter Ace
Luftwaffe Fighter-Bombers over Britain
Luftwaffe Fighters and Bombers
Massacre at Tobruk
Mechanized Juggernaut or Military
　Anachronism?
Messerschmitts over Sicily
Michael Wittmann, Vol. 1
Michael Wittmann, Vol. 2
Mission 85
Mission 376
Mountain Warriors
The Nazi Rocketeers
Night Flyer / Mosquito Pathfinder
No Holding Back
On the Canal
Operation Mercury
Packs On!
Panzer Aces
Panzer Aces II
Panzer Aces III
Panzer Commanders of the
　Western Front
Panzergrenadier Aces
Panzer Gunner
The Panzer Legions
Panzers in Normandy
Panzers in Winter
Panzer Wedge, Vol. 1
Panzer Wedge, Vol. 2

The Path to Blitzkrieg
Penalty Strike
Poland Betrayed
Red Road from Stalingrad
Red Star under the Baltic
Retreat to the Reich
Rommel's Desert Commanders
Rommel's Desert War
Rommel's Lieutenants
The Savage Sky
Ship-Busters
The Siege of Küstrin
The Siegfried Line
A Soldier in the Cockpit
Soviet Blitzkrieg
Stalin's Keys to Victory
Surviving Bataan and Beyond
T-34 in Action
Tank Tactics
Tigers in the Mud
Triumphant Fox
The 12th SS, Vol. 1
The 12th SS, Vol. 2
Twilight of the Gods
Typhoon Attack
The War against Rommel's Supply Lines
War in the Aegean
War of the White Death
Winter Storm
Wolfpack Warriors
Zhukov at the Oder

THE COLD WAR / VIETNAM
Cyclops in the Jungle
Expendable Warriors
Fighting in Vietnam
Flying American Combat Aircraft:
　The Cold War
Here There Are Tigers
Land with No Sun
MiGs over North Vietnam
Phantom Reflections
Street without Joy
Through the Valley
Two One Pony

**WARS OF AFRICA AND THE
MIDDLE EAST**
Never-Ending Conflict
The Rhodesian War

GENERAL MILITARY HISTORY
Carriers in Combat
Cavalry from Hoof to Track
Desert Battles
Doughboy War
Guerrilla Warfare
Ranger Dawn
Sieges
The Spartan Army

PANZER WEDGE

VOLUME TWO

The German 3rd Panzer Division and Barbarossa's Failure at the Gates of Moscow

**Lt. Fritz Lucke,
with Robert Edwards and Michael Olive**

STACKPOLE
BOOKS

English translation © 2013 by Battle Born Books and Consulting

Published in 2013 by
STACKPOLE BOOKS
5067 Ritter Road
Mechanicsburg, PA 17055
www.stackpolebooks.com

Printed in the United States of America

10 9 8 7 6 5 4 3 2 1

ISBN 978-0-8117-1205-7

The Library of Congress has cataloged the first volume as follows:

Lucke, Fritz.
   [Panzerkeil im Osten. English]
   Panzer wedge / Fritz Lucke ; with Robert Edwards and Michael Olive.
      p. cm.
   Translation of: Panzerkeil im Osten : Gedenkbuch der Berlin-mdrkischen Panzer-division. Berlin : Verlag "Die Wehrmacht, 1942.
   ISBN 978-0-8117-1082-4
   1. Lucke, Fritz. 2. Germany. Heer. Panzer-Division, 3. 3. World War, 1939–1945—Personal narratives, German. 4. World War, 1939–1945—Regimental histories—Germany. 5. World War, 1939–1945—Campaigns—Eastern Front. 6. World War, 1939–1945—Tank warfare. I. Edwards, Robert. II. Olive, Michael. III. Title.
   D757.563rd L8313 2012
   940.54'1343—dc23
                                                         2012032603

Contents

CHAPTER 1

Armored Blocking Position to the South

THE FIGHTING IN AUGUST BETWEEN THE DNEJPR AND THE DESSNA

After the second major interval in the campaign in the East, the breakthrough through the Stalin Line, the following situation had arisen in the middle portion of the gigantic front (rough overview). The center field-army group of the Soviets was positioned in a broad salient around Smolensk, which was open to the west. The salient started in the north, about in the area around Welikije Luki, arced to the south, pivoted sharply to the west to the Dnjepr, crossed the Dnjepr and the Beresina, and then ran into the Pripet Marshes. The Bolshevik leadership, which took the loss of the Minsk–Smolensk–Moscow Highway hard, wanted to exploit its flanking position—as evidenced by prisoner statements and other enemy material—and retake the western key point along the Beresina, the old fortress of Brobruisk, and, above all, Smolensk. Bringing in strong new field armies, the Soviets conducted extremely violent attacks throughout the second half of July and into the beginning days of August. All of them collapsed and sustained heavy losses.

In order to eliminate that constant threat to the flanks, a number of smaller operations were executed by the German command at the beginning of August. They found their conclusion in the special report from the German Armed Forces High Command on 20 August concerning the fighting at Gomel. The fighting led to the complete collapse of the enemy flanking positions and the destruction of several Soviet field armies, with corresponding extremely heavy losses in life and prisoners. The formation of several pockets, especially at Roslawl, Miloslawitschi, and southeast of Rogatschew, once again proved the superior abilities of the leadership and soldiers. The fact that the enemy completely realized the seriousness of the danger that faced him there is shown by the following:

1. The headquarters of the Soviet commander in chief in the central portion of the front, Timoschenko, was moved to that sector.

2. Orders demanding positions be unconditionally held and desperate attempts to regain lost positions.

3. Finally, the statements of captured staff officers that Moscow placed special importance on the front north of the Dnjepr.

It should also be mentioned at this point that the operations of the German formations employed went well beyond the originally designated objectives, which was largely thanks to the rapid, personal decisions of the subordinate commanders, who exploited every weakness the enemy presented and achieved long-range effects with the limited forces at their disposal.

Especially admirable in this connection was the operations of one armored formation that was employed on the extreme left wing of the entire operation. That formation had formed the pocket of Miloslawitschi southwest of Roslawl in the days around 10 August. It took 20,000 prisoners out of that pocket. It then moved out a few days later to advance to the south. In two and one half days, it had moved 120 kilometers south, considerably beyond the then-current front. It should be mentioned here that the term "front" in the Eastern campaign is not an exactly accurate term, since the operations there, even in the sector of a single field army, never come to a complete standstill. Second, even in the "quiet" sectors, the two opponents are not positioned along clear-cut lines. Instead, they face one another across deeply echeloned, intertwined areas. That changes nothing about the fact, however, that our armored formation found itself all "alone in the valley" and deep in the enemy rear by the evening of the second day of attack. Even to the west, there were more than 200 kilometers to the Ssosh River Valley, where a neighboring German field army had also moved out in the direction of Gomel.

The armored advance to the south took place in terrain that exceeded by a long shot all of the bad experiences that the tankers had had in the East up to that point. The terrain between the Ssosh and Dessna Rivers was broken up by woods, marshy vegetation, treacherous stretches of sand, and correspondingly bottomless country roads. The villages were widely scattered and unspeakably impoverished. It is well known that a tank is not limited to roads and neither are its constant brothers-in-arms, the motorized rifle regiments, but the majority of the supply system is. Many formations of an armored corps move by wheel, not by track, and the speed of their forward progress determines the tempo of the entire formation during wide-ranging operations. In addition, there was the fact that the broken nature of the terrain also forced the tracked vehicles to generally move in a single column, one behind the next, as opposed to the normal armored attack across a broad front. This meant that the armored thrust to the south had the most unforgiving natural restrictions imaginable and placed unbelievable demands on both leaders and soldiers.

Despite that, the mission was accomplished. Indeed, as has already been mentioned, it was accomplished in a manner that even the higher command had not even initially contemplated. On the third day of the attack, the lead elements of the left wing were 120 kilometers south of their attack objective. Among the three attack columns, as well as in the open flanks of the entire formation, there were many numerically superior and almost untouched enemy corps and divisions.

It is a sign of the current state of the Soviet army that it was unable to bring about a well-thought-out defense against that lance in the middle of its front. Instead—apparently without any unified command—it only initiated the movements of smaller and larger formations, which quite clearly demonstrated that it only had confused reports and estimations concerning the enemy situation. As a consequence, our armored formation saw itself exposed to breakout attempts at many and constantly changing places. Despite the thinness of the German lines, they were turned back everywhere and, after a short time, dammed up. The railway hub of Unetscha, which was approximately in the center of the entire battlefield, was the target of systematic Soviet attacks by strong forces for an entire day. In the successful defense of that locality, which took place under the eyes of the commanding general, who was present, individual deeds were accomplished that are reserved for an account later on. In this overview, we need to restrict ourselves to the remark that the overall performance of this armored formation, which had either been fighting or advancing ever since the start of the campaign in the East, was beyond all praise. The quality of the German equipment—including countless vehicles—was subjected to such a brutal test on the impossible roads between the Ssosh and the Dessna, the likes of which have seldom, if even, been seen. The test was passed!

If you take the old "front" along the Rogatschew–Roslawl line as a basis, then the armored thrust south and the almost simultaneous offensive of the western neighbor in the direction of Gomel resulted in a rectangle, open to the south, of nearly 50,000 square kilometers. Since it was only considered a secondary operation with a limited tactical objective, there was no thought given to hermetically sealing the fourth side. To do that would have required several field armies! The enemy proved not only incapable of breaking open the eastern side of the rectangle, he also failed to pull his numerous corps out to the south in halfway good order, despite the presence of his commander in chief. What he was capable of saving between Gomel and Starodub was a completely defeated and badly battered remnant of his formations. What he lost has since been announced by the Armed Forces High Command in a special report.

That which was accomplished in the Battle of Gomel with the armored thrust to the south was done with the slightest of means and under the most difficult of circumstances in just three days. It fills every participant or witness to the fighting with a feeling of almost certain superiority and confidence in the continuation of the War in the East.

THE HISTORY OF *PANZER-REGIMENT 6*

The regimental history of *Panzer-Regiment 6* records the events of this chapter as follows:[1]

On 15 August, the regiment received radio traffic from the division that indicated that several days of rest were coming up. But another radio message followed at 1200 hours, stating that the regiment was to be alerted and be prepared to advance south by 1500 hours. What had happened?

The decision of the highest level of command to encircle the very strong enemy forces around Kiev before the advance east was continued forced *Generaloberst* Guderian to pivot his field army to the south, even though he was vehemently opposed to it. In his opinion, it was imperative to gain ground to the east as rapidly as possible so as to be able to take Moscow before the onset of winter. The new orientation—turning away from the operational direction of Moscow—would later have calamitous effects on further operations in the Eastern campaign.

---

1. Munzel, 84–86.

At that point, the *XXIV. Armee-Korps (mot.)* moved out as quickly as possible to the south with the *4. Panzer-Division* on the right, our division on the left, and the *10. Infanterie-Division (mot.)* following.

The regiment was ready to move at 1500 hours. The 2nd Battalion moved to the head of *Gruppe von Manteuffel* and reached the town of Mglin, forty kilometers away, later that evening, despite delays caused by the clearing of mines, the repair of bridges and the reconnoitering of routes. The remaining elements of the regiment followed at 2045 hours as part of *Marschgruppe Kleemann.* Due to unimaginable delays on the roads, it only moved a few kilometers before spending the rest of the night on the road.

It was not until 0645 hours on 17 August that the march started to make progress again, moving fairly rapidly to the south and reaching the Bessely River, where the march was again held up due to bad bridges and marshy flood plains. The regiment had to bivouac on both sides of the road. The town of Kotimsk along the river went up in flames due to enemy bombers. After improving the bridges, the regiment received orders to advance on Degtjarewka along the Jputi River, "exercising right of way over all forces."

Those types of orders were illusory in those types of situations, since it was impossible to pass along those bad routes. As a result, the wheeled vehicles got stuck, and only the tanks finally reached the designated locality, where it was impossible to move further because the wooden bridge was too weak. During the night, some of the supply vehicles closed with the tanks, thanks to the incredible sense of duty of the crews, but most of them had to be recovered at first light by prime movers. That stretch of road was the worst the regiment had experienced up to that point. Moving far ahead, the 2nd Battalion had taken the locality of Mglin south of the Sput during the evening.

After seemingly endless waiting, the regiment moved out over the bridge over the Sput, which had been repaired during the night, in the direction of Mglin on 17 August. But before the Roslawl–Mglin road could be reached, the wheeled vehicles had become hopelessly stuck. Only the tanks reached the town of Mglin at 0945 hours; there they finally had an improved road. It wasn't until hours later that the wheeled vehicles could be brought forward by prime movers. In the meantime, the 2nd Battalion had advanced farther south at the head of its *Kampfgruppe* and approached the important railway hub of Unetscha. The enemy took pains to stop the advance by uninterrupted employment of his air force. As a result, the 2nd Battalion sustained some losses. In the fight against an enemy antiaircraft battery, young *Leutnant* Bertram had to give up his life.

The resistance was especially tough when Unetscha was entered. The resistance could only gradually be broken, after all elements of the regiment were able to reach Unetscha, coming from Mglin, at 1230 hours. The 2nd Battalion was released from its attachment and returned to the regiment, with the 3rd Battalion then being attached to von Manteuffel's advance guard. At 1930 hours, it moved out in the direction of Starodub, some thirty kilometers distant, while Unetscha was still being cleared of the enemy. Quantities of captured Russian goods helped enrich the rations, especially the large number of eggs.

At first light on 18 August, the 3rd Battalion, together with the *II./ Schützen-Regiment 3*, moved out as the advance guard from Rjuchoff, which had been occupied during the night. Moving south, it took the city of Starodub at 0915 hours, after putting down tough resistance, especially from Soviet youth groups. The remaining elements of the regiment arrived at noon, as well as other elements of the division. Spoils of war were also found in that city, a sign that we were in the middle of the Russian supply area. As it started to turn dark, Russian bombers attacked practically every hour until first light. The flares dropped in series by the enemy lit up the like daylight. One could observe the orientation searchlights that continued to circle at a Russian airfield only a few kilometers away. The enemy bombers took off from there at short intervals. Russian prisoners were convinced that our units were airborne elements, since an appearance so far east by land was unthinkable.

During the night of 18–19 August, the situation for the lead elements of the *3. Panzer-Division* turned critical. In the course of the night, the enemy had inserted himself between our two armored divisions and interdicted the line of communications between Unetscha and Mglin. *General Freiherr* Geyr von Schweppenburg [the commanding general] was in Unetscha with elements from his corps, when the Russians attacked from the west at first light. It was only thanks to three damaged tanks, which were in Unetscha awaiting the arrival of the maintenance company, that the first Russian attack was turned back. The three damaged tanks knocked out the first three T-34's, whereupon the enemy attack started to waver. A fourth Russian tank reached the city, however. It could only be stopped by one of the German tanks ramming it. It was then destroyed by a satchel charge tossed on the engine compartment by *Leutnant* Störck (engineer platoon of *Schützen-Regiment 394*).

Based on the reports coming from Unetscha that the corps headquarters had been encircled by enemy forces, the division ordered the 2nd Battalion, which was already twenty kilometers farther south, to turn around and return to the city immediately. The regimental headquarters and the 1st Battalion, which had taken over a long-extended screening area at Janikowa, seven kilometers north of Starodub, were also ordered back. By then, however, the 2nd Battalion had completely cleared up the situation by its rapid actions. Several poorly led Russian attacks were turned back. Unfortunately, the battalion lost one of its most experienced tank commanders during that round of fighting, *Oberfeldwebel* Wacker. He had been a tanker since Spain. As a result of the broken terrain, he was standing in the cupola of his tank directing his gunner when he was mortally wounded.

In the evening, the regimental headquarters and the 1st and 2nd Battalions bivouacked at the edge of Unetscha to secure the city. The 3rd Battalion remained far out in front in Starodub. Both of the cities were attacked by enemy bombers throughout the night.

The situation remained critical during the night of 19–20 August, since there was still no communication to the rear with the division and to the *4. Panzer-Division.* It was not until the following morning that the lead elements of the *4. Panzer-Division* approached Unetscha and started securing that sector. The 1st and 2nd Battalions, as well as the regimental headquarters, could then head south. But that effort soon came to an end, since the Russians attacked along the road north of the locality of Rjuchoff with strong forces and blocked the only avenue of advance. Due to the completely unclear enemy situation, there were many individual engagements in the broken terrain, which was covered with woods and vegetation. The 1st Battalion succeeded in ejecting the enemy from both sides of the road and then, supported by two tanks from the 2nd Battalion, to penetrate into Rjuchoff, clearing it. In that fighting, *Oberleutnant* Meyrhofer showed a great deal of bravado. Prior to the start of the attack, he had gone into the woods some distance in order to reconnoiter for a detour. He became lost and was no longer able to link up with his company. His tanks had to be attached to other companies. When the battalion approached the locality of Rjuchoff, its commander (*Oberstleutnant* Schmidt-Ott) noticed a heavy enemy tank that two men were working on. Just as he was directing his gunner onto the target, he received the report that the tank was manned by German soldiers. It turned out that *Oberleutnant* Meyrhofer had discovered the abandoned tank during his reconnaissance, had fetched two men from a nearby *Flak* and took the Russian crew prisoner. He then got the 7.62-centimeter main gun operational again and participated in the fighting, in which he fired forty rounds against the enemy tanks and columns fleeing from the locality. It wasn't until Rjuchoff was taken that he returned in one piece to his battalion.

The situation along the road continued to remain critical. The road was under fire from individual machine guns, several artillery pieces, and a heavy tank, which was right next to the road but could not be seen. Despite all that, the regimental commander succeeded in getting through to Rjuchoff with several *Kübelwagen* and motorcycle messengers by exploiting an extended row of vegetation next to the road. They then went on to the division command post in Askolki, where he rendered his report and returned with an order for all elements of the division in the vicinity of Rjuchoff to attack. It had been directed for the enemy-occupied, thick stretch of woods between the road and the Unetscha–Starodub railway line further to the west to be cleared. The attack had to be postponed to the next day, however, since it had already turned dark and the 1st Battalion was fighting a Russian breakout attempt at Rjuchoff. In addition, the 2nd Battalion, which still had not reached Rjuchoff, was involved in hard defensive fighting against the enemy pressing in from the west. The situation at the location of the combat trains of the regiment, which had taken up an assembly area in the woods just south of Unetscha, was also critical ever since the afternoon. The men of the trains had to defend themselves in close combat. In the process, they captured numerous Russian trucks and took a number of prisoners. It still could not be avoided, however, that the enemy was able to flee to the east in groups on foot during the night.

The advance of the *XXIV. Armee-Korps (mot.)* to the south continued on 25 August. Moving along a line defined by Cholmy–Nowgorod Sewerski, it had been directed to cut off the retreat route for the enemy to the east southwest of Gomel and link up with the German forces thrusting to the south.

THE DIVISIONAL HISTORY

The divisional history records the events of this chapter as follows:[2]

At noon on 15 August, the division issued a warning order for the resumption of the advance. The commanders were summoned for conferences, the maps were issued and the new march routes marked on the maps. Everyone was amazed: This time, they were headed south! The warning order was short and to the point:

"The *XXIV. Armee-Korps (mot.)* moves out to the south on 16 August with the *4. Panzer-Division* on the right, the *3. Panzer-Division* on the left and the *10. Infanterie-Division (mot.)* following, in order to cut off the retreat route of the withdrawing enemy in front of the attack of the *2. Armee* to the east."

The elements of the *3. Panzer-Division* were to be ready to move starting at 1600 hours. At 1700 hours, the actual order was issued.

The nighttime approach march in the new direction could only be executed with a great deal of effort and delay. The many narrow routes were so full from the many columns that the vehicles could only advance at a walking pace. The lead elements of the division barely made it past Gabitschi; it was only the motorcycle battalion of *Major* von Corvin-Wiersbitzki that was able to reach Chotimsk by first light. But the bridges had to be reinforced there, so that the heavy vehicles could continue. *Kradschützen-Bataillon 3* was able to cross around 0800 hours, reaching the five-kilometer-distant Warwarowka in a rapid move. The motorcycle infantry and reconnaissance soldiers did not spend time there; they moved on. In the meantime, the men of the two engineer companies that were marching towards the front cleared mines so as to enable the continuation of the move past Chotimsk. Because of the mines, the *II./Panzer-Regiment 6* was also halted in Warwarowka, so as to avoid unnecessary losses.

The lead group under *Oberst* von Manteuffel made it to Degtjarewka on the Iputj. Enemy resistance was broken, and the first bridgehead was formed after crossing in inflatable craft. *Hauptmann* Ziervogel and *Major* von Corvin-Wiersbitzki immediately pressed on with their companies. The engineers under *Hauptmann* Winkler and *Oberleutnant* Brandt started to

---

2. *Traditionsverband,* 149–57.

erect a bridge. The bridging column was ordered to move us as quickly as possible. By 1700 hours, it had completed a 100-meter-long engineer bridge by constructing a 9.6-meter end section.

After a crossing point was created for the heavy vehicles—the terrain otherwise consisted of sandy forest soil—the *II./Panzer-Regiment 6* (*Oberstleutnant* Munzel) continued its march from Warwarowka starting at 1315 hours. Two hours later, the entire regiment received orders to move out and reach Degtjarewka as soon as possible. Once again, the *3. Panzer-Division* had spread out over the distance of many kilometers. The lead group was already advancing through Zynka along the good, improved road from Roslawl to Mglin, while the 1st Battalion and the 3rd Battalion of the tank regiment were churning through deep sand and marshy spots. All the while, the sun was burning hot, with the thermostat registering more than 30 degrees [86 Fahrenheit]! The 2nd and 3rd Companies of *Schützen-Regiment 3* were employed screening a fifteen-kilometer stretch of road between Chotimsk and Degtjarewka.

Kampfgruppe von Manteuffel was on the road leading to Mglin. A competition to see who could move the fastest started among the tankers, the motorcycle infantry, the reconnaissance soldiers, the cannoneers and the engineers. Enemy resistance on the road was quickly broken. The Russians frequently didn't have time to defend and had to race head over heels" into the closest patch of woods. Enemy forces grew in size outside of Mglin. The *Kampfgruppe* halted briefly and prepared to attack, while the batteries of *Oberstleutnant* Wellmann sent their fiery greetings into Mglin. The *II./Panzer-Regiment 6*, *Kradschützen-Bataillon 3*, *Aufklärungs-Abteilung 1* and the more slowly following *II./Schützen-Regiment 3* moved out, entered the city quickly and immediately transitioned to an all-round defense.

The main body of the division was more than twenty kilometers farther to the rear and secured the bridgehead over the Iputj from the high ground at Degtjarewka. The wheeled vehicle columns of *Kampfgruppe Oberst Kleemann* closed up there during the night. *Kampfgruppe Oberstleutnant Audörsch* found itself an additional twenty kilometers farther back. The great distances, of course, could not be completely screened. As a result, Soviet partisans succeeded in attacking the village of Chotimsk during the night and burning it completely to the ground.

After the cool night started to yield to the first faint rays on the horizon, which indicated another hot day, *Kampfgruppe von Manteuffel* immediately moved out. The *7./Panzer-Regiment 6* arrived in Mglin at 0500 hours. At the same time, the remaining two battalions of the tank regiment left their bivouac areas along the Iputj, after almost all the engineer companies had improved the roads through ceaseless effort. Since the bridges over the river were still incapable of supporting tanks, the fighting vehicles forded the river and advanced without stopping to Mglin, which they reached at 1000 hours.

At the same time, *Oberstleutnant* Munzel was advancing south with his companies and the motorcycle infantry and reconnaissance elements attached to him. The advance guard was able to get as far as the southern edge of the large forested tract outside of Unetscha without enemy contact. At that point, a Russian antiaircraft battery prevented a further advance through well-aimed fire. The fighting vehicles of the battalion formed up to conduct a concentric attack against the battery. At that point, Russian aircraft attacked the columns at low level; they were unable to defend themselves. *Leutnant* Bertram, *Gefreiter* Grund, and *Gefreiter* Sobeck were killed in the fighting.

The *1./Schützen-Regiment 3* (*Oberleutnant* von Zitzewitz) was moved forward, and the last resistance was finally broken with its assistance. The tanks immediately entered the city of Unetscha and moved to the far end without regard for any other pockets of resistance that were still holding out. Unfortunately, they were a few minutes too late: a long, fully loaded freight train left the railway station in front of their eyes and snorted away.

In the next two hours, the enemy remaining in Unetscha was eliminated. In the process, a portion of the city burned down. Towards 1630 hours, *Oberstleutnant* von Lewinski arrived with the other two battalions, and a short while later, *Major* Wellmann and his riflemen also arrived. The Russians did not want to give up Unetscha so easily. Soviet fighter-bombers attacked the already burning city and the entering German columns repeatedly until it turned dark. At 1930 hours, the *III./ Panzer-Regiment 6* (*Hauptmann* Schneider-Kostalski) moved out with the *II./Schützen-Regiment 3* as the advance guard in the direction of Starodub. The quick onset of night forced the advance to be halted in the vicinity of Rjuchoff around 2300 hours. The advance guard set up for defense and waited for the morning.

The advance of the *XXIV. Armee-Korps (mot.)* again turned fluid on 17 August. In the process, the *3. Panzer-Division* had gained a surprising amount of ground to the south and was just to the east of Gomel. The *4. Panzer-Division* was able to take Gelynkowitschi and followed the *3. Panzer-Division*. The *10. Infanterie-Division (mot.)* was inserted into the line to the right of the *3. Panzer-Division* in order to establish contact with the infantry divisions, which were hanging back far to the northwest.

Generalleutnant Model issued orders at 0115 hours for the further pursuit south. The supplemental order issued by *Panzer-Regiment 6* started with the sober statement: "*Gruppe von Lewinski* reaches the area around Starodub, starting out at 0530 hours."

At that precise moment, *Oberstleutnant* von Lewinski moved out with his strong force from the area south of Unetscha. In the lead were the companies from the *I./Panzer-Regiment 6*, followed by the vehicles of the *1./ Flak-Regiment 94* and the two antitank battalions. The companies of the *I./ Schützen-Regiment 3* followed that group, with the batteries of the *I./Artillerie-Regiment 75*, the *2./Pionier-Bataillon 39* and the *1./Kradschützen-Bataillon 3* bringing up the rear of the column. *Major Freiherr* von Türckheim, the commander of *Panzerjäger-Abteilung 543* took up the security of the avenue of advance with his guns and the attached *3./Schützen-Regiment 3*. In the process of executing that mission, his gunners knocked out seven light Russian fighting vehicles.

The advance guard of *Hauptmann* Schneider-Kostalski moved out south from Rjuchoff at 0630 hours. The *9./Panzer-Regiment 6* took the lead. The lead fighting vehicles arrived outside of Starodub, the large transportation hub halfway between Gomel and Brjansk, around 0900 hours. The Russians had quickly set up defenses at the outskirts and were prepared to defend the city. Our tanks did not allow the enemy any time and headed immediately in the direction of Starodub. The Soviet resistance was very tough in some places, especially where a formation of *Komsomol*, a youth group of the Communist Party, defended. The enemy could be ejected everywhere, however. At 0915 hours, the city was in German hands! The Russians were so surprised by the sudden appearance of the German tanks that they thought there were dealing with airborne forces.

Kampfgruppe von Lewinski reached the city three hours later. While the tank companies screened and established bivouac sites in the southern and western portions of Starodub, the riflemen set up for the defense to the east and north. The forward groups of the *3. Panzer-Division* set up hedgehog defenses. They were all by themselves, since the advance route of the division stretched all the way from Starodub to Mglin. The *4. Panzer-Division* was unable to advance as quickly that day. For that reason, elements of *Schützen-regiment 394* had to remain behind and only slowly made their way forward.

Kampfgruppe Audörsch reached Mglin and received orders there to continue on to Unetscha, a large railway transportation hub on the Moscow line. Upon reaching Unetscha, the Division Commander, *Generalleutnant* Model, issued orders to *Oberstleutnant* Audörsch to hold the town, although the *II./Schützen-Regiment 394* was to continue marching in the direction of Starodub to support the elements of the *3. Panzer-Division* employed there.

At the same time, Soviet bombs were falling on Starodub, where *Kampfgruppen von Manteuffel, von Lewinski,* and *Kleemann* had either arrived or were arriving. The enemy aerial attacks lasted the entire night and did not abate until first light on 19 August.

The Soviet command knew all too well that the breakthrough of German armored forces to the south constituted a great danger to their own front, which was still oriented to the west. For that reason, everything was then geared to defeating or at least holding up the *XXIV. Armee-Korps (mot.)*.

After *Generalleutnant* Model had taken off in the direction of Starodub, reports filtered in to *Oberstleutnant* Audörsch from the reconnaissance efforts that had been dispatched that the woods in the vicinity of Unetscha and the roadway to the rear had been occupied by Russians. At that moment, the commanding general, *Generalleutnant* Geyr von Schweppenburg, arrived at Audörsch's command post and Audörsch filled him in on the latest reports. Von Schweppenburg ordered that the *II./Schützen-Regiment 394*, which was marching through Unetscha at the time, was to remain there. The commanding general decided to remain at Audörsch's command post, since all of the roads to the corps command post were occupied by the enemy. Since it was expected that the Russians would attack Unetscha the next morning, all necessary measures for the defense of the town were taken. At first light on 19 August, the positions of *Schützen-Regiment 394* were placed under heavy Russian artillery fire; an attack by fifteen Russian fighting vehicles attempted to break through the positions. The attack hit the company of *Leutnant Dr.* Lotze (the *2./Schützen-Regiment 394*) especially hard, but it did not allow itself to be shaken and bravely conducted its defense. *Oberstleutnant* Audörsch employed the three tanks that had remained in Unetscha, some of which were immobilized. *Leutnant* Büschen conducted a successful defensive engagement with his two *Panzer III's* and single *Panzer IV*. After three T-34's had been knocked out, the Soviets turned away. Some of them bogged down in the marshland, where they remained stuck.

A Russian infantry attack then started against the command post of the *Kampfgruppe*, where the commanding general then found himself. It was supported by heavy artillery fire. All available forces, including clerks and liaison officers, were used in the defense. The commanding general personally got involved in the fighting, armed with a submachine gun. The general's liaison officer, standing next to the commanding general and *Oberstleutnant* Audörsch, was badly wounded. The enemy attack was turned back.

The fighting then continued with unrelenting harshness. The responsible *Kampfgruppe* leader, *Oberstleutnant* Audörsch, received constant reports of renewed enemy attacks or small penetrations into the positions.

It was almost miraculous that the corps landline leading forward to the *3. Panzer-Division* had not been discovered by the Russians. The commanding general was thus able to speak with *Generalleutnant* Model and ordered the immediate sending of two tank battalions to Unetscha, since that important railway hub could not be lost under any circumstances. After that conversation, Model spoke with Audörsch and asked him the following question: "Are you going to hold Unetscha or not?" After Audörsch answered the question in the affirmative, Model decided not to send the second tank battalion to Unetscha. *Oberstleutnant* Munzel and the *II./Panzer-Regiment* 6 were then sent to Unetscha.

The difficult defensive fighting of *Schützen-Regiment 394* continued. The disquieting information reached the command post that a fifty-two-ton fighting vehicle had just succeeded in crossing a bridge into Unetscha, after it had eliminated the German guard force on the bridge with its main gun. Audörsch gave *Leutnant* Störck (engineer platoon) the mission of destroying the tank. The heavy tank was careening around the streets of the city, firing wildly. Previous efforts to take care of the tank with satchel charges had failed. *Leutnant* Störck jumped onto the rear deck of the tank with a satchel charge. *Gefreiter* Baldes likewise jumped up onto the rolling tank and blocked the vision ports of the turret with his hands. Störck threw open an engine compartment access grate and tossed the satchel charge inside. Both of the engineers jumped off and went into cover behind the corner of a house. The charge detonated and destroyed the tank; the Russian crew was able to dismount without any serious wounds. Störck reported to the commanding general laconically: "Tank destroyed; I brought the Russian crew." The general removed his own Iron Cross, First Class, and pinned it to the chest of *Leutnant* Störck for his brave deed.

The attacks of the Russians did not let up; they were turned back everywhere by the brave riflemen, however. The difficult fighting cost many casualties. *Hauptmann* Schmidt, the commander of the *4./Schützen-Regiment 394*, and the battalion physician of the *II./Schützen-Regiment 394*, *Assistenzarzt* Bosien,[3] were killed. *Sanitäts-Feldwebel*[4] Holler took his place. *Assistenzarzt Dr.* Türk was practically helpless in the face of all the wounded, but he was able to master the situation, as he so frequently did, with the assistance of his medical personnel. Towards noon, the heavy fighting abated somewhat, with only smaller attacks being conducted by the Russians, which were effortlessly turned back by the riflemen. *Oberstleutnant* Munzel's *II./Panzer-Regiment 6*, which arrived around noon, turned back the last Russian attacks; the riflemen, who had been in extremely difficult but ultimately successful defensive fighting since the early morning, were happy that the tanks had arrived to provide some relief for the situation.

At 0945 hours, *Oberstleutnant* von Lewinski pulled his *Kampfgruppe* a few kilometers back from Starodub, so as to set up a screening position further to the north at Janjkowa, so that contact was not lost between the two cities. Unfortunately, the enemy was so strong and our supply situation with fuel and ammunition so weak that the Soviets could no longer be driven from the road. After the armored *Kampfgruppe* had pulled out of its screening position between Unetscha and Starodub, the division moved another *Kampfgruppe* into the area to prevent the enemy forces battered at Unetscha from also attempting to separate those two cities. *Oberstleutnant Dr.* Weissenbruch, the commander of the *I./Artillerie-Regiment 75*, was given the mission of forming the screening *Kampfgruppe*. The *1.* and *2./Schützen-Regiment 3*, as well as elements of *Panzerjäger-*

---

3. A medical officer rank equivalent to *Leutnant*.
4. Enlisted medical personnel generally had their specialty (medical = *Sanitäts-*) placed in front of their rank.

Abteilung 521 and Weissenbruch's own battalion moved out of Starodub at noon and occupied positions at Asskoli, ten kilometers north of the city. *Generalleutnant* Model was also at that location. The men of *Pionier-Bataillon 39* also mined the railway line and the 2nd Company of the engineer battalion built a sixteen-ton bridge in Rjuchoff. The *III./Panzer-Regiment 6* and elements of *Kradschützen-Bataillon 3* and *Aufklärungs-Abteilung 1* remained in Starodub, where they conducted patrols in all directions in the course of the day in an effort to keep the southern wing of the division from being surprised. *Kampfgruppe Major Frank—Kradschützen-Bataillon 3,* the *1./Panzerjäger-Abteilung 521,* a battery from *Artillerie-Regiment 75,* and the 4th Platoon of the *3./Pionier-Bataillon 39*—captured three artillery pieces and took fifty prisoners, among other spoils of war.

The enemy movements continued through the night and hit the widely extended *3. Panzer-Division,* which was fighting in all directions, with full force early on the morning of 20 August. Strong Soviet forces rolled across the crossroads north of Shetscha at 0400 hours, heading from the northwest to the southeast. Additional columns followed those initial forces in the area around Rjuchoff. Coming from *Kampfgruppe Oberstleutnant Dr. Weissenbruch,* elements of differing battalions under *Major* Wellmann immediately went into position south of Rjuchoff and engaged the enemy. The *1./Schützen-Regiment 3* encountered an enemy antiaircraft battery in the process of attempting to break through. *Obergefreiter* Schrader's rifle squad took up the fight. The soldiers approached the enemy with aggressiveness, eliminated the battery and took 192 men prisoner.

The engineers in position at Rjuchoff had a worse time of it. They had been surprised by a lightning-like attack by the Russians and lost four dead, five missing and one wounded. At the last moment, *Unteroffizier* Münchow was able to escape encirclement with four vehicles and reestablish contact with Bridging Column 1. *Major* Beigel immediately employed a motorized patrol under *Leutnant* Seefeld (the *3./Pionier-Bataillon 39*) to see what had happened. Unfortunately, the engineers were unable to make it through to their encircled comrades and had to return without any tangible results.

Generalleutnant Model directed friendly tanks to intervene as soon as possible. The *I./Panzer-Regiment 6* rolled in the direction of Shetscha. From there, the *1./Panzer-Regiment 6* was employed in an enveloping maneuver to the left two hours later, while the remaining companies attacked Rjuchoff from the north and felt their way forward along the road heading south that bypassed the city to the west. Two Russian fighting vehicles—T-26's—as well as an artillery piece were destroyed during the reconnaissance-in-force. The lead vehicles then linked up with the first couple of tanks from the *III./Panzer-Regiment 6*, which had moved out from Starodub to the north. As a result, contact between the divided division was reestablished at 1315 hours!

Around 1400 hours, the situation around Rjuchoff cleared up somewhat. The Soviets had disappeared from the road. They had pulled back into the thick woods between Rjuchoff and Shetscha. From there, they continued to present a danger to the columns advancing along the road. At that point, the *I./Panzer-Regiment 6* only had seven *Panzer II's*, three *Panzer III's* and a single *Panzer IV* at its disposal. It was impossible for it to attack the enemy. The forces had to transition to the defense everywhere.

Kampfgruppe Audörsch left Unetscha around 1400 hours on 20 August with the *II./Panzer-Regiment 6* in the lead after elements of the *4. Panzer-Division* had assumed security there. The lead company encountered its first Russian formations four kilometers south of the city; they had advanced as far as the road again. The enemy had even brought artillery into position and took every vehicle under fire. The tanks succeeded in breaking through.

Schützen-Regiment 394 followed the tank battalion and, protected by it, continued its march south. All of a sudden, aircraft with the Red Star appeared above the column. The first bombs fell soon afterwards, and a short while later, enemy artillery again fired into the ranks of the regiment. Exploiting the situation, the enemy came out of the woods with tanks and riflemen, scattered the *I./Schützen-Regiment 394* and pressed on further to the east.

The next halt was at Shetscha. A camouflaged fifty-two-ton tank was positioned under trees near the roadway. It took every vehicle that rolled past under fire from pointblank range with its main gun. The first vehicle was set alight; the second one ran into it; the third one tipped over. Everything came to a standstill, and there was total confusion. The friendly infantry weapons were powerless against the steel monster.

Oberstleutnant Schlutius, the commander of the *III./Artillerie-Regiment 75*, immediately ordered a 15-centimeter battery forward. Unfortunately, the guns could not be brought into position to destroy the tank under direct fire. *Major* Haas employed the battery on both sides of the road. The riflemen were unable to advance, since the Soviets were constantly bringing up reinforcements and appeared to have appreciable amounts of ammunition.

The Soviets attacked the German outposts at 1900 hours in an effort to force a breakthrough to the east. The *III./Artillerie-Regiment 75*, the *4./Artillerie-Regiment 75* and the *6./Flak-Regiment 59* fired with everything they had. In addition, there was the bark of infantry guns and mortars. It was a hellish concert in those gloomy woods, over which Northern Lights played that night in the bloody-red heavens. The enemy only pressed forward with riflemen. That effort could be turned back, with some of the enemy running into mines that had been laid by the *5./Schützen-Regiment 394*. The Russians did not employ any tanks that time. Towards evening, the fighting slowed down somewhat. The Soviets had suffered heavy casualties, but the friendly losses also weighed heavily. The *I./Schützen-Regiment 394* lost eight dead, including *Leutnant* Schellong, who had only been given acting command of the 3rd Company a few days earlier.

That evening, *Oberstleutnant* Audörsch received orders to immediately clear the woods of the enemy between Rjuchoff and Stietscha. Audörsch reported to the division that the orders could not be carried out in the darkness and that the attack would take place in the morning. The division placed extreme importance on driving the enemy from the road and firming up the friendly front enough so that no more Russians got through.

Audörsch, who had two tank battalions (the *I.* and *II./Panzer-Regiment 6*), as well as artillery, attached to him for the operation, scheduled the attack for 0500 hours. The planned attack had to be postponed indefinitely, however, since heavy fog took away all visibility in the bottomlands and in the woods. The batteries of *Artillerie-Regiment 75* did fire heavily into the huge woods, however, and it started to burn brilliantly in places.

Panzer-Regiment 6 had set up its screening positions as follows: The *I./Panzer-Regiment 6* along the Unetscha–Starodub railway line, blocking the woods from the west; the *II./Panzer-Regiment 6* screened along the eastern side of the woods. *Oberleutnant* Klöber, the brave commander of the 7th Company, was killed within a few minutes by a shot to the throat from short range by a sniper. The *III./Panzer-Regiment 6* continued to remain in Starodub that day to protect the division to the south and, from Merinowka, to the east.

During that lull in the fighting, Model appeared at Audörsch's command post and was initially highly annoyed that the attack had not yet started. After Audörsch had rendered his report on the situation, however, Model left it up to him to determine the time of the attack. Model waited for the attack to begin. It started at 1100 hours in brutal heat after the fog had cleared. *Schützen-Regiment 394* advanced on a broad front from the east along all forest trails and roadways into the large expanse of vegetation and trees. The tanks of the *II./Panzer-Regiment* rattled closely behind. The Russians had camouflaged themselves and dug in magnificently. Heavy fighting developed in some sections of woods. The enemy slowly turned weak and wanted to flee to the west. It was there that he ran into the deployed *I./Panzer-Regiment 6*, whose concentrated fires caused even more casualties among the Russians attempting to break out. Eleven guns, including eight of 15-centimeter caliber, were destroyed by German rounds. After four hours of bitter fighting, the lead elements of *Schützen-Regiment 394* were at the western edge of the woods. The last enemy resistance collapsed at 1800 hours. Forty Russian artillery pieces and tanks—most of which had gotten stuck in the marshes—were captured. More than 900 prisoners started their way to the rear.

Under sunny and warm skies, the next day promised to be somewhat more "peaceful." The division informed all of its elements telephonically at 0900 hours that a fairly long break was in the works. The enemy, however, continued to attempt to find a "hole" somewhere along the front of the *3. Panzer-Division*. Early in the morning, a Russian column attempted to break through in the sector of the *3./Schützen-Regiment 3*. The attack collapsed in the defensive fires of the riflemen. One artillery piece, four trucks, one quad antiaircraft gun, and one unit flag remained in German hands.

Along the road to Rjuchoff, *Schützen-Regiment 394* combed through the woods one more time. In the process, there were additional skirmishes.

Over the next few days, the Soviets gave up their attempts to break through out of the area around Gomel and intended to escape German encirclement by going across the Dessna farther south.

The *2. Armee* had crossed the Ssosh on a broad front to the south with its infantry divisions, whereby the *1. Kavallerie-Division* on the right wing was already not too far from Gomel. The *10. Infanterie-Division (mot.)* continued to maintain contact with the forward elements of the *XXIV. Armee-Korps (mot.)*. The *3. Panzer-Division* screened from the areas it had reached and pulled its own forces closer to Starodub, since the *4. Panzer-Division* had assumed the protection of Unetscha. Behind it was the *17. Panzer-Division*, that was marching down from the northern sector of the armor field army, reaching Mglin. In the course of the individual screening engagements, patrolling activities and combat raids, the *I./ Schützen-Regiment 3*, together with *Kradschützen-Bataillon 3*, was able to bring in 200 more prisoners. The *9./Panzer-Regiment 6* was able to occupy Mischkowa and Dochnowitschi to the southeast of Starodub., capturing 10 Russian howitzers in the process.

Heeresgruppe Mitte issued orders on 22 August that its field armies were to move out to the south from the line running Gomel–Starodub, whereby *Panzergruppe 2* was to envelop east to prevent the enemy from escaping.

CHAPTER 2

Taking the Dessna Position by Surprise

THE POCKET BATTLE EAST OF KIEV GETS UNDERWAY

The smaller-scale operation of the field army and the armored group had finally eliminated the danger of a Soviet thrust into the flanks in the salient between the Minsk–Smolensk Highway and the upper waters of the Dnjepr. The dented curve of the German front in the East had been transformed into its opposite and the flank thrust to the south had opened new opportunities. The Dessna River Line, which had been feverishly worked on and improved over the previous weeks by the Bolsheviks, was within grasp of the formations that had advanced south and, with it, the Kiev–Moscow railway line.

There was an order from corps at the command post of our division: The division was to move out early the next morning in the direction of Nowgorod-Ssewersk on the Dessna. The orders were prepared during the night for the regiments . . . for the tanks . . . for the motorized riflemen . . . for the motorcycle infantry. The battle staff of the division also moved out at first light. I swapped my seat in the staff car for one in the *Kübelwagen* of the *Ic*.[1] At the very front were the *Kübelwagen* of the general, two motorcycles, the radio vehicle, our vehicle, and an armored car. The direction of march was to the south.

During the first hour, we passed some of the main body, which had departed earlier. We got to the very front and halted. The maps were spread out in a stubble field next to a windmill. The first reports were

---

1. Intelligence officer. The *Ib* was the division logistics officer, and the *Ia* was the division operations officer.

received via radio and messenger. The first prisoners were brought in and quickly interrogated on the most important points. They were personnel from enemy formations we had known about for a long time, the remnants of repeatedly smashed divisions that were divisions in name only. The prisoners were mostly men in age from thirty-five to forty, largely without rank, barely trained or not at all, brought to the front just a few days previously. All of them were happy that the war was already over for them, even a couple of young officers: "Rations miserable; leadership poor; headquarters scattered; we couldn't do anything." But they still had huge quantities of weapons, and good ones, especially artillery.

The same scene repeated itself the entire day: We passed the marching division, stopped for a new orders conference and then passed the division again. Patrols had determined that the main route of advance was difficult to negotiate in places. We took a detour through the woods. We were already some fifty kilometers in enemy territory. There could have been untold amounts of enemy formations in the woods to the left or right. No one paid any attention. That was the new way of conducting war!

It was not until we were right next to the Dessna that strong resistance was reported. We stopped briefly in the last village outside of Nowogrod-Ssewersk, but the general was restless. He wanted to personally see what was going on with the lead elements. Right behind the village was an extended ridgeline. We passed the lead elements of the tanks; the motorcycle battalion had pushed outposts out in front. There were exchanges of some light fire with enemy riflemen and machine guns. Cannon went into position behind us; a heavy battery moved up to the northern edge of the village.

Through the binoculars, you could see enemy columns moving westward along a parallel road about two kilometers to the south. They were apparently headed for some extended woods in our flank. Enemy artillery fire was soon coming from that direction; our cannon tried to locate it. A short while later, heavy rounds were impacting that came from the direction of Nowgorod-Ssewersk. In addition, there was mortar fire from the rifle positions a few hundred meters in front of us. Lucky hits caused painful casualties. The division commander was slightly wounded on the hand by artillery shrapnel. He had a field dressing applied; the matter was over. The artillery commander was killed. We helped apply dressings to a few wounded and got them out of the beaten zone on motorcycles and field ambulances. Soviet fighter-bombers used the opportunity, whenever there was a break in the cover provided by our zealous fighters due to their flying in or out, to bomb and strafe our high ground and the village. Our light *Flak* prevented them from taking exact aim. Nevertheless, there were still some wounded.

The impression we had garnered, reinforced by the reports rendered by the tankers, motorcycle infantry, and patrols, as well as the message drops by the aerial reconnaissance—which the tankers followed devotedly—was this: The enemy appeared determined to defend the Dessna and, to that end, had established deep bridgeheads on this side of the river at the main crossing points at Nowogrod-Ssewersk and at other points in front of the neighboring division. The two bridges in our sector were still intact. The Dessna Valley was a very good natural obstacle. It was 500 to 1,000 meters wide, full of oxbow lakes and marshy. It was thus the main goal of the division commander to take the bridges—or at least one of them—intact. He prepared his attack plans.

It was directed that the forces were to move out at 1900 hours. It was already towards the end of twilight when the armor regiment, which we were with, started to roll out. It turned dark very quickly. The terrible routes held up the neighboring column, which was supposed to approach Nowogrod-Ssewersk at the same time. The motorcycle battalion, which was advancing to the right, was also unable to proceed due to the growing darkness. The attack was postponed until the morning. The main effort was shifted to the second bridge, which was about ten kilometers farther downstream. That had all taken place the previous day.

This morning, at 0500 hours, we were up from with the commander of our armored regiment. The first few deserters came out of the stubble field; there were soon 200 of them. Off to the right of Nowogrod-Ssewersk, a huge explosive cloud rose at 0600 hours: The second bridge had been blown up! (Not too good of a job, however, as was later determined.) We advanced to a railway embankment just outside of Nowogrod-Ssewersk with the regimental staff. A small liaison armored vehicle approached and the radiant face of a *Leutnant* reported: The tank company had just surprised and set alight a brand-new heavy 15-centimeter battery on the far side of the embankment. It was the same one that had hit some of our comrades the previous evening. It was in the process of pulling out with its tractor prime movers. When we passed the battery half an hour later, the oil from the tractors was still burning brilliantly. We had to move quickly, since the ammunition was going up with a huge racket at regular intervals.

Report from the neighboring column: Lead elements penetrating into Nowogrod-Ssewersk; contact established with our patrols. We were on the opposite edge of the city, in the process of sending a rifle battalion with tank support to the second, more southern bridge. At that moment, the *General* arrived and ordered us into his vehicle. We then moved clear through the city, which had only been occupied a short while ago by initial forces, to the neighboring group. We then got a big surprise: The main bridge was intact and had just been taken by *Leutnant* Störck,[2] a Knight's Cross recipient, and four men in the face of heavy artillery fire. They had prevented its demolition at the last moment! Thirty Bolsheviks, who were still running around underneath the bridge with cans of fuel, were eliminated by the lead tank.

The *General* moved to the bridge. As we left the rows of houses, we saw a magical picture from the high right bank: At our feet was the broad, green Dessna Valley. On the far side, the view extended more than thirty kilometers into Ukrainian soil. There was a magnificent late-summer sky, broken up by high, white cloudbanks. And the nicest thing for a military man's eye: The large wooden bridge over the Dessna in its entire length— completely intact! The *General* immediately moved over the bridge. On the far side, we congratulated the small section of engineers, with its *Leutnant*, a man of more mature years, who had achieved that priceless success. A large crowd of prisoners surrounded us; they had been called up only fourteen days previously and had arrived just in time to be taken prisoner.

The Dessna had been forced. Eighty kilometers in exactly thirty hours. That short statement concealed an almost superhuman efforts on the part of commanders and men—efforts that could only be measured in their completeness and harshness by an eyewitness.

---

2. Georg Störck received the Knight's Cross on 22 September 1941. At the time, he was credited with being the platoon leader of the engineer platoon of the headquarters company of *Schützen-Regiment 394*.

THE DIVISIONAL HISTORY

The divisional history records the events of this chapter as follows:[3]

On 24 August, the field army group ordered the attack of the *Panzergruppe* to the south and into the rear of the Soviet 5th Army, which was holding out in front of Kiev. The *XXIV. Armee-Korps (mot.)* was to be the steely point of the field army once the Dessna was crossed. The corps directed the *10. Infanterie-Division (mot.)* to advance on Cholmy–Awdejwka and the *3. Panzer-Division* to force a crossing over the Dessna, while the *4. Panzer-Division* was to initially clear the west bank of the river and follow the *3. Panzer-Division.*

The *3. Panzer-Division* was about 600 to 1,000 meters in front of the broad valley of the Dessna. The city of Nowgorod-Sewersk separated the division from the river. The division closed up to the river during the night. *Oberst* Kleemann arrived with his headquarters, as did the *I./Panzer-Regiment 6, Kradschützen-Bataillon 3* and *Aufklärungs-Abteilung 1.* It took longer for the batteries to make their way through the sandy roads and the deep woods in the defiles in front of the city. The commanders discussed the attack in the hours that followed. It was scheduled for 0500 hours the following morning. Since the bridge over the Dessna was marked on the bad maps available as being at the northern entrance of Nowgorod, it was directed that a reinforced tank company under *Oberleutnant* Vopel (commander of the *1./Panzer-Regiment 6*) take the bridge in a *coup de main.* The remaining companies of the *I./Panzer-Regiment 6* were to give covering fire from the high ground in front of the city while that was being done. *Kampfgruppe Oberst Kleemann* would advance against the southern entrance to Nowgorod-Sewersk, while *Kampfgruppe von Lewinski* would come in from the west.

The advance guard of *Oberleutnant* Vopel—reinforced by the *1./Schützen-Regiment 394*, the *3./Panzerjäger-Abteilung 543* and the engineer platoon of *Schützen-Regiment 394*—left its staging area at 0345 hours. The tanks and personnel vehicles were hit by artillery and mortar fire as they approached. They did not allow themselves to be deterred. The Rome Bridge was crossed and, about one kilometer to the southeast, the first Soviet roadblock broken through. The advance guard then moved two kilometers through a defile, which was dominated by enemy infantry-gun

---

3. *Traditionsverband*, 160–63.

fire. The fighting vehicles approached the enemy guns at full speed and overran them.

The enemy's resistance stiffened a bit later at the fork in the road 3.5 kilometers northwest of the city. The fighting vehicles had to halt there, and the riflemen had to dismount to force the Russians to pull back in a hand-grenade duel. *Leutnant* Aye, a platoon leader in the *1./Schützen-Regiment 394,* was killed, while he was negotiating with Soviet emissaries. A short while later, the lead fighting vehicles were at the northern outskirts of Nowgorod-Sewersk. Although there were a few machine-gun nests, they were overrun in short order. But where was the bridge?

By then, *Oberstleutnant* Schmidt-Ott had worked his way forward to the high ground with his other companies. The men were offered a magnificent picture from there. To the left was the broad bed of the Dessna, with its two arms. On the right side was the pretty city, extended along the steep high ground. Behind that—about four kilometers distant—was the high bridge, over which an unending stream of trucks and *Panje* carts was crossing. The artillery liaison officer said he was not capable of engaging the bridge, since the batteries were so far back. At that point, Schmidt-Ott had *Kampfgruppe Vopel* informed by radio of the exact location of the bridge and issued orders that it was to be taken immediately.

The tanks, personnel carriers, and motorcycles moved out again. This time, they were hit by Russian fighter-bombers, but little damage was done. *Kompanie Vopel,* followed by the antitank elements and the riflemen, rattled in the direction of the bridge. Wherever resistance was offered, it was answered in the steely language of the main guns and machine guns. A Russian truck was destroyed right in front of the bridge. The tanks were in front of the high bridge, some 700 meters long! The clocks registered 1000 hours.

While the forwardmost elements of *Kampfgruppe Kleemann* arrived quickly at their objective, *Kampfgruppe von Lewinski* had approached the southern outskirts city from the west. The *II./Panzer-Regiment 6,* along with its attached elements, had departed Forostowitschi around 0700 hours. Artillery fire descended on the roads and defiles. The *Kampfgruppe* reached the stubble fields, which were full of machine guns and guard outposts. While the tanks continued their way east uninterrupted, the men of the *II./Schützen-Regiment 3* swarmed out across the fields and smoked out the individual enemy groups, one after the other. The battalion was once again being led by *Major* Zimmermann, who had been released from the hospital. His predecessor, *Hauptmann* Engelien, was sent to Eberswalde, to complete General Staff Officer training.(He ended the war as a regimental commander in Kurland.)

Oberstleutnant von Lewinski conducted a commanders' conference with the commanders of his *Kampfgruppe* around 0900 hours in one of the many defiles. Coordination with the batteries was emphasized, since they could only move forward in the local terrain with difficulty. Soviet fire fell on the group of officers. The commander of *Artillerie-Regiment 75*, *Oberst* Ries, was killed. With him died another member of the divisional artillery, *Leutnant* Wöhlermann of the regiment's 1st Battery. *Unteroffizier* Lipschitz, who later became the senator for internal affairs in postwar West Berlin, was badly wounded and lost an arm.

Within *Kampfgruppe von Lewinski*, the *7./Panzer-Regiment 6* took up point again. It crossed a railway embankment just before the first houses of the city. As the tanks crossed the tracks, they ran into the positions of a Russian 15-centimeter battery. The Soviets were in the process of limbering the guns to the tall, ungainly tractors with the wide tracks that served as prime movers. The main-gun rounds crashed into the guns and the vehicles and left behind only steel skeletons and a cloud of burning oil and fuel.

A short time later—1030 hours—*Kampfgruppe von Lewinski* advanced into Nowgorod-Sewersk. *Generalleutnant* Model had moved to the head of the column in his open staff car and ordered contact be established between the two battle groups. The *II./Panzer-Regiment 6* was able to clear the area around the railway station. The division then sent the tank battalion further to the south, in the direction of Juchnowa, to take the bridge there.

Oberleutnant Vopel's reinforced advance-guard company of the northern *Kampfgruppe* was at the river. The terrain sloped steeply downward and rose equally steeply on the other side. The bridge stood there as the connection between the two points, jutting high into the sky on four large pilings. All of a sudden, there were bursts of machine-gun fire from the bridge guards. The two tanks in front took up the fight and shredded the machine-gun positions. Twenty to thirty Russians fled to the base of the bridge.

Leutnant Störck of the engineer platoon of *Schützen-Regiment 394* turned out to be quicker, however. He maneuvered his way through the front line of fighting vehicles and raced towards the bridge. Soviet artillery, mortars and machine guns fired from the opposite banks. *Oberleutnant* Vopel had his tanks spread out to lend support and the tinny reports of the main guns and machines could be heard firing against identified enemy positions. The engineer vehicle halted sixty meters in front of the approach ramp to the gigantic, immense bridge. Störck jumped down from his vehicle. Following behind him were *Feldwebel* Heyeres, *Unteroffizier* Strucken, *Obergefreiter* Fuhn and *Gefreiter* Beyle. The men hurried towards the bridge, racing bent over along the wooden planks, while the rounds of the tanks kept the enemy down. Störck and Beyle paid no attention to them. Their eyes were looking for demolitions and, indeed, they found them. The *Leutnant* discovered the first charge on one of the vertical pilings on the box-like superstructure of the bridge. The engineers dove on it, tearing the lines out and throwing the box into the water. Störck hastened on, found the second charge . . . then the third . . . then the fourth.

The rounds of individual Russian machine guns headed towards them and forced the engineers to take cover. A few Russian soldiers attempted to flee from the bridge and reach the safety of the far shore. The tank gunners took up aim and fired. Störck was then able to continue. Another charge was flung into the water, followed by another. Valuable time ticked by; no one knew how many charges were still on the bridge. Then they did it! *Oberleutnant* Vopel decided to exploit the confusion among the enemy and not wait until the engineers had completed their dangerous work. The bridge could have gone up at any minute . . . the *Oberleutnant* recognized the opportunity that was being offered. He ordered: *"Panzer— Marsch!"*

The vehicles rolled out. The rattled towards the bridge, moved past *Leutnant* Störck, who was still in the process of removing charges, and reached the far side. *Unteroffizier* Borowczek of the *4./Panzer-Regiment 6* led the first tank. With him was *Leutnant* Hiltmann, the liaison officer from the rifle brigade. Vopel followed close behind with all tanks capable of moving. Close behind were the men of *Pionier-Bataillon 39* under *Leutnant* Harzer.

It was 1100 hours when the German tanks reached the south bank of the Dessna! The Soviets were so surprised they fled their positions. *Oberleutnant* Vopel intended to advance farther. He advanced through the fleeing columns with his reinforced company so as to take the high ground, some 800 meters away. While the Russian infantry fled, enemy artillery and 7.62-centimeter antitank guns started firing into the approaching tanks. One fighting vehicle was lost to a direct hit from an antitank gun; the vehicle of the *Oberleutnant* was also hit. *Generalleutnant* Model arrived at the bridge at that moment and had *Oberstleutnant* Audörsch brief him. He could hardly believe that the large bridge had fallen into our hands intact. He ordered that Störck be recommended for a Knight's Cross immediately; he later received it from the hands of Model outside of Orel.

The Soviets then noticed the great danger the loss of the bridge placed them in. They placed one artillery fire mission after the other on the bridge and the approach road. It was already too late. *Oberstleutnant* Schmidt-Ott was already there with his remaining companies. The battalion commander was the first one to race over the 700-meter-long stretch. Behind him was *Oberleutnant* von Kriegsheim with the other tanks. A fighting vehicle was hit by an antitank gun, but it was able to continue moving under its own power. One of the charges went off that the engineers had overlooked. Fortunately, it only caused light damage to the wooden beams.

The *1./Panzer-Regiment 6* underwent heavy artillery fire on the high ground 800 meters on the other side of the bridge. The rest of the battalion arrived in a timely manner, bring palpable relief. The *4./Panzer-Regiment 6* took the woods on both sides of the road under fire. The Russians quickly pulled back. At that point, the first riflemen arrived. The *1./Schützen-Regiment 394* relieved the hard-fighting tank company. Over the next few hours, *Oberstleutnant* Audörsch brought his entire regiment across to the east bank! The riflemen expanded and fortified the rapidly won bridgehead. In the process, they engaged an enemy artillery position, capturing a few guns and antiaircraft guns and taking some prisoners.

THE HISTORY OF *PANZER-REGIMENT 6*

The regimental history of *Panzer-Regiment 6* records the events of this chapter as follows:[4]

The other two battle groups also approached Nowgorod-Sewersk during the night. The division had covered more than 2,000 kilometers by that point.

At 0700 hours on 26 August, the 1st and 2nd Battalions advanced against the stubbornly defending enemy from the north and the west. Numerous artillery pieces had to be eliminated at the edge of the city. The 1st Battalion was especially successful in doing so. When the large bridge over the Dessna—almost one kilometer long—became visible, the 1st Company of *Oberleutnant* Vopel immediately set a course for the crossing. Although the company was covered with artillery and antitank-gun fire from all sides, it reached the approaches to the bridge, deployed its tanks and opened fire on the enemy on the opposite bank. The engineer platoon of *Schützen-Regiment 394* under *Leutnant* Störck approached, lunged onto the bridge and started to eliminate one charge after the other, tossing them into the river. *Oberleutnant* Vopel did not wait until all of the charges had been removed. Instead, he ordered: *"Panzer marsch!"* With the tanks of *Unteroffizier* Boroczek and *Oberleutnant der Reserve* Hiltmann in the lead, Vopel and his entire company raced across the bridge. One tank was destroyed by a direct hit and another had its cupola shot off, but the company got across, and the enemy fled, horrified, from his guns. *Oberleutnant* Vopel gave him no rest. Instead, he assaulted up the 800-meter-long steep slope on the south back with his tanks, moving among the fleeing Russians and into the antitank-gun and artillery positions. The enemy then recognized the danger. He concentrated his artillery and fired on the bridge and road. But *Oberstleutnant* Schmidt-Ott was already across with all of his elements and advancing. The guns along the way were destroyed and the next section of terrain along Iwotka Creek reached. Once again, the combat vehicles had to be towed across the sometimes sandy, sometimes marshy roads. The battalion set up an all-round defense on the south bank and assisted the vehicles of the division that were following, whenever bunkers not identified during the rapid advance opened fire. During the afternoon of the same day, the 3rd Battalion was sent marching as part of *Gruppe von Lewinski* to take

---

4. Munzel, 84–86.

another large bridge over the Dessna. It was ten kilometers away. When the *Kampfgruppe* arrived, however, the bridge had already been destroyed. Heavy fire was received from the far bank. The 3rd Battalion remained there, while the regimental headquarters and the 2nd Battalion screened from the southern edge of Nowgorod-Sewersk.

The commander discusses details of the advance at the forward division command post. Seen here is *Generalmajor* Breith with staff officers, placing this photograph at sometime after October 1941.

Off to the south—to close the giant pocket at Kiev.

New orders leave the signals center for the units to execute their thrust to eliminate the enemy.

On the northern border to the Ukraine: the crossing of the advance guard over the Iputj, north of Meglin.

Our *Flak* was always ready—if it worked out, security duties were combined with a little sunbathing. A *3.7-cm Flak 36/37* on an interesting improvised mounting.

In liberated Meglin, the populace was able to attend religious services for the first time in nineteen years.

Infantry approach a wooded area where the enemy has dug in.

The enemy attempted to hold up our flank attack at Unetscha with the heaviest of weapons. We flushed it out, but it got stuck. One of the destroyed tanks, an early version of the T-34, probably the 1940 variant.

A skirmish line of riflemen clears terrain in a gigantic Ukrainian field. The vastness of the land can be seen to good advantage in this photograph.

Riflemen feel their way forward in a relatively large village that has fortified positions. A few prisoners have already been collected.

The old fortified monastery in conquered Novgorod-Ssewersk on the Desna.

View from the edges of the beautiful Dessna flood plain across the river at Novgorod-Ssewersk.

In a bold *coup de main*, the strategically extremely important bridge at Novgorod-Ssewersk was taken. It spans a valley several hundred meters in width at that location.

All of the men in a village were often dragged along with the fleeing Bolsheviks: women bring in the harvest under the protection of German forces.

Right through the woods—the main thing is that the enemy is not given the chance to dig in again. This appears to be a mortar section, since the soldier bringing up the rear is carrying a base plate.

Attack! Infantry catch a ride on a *Panzer II*. Other armored vehicles can be seen forming up in the background.

An earlier-model Panzer IV—most likely a "D" version—which was armed with a short-barreled 7.5-centimter main gun. This was the biggest tank the Germans employed in "Barbarossa" although it was intended to be used in a support role, since its main gun was incapable of defeating heavily armored targets. It is believed this particular *Panzer IV* was assigned to the *10. Panzer-Division.*

Luftwaffe Flak gunners provide point defense for the bridge in the background, while a tank commander in a *Panzer II* scans the terrain to the front. River-crossing operations were always inherently difficult, and the capture of an intact bridge was always of tactical importance.

CHAPTER 3

The Iron Curtain Closes behind Budjenny's Field Armies

WITH A PATROL RIGHT THROUGH THE MIDDLE OF THE ENEMY
The armored forces of *Heeresgruppe von Bock* under the command of *Generaloberst* Guderian unexpectedly advanced south from the center sector of the front and into the Ukraine. The enemy attempted to thwart that operation, whose importance he immediately recognized, by offering a bitter defense along the Dessna and Sejm flood plains. Both of the rivers offered a large natural obstacle due to their broad stretches of marshland along their banks, especially well suited to the defense. Despite that, the attacking mobile forces, with tremendous support from the *Luftwaffe*, were able to force crossings over the Dessna and the Sejm and then break through the lines of the enemy.

The advance of the German armor forces severed the lifeline of Kiev and the large two-tracked rail line from Kiev to Moscow, as well as hitting the two Bolshevik field armies of Timoshenko and Budjenny at their boundaries. The advance struck deep in the rear of the field armies of Soviet Marshall Budjenny, who was defending the northern Ukraine to either side of Kiev behind the Dnjepr with his divisions.

The German advance was made difficult by terrible and continuous cloudbursts, which transformed all of the roads into knee-deep rivers of mud. One vehicle had to tow the next. Even heavy prime movers got stuck, one that otherwise never knew any obstacles. The plagued motorcycle infantry were finally reduced to hitching up peasant horses in front of their motorcycles and being pulled through the pools of mud that extended for kilometers on end. But despite all of the obstacles, the advance continued inexorably forward, even if every meter was a contest against nature and frequently against bitter enemy resistance as well.

As long as there was still light in the day, the marching continued. The nights were spent in the vehicles along the avenue of advance; the engines turned over to continue the march at first light.

That was how the advance guards reached the northern Ukrainian communities of Romny and Lochwiza. The route led along a blocking position that had been carefully established and thoroughly prepared. The German outposts were able to use it to hold up the enemy forces attempting to get out of the Kiev Pocket and prevent them from escaping east. Deep tank ditches, obstacles and bunkers in the Budjenny position were being used against their original owners. Whoever digs a grave . . .[1]

Approaching the thrust from the north from *Heeresgruppe Feldmarschall von Bock* was an armored thrust from the south from *Heeresgruppe Generalfeldmarschall von Rundstedt.* On Sunday, 14 September, there was still a gap of fifty kilometers between the two field army groups. Aerial reconnaissance indicated the Bolsheviks were still trying to guide columns through it to the east. The gap had to be closed in any event so as to close an iron curtain behind Budjenny's field armies in the northern Ukraine.

On Sunday, around 1100 hours, a powerful force set out from the north in order to establish contact with the armored division from the southern field army group. In a long, extended column, one vehicle behind the next, they moved out on the journey of discovery. They knew that they would have to go right through the middle of the enemy. After saying good-bye to their comrades, the last German outposts were passed. A final escort was provided by large swarm of *Stukas* returning form a sortie. They circled above the march column at low level. They also disappeared a short while later on the horizon. Surrounding the column all around was the fruitful Ukrainian countryside. The only contact remaining with the battalion in Lochwiza was radio. Occasionally, locations of the force were reported. Based on the inquiries that reached *Oberleutnant* W., it could be seen how attentively the progress of the patrol was being followed on the map.

There was already enemy contact in the first village that had to be moved through. The tanks ran into Bolshevik supply columns, from which the drivers fled in wild haste: behind the straw-thatched white peasant huts; within the leafy perennials of the home gardens; and into the fields of sunflowers. Cavalrymen sprang from the edge of the advance

---

1. A German aphorism: *Wer anderen eine Grube gräbt, fällt selbt hinein*—"Whoever digs a grave for others falls into it himself."

route and attempted to find concealment behind haystacks. On the high ground above the village, the wings of a windmill suddenly started turning. One could assume that they were signaling the approach of the German formations by the movement at the windmill. That meant we had to be careful. In any event, the tank main guns and the machine guns of the riflemen had already issued a powerful statement in the first locality. The rounds reached a few of the fleeing Bolsheviks. And the windmill stopped spinning. Orphaned vehicles, *panje* carts, and steeds remained behind the patrol. The enemy column had been scattered.

Unfortunately, as the result of mechanical problems, a personnel carrier, a smaller tank, an antitank element, and a motorcycle had to be left behind. Some of the personnel were taken aboard the remaining vehicles of patrol, which had been greatly weakened. The others remained behind, and the battalion was requested by radio to render assistance to the stranded vehicles.

Right behind the next rise, we ran into another surprised Soviet truck column as it approached us. The drivers scrammed into the nearby fields as best they were able to. Since it was impossible to tow the vehicles along with us, they were rendered non-operational by means of a few rounds. And that's the way it went: enemy rider patrols; artillery columns; trains elements; construction battalions; airfield ground personnel; administrative and logistical services of all types; fuel columns that consisted of tractors with coupled *panje* carts on which were stacked barrels of gas and oil. Those were the spoils of war of the patrol. An especially juicy morsel was a truck column that stretched for kilometers on end, which innocently crossed the march route in some bottomland. The main-gun rounds and machine-gun bullets harvested among the large vehicles of the enemy. Bolting horses ran across the fields, which were covered by clouds of dust and smoke. Scattered around were burning or tipped-over trucks.

The Bolsheviks seemed to have no idea how close the Germans were and blundered into our troops again and again. It would have been easy for the tanks and vehicles of the riflemen to take out additional columns of the enemy on that sunny, beautiful September day, but the patrol needed to stick to its mission: "Establish contact with the armor division approaching from the south." It thus had to force it self to disengage each time from the enemy and continue of its march.

The march route had considerable difficulties. It led through terrain that tankers did not like: defiles, marshy flood plains, and thick woods. The tachometer registered increasingly greater numbers, and there was enemy everywhere. No matter where you looked, there were enemy columns. Friendly forces were nowhere to be seen. Although the sound of fighting could be heard in the distance—based on the direction, it could only have been coming from the forces fighting their way up from the south—there were no white signal flares being fired into the air as recognition signals. In such a situation, you could only draw the enemy's attention to the patrol. Correspondingly, we felt our way forward carefully. Then, when we lost radio contact with the battalion in terrain filled with defiles, a certain feeling of loneliness swept over us. "Just don't break down now!" That was most certainly the thought of every officer and enlisted man of the patrol.

We had already moved more than fifty kilometers. The day was drawing to a close when the silhouette of a city rose from the evening sky in the distance in front of the patrol. A deep defile separated us from the settlement, which was burning in places and from which the sound of heavy fighting could be heard. The fighting vehicles of the patrol carefully snuck forward through stacked grain. They were trying to find out whose position they were actually approaching. Were they in the rear of the enemy or in his flank? Where was the enemy? Where were the friendly forces? Should we try the white signal flares at this point? Those were the questions that preoccupied the leaders and the vehicle commanders, when an aircraft showed up in the skies. A German reconnaissance aircraft. If we succeeded in establishing contact with it, then everything would be fine. The white signal flares hissed skywards from the cupolas of the tanks and, in fact, the aircraft's attention was drawn towards us. It flew around the tanks in circles that started wide but grew ever tighter. Apparently, the pilot wanted to first establish that he was dealing with friendly tanks. Eventually, he landed between the tanks and the cornstalks. Tankers and aviators shook hands. They oriented each other quickly, and the pilot promised to alert the comrades to the south of the presence of the patrol. Then he started up again. A short while later, we saw him dive down to drop a message, where he told the tankers the friendly forces were located. A few minutes later, the signal flares rose from there as an attempt to communicate. First contact had been established! At that point, the only thing separating the forces of the German field army groups was the defile at Lubny. That was the name of the city in front of us; there was still fighting along its western edges. That resistance was also soon overcome, and the first German soldiers could be seen on the opposite slope. Those were engineers, who were advancing. They became the first ones to encounter the scouts, who had gone clear across the northern Ukraine, through fifty kilometers of enemy territory, to get to *Heeresgruppe Rundstedt*. With a handshake between the patrol leader and the company commander of the engineers, the pocket of Kiev was symbolically closed. The following morning, large combat formations headed out from both directions in order to cut off and block the last east-west connection from the pocket for Budjenny's encircled field armies.

All of the officers and soldiers of the patrol were "passed around" by their comrades coming from the south. Everyone wanted to do something good for them. They received things to eat, drink, and smoke; they received help for their vehicles and fuel. Everyone was aware of the meaning of that historical event, which had been planned in the *Führer* Headquarters and the Army High Command, which had been realized by the field army commanders and which had been executed by a patrol of the Brandenburg armor division.

In the gardens of the quarters of a tank regiment, which had been graciously offered to the comrades from the north, were the camouflaged tanks with the large "G" of *Generaloberst* Guderian. They were parked next to the tanks with the "K" of *Generaloberst* von Kleist. Two armored field armies had arranged to meet in the midst of the enemy; the iron curtain behind the Northern Ukraine, behind Kiev and behind hundreds of thousands of enemy soldiers and gigantic amounts of war materiel had been pulled shut. The history of the war for German freedom had been enriched by another laurel.

THE DIVISIONAL HISTORY

The divisional history records the events of this chapter as follows:[2]

The new day, 14 September, brought a clear morning and sunny weather. The banks of fog from the Ssula were still over Lochwiza, when the fighting started anew. *Major* Wellmann was unable to grant his riflemen a whole lot of time to sleep; he had been directed to clear the entire city on that day. Both of his companies and the fighting vehicles attached to

---

2. *Traditionsverband*, 179–80.

him from the *III./Panzer-Regiment 6* moved out at first light around 0500 hours to attack the identified Russian pockets of resistance. What they had been unable to accomplish the previous day, was accomplished that day. The *3./Schützen-Regiment 3* of *Hauptmann* Peschke assaulted surprisingly fast through the city and took the large northern bridge in a *coup de main*. To the amazement of the German soldiers, there were six heavy antiaircraft guns in front of the bridge, wheel-to-wheel across the entire width of the street. They were unmanned. The riflemen charged the guns with a "Hurra!" and pulled the crews, which were still sleeping, out from under their blankets! As quickly as that action was completed, Lochwiza was also cleared that morning, which had turned into a beautifully sunny day. The fighting vehicles of the *III./Panzer-Regiment 6* were able to enter the city without incident around 1030 hours!

The *I./Schützen-Regiment 3* advanced across the bridge and occupied the high ground outside of Jaschniki, to the north of Lochwiza, with its 3rd Company. The 2nd Company set up on the high ground at Charjkowzi west of the city. The remaining elements of the advance guard spread out to all sides to hold open Lochwiza for *Kampfgruppe Oberst Kleemann*, which was closing on the city. It entered the locality around 1020 hours with the *II./Panzer-Regiment 6* and the *II./Schützen-Regiment 3*.

At the same time, the division ordered *Panzer-Regiment 6* to form a strong combat patrol, which was to immediately advance to the south to establish contact with the *16. Panzer-Division*, which had taken Lubny the previous day. *Oberleutnant* Warthmann, the commander of the *9. Panzer-Regiment 6*, was given the mission. Only a single fighting vehicle, a *Panzer III*, was available. Functioning as the communications center was the regimental commander's tank and a few personnel carriers. The necessary fuel had to be taken from wheeled vehicles, since the supply columns had not yet closed on the city. The patrol consisted of a total of forty-five men, including the two *Oberleutnants*, Warthmann and Müller-Hauff (commander of the *3./Panzer-Regiment 6*) and the war correspondent, Heysing, who experienced everything from the commander's tank. At that point, a short episode started in the history of the *3. Panzer-Division*, which exemplified the boldness of the German armored arm in that summer of 1941. The action that was initiated led to the closing of one of the greatest pocket battles in history!

The *Kampfgruppe* started its march at the designated time. *Oberleutnant* Müller-Hauff took the lead. The weather was sunny and clear; the roads were firma and showed only a few spots of clinging mud. On top of that it was Sunday—perfect "riding weather" or, in this case, "tank weather." The tanks and personnel carriers soon left behind the forward-most outposts of Frank's advance guard at Iskowzy-Ssentschanskije and had the slightly rolling Ukrainian countryside in front of them. The enemy was somewhere, but no one knew his strength or his weaponry. Contact with the division could only be maintained by radio.

The village appeared after moving for three hours. It was bypassed. A Russian transport column was on the road. When the German vehicles approached, the drivers abandoned their *panje* carts and fled into the nearby sunflower fields. When some high ground was crossed, enemy trucks were crossing the road. Once again, the machine guns did the talking. And so *Lützows wilde, verwegene Jagd*[3] continued. Once again, Soviets appeared. This time it was a gigantic column consisting of batteries, trains elements, construction battalions, limbers, *panje* carts, tractors, two fighting vehicles, and some Cossacks on horseback added to the mix. The machine guns whistled again and shot a route through the Russian column. The tanks and other vehicles raced through the stream of vehicles at high speed.

Oberleutnant Warthmann and his men knew only one thing: Get through! And so the vehicles rolled through defiles, marshy flood plains, woods and fields and across several fragile bridges. The column crossed the Ssula in the vicinity of Titschi—that was half the way! All of a sudden, radio contact was lost with the division. The friendly vehicles were in a defile. Once they worked their way out again, the radio contact could be reestablished. In the rear, at Romny, *Generalleutnant* Model and *Major i.G.* Pomtow breathed an audible sigh of relief when they heard: "As far as Luka at 1602 hours."

The sun had already gone down, a reddish gold. Finally, however, the *Kampfgruppe* was able to halt on a plateau and conceal its vehicles under piles of grain. The men gazed over to the silhouette of a city though binoculars, which was still offset from the evening sky. Haze and clouds of

---

3. "Lützow's wild, daring hunt," a popular military song. Lützow was the stuff of German military legend in his various exploits against Napoleon.

smoke crossed over the houses; in between was the whistling of machine guns and the crash of impacting artillery. There was no longer any doubt: The patrol was right behind the Russian front and a few kilometers further on were the lead elements of *Heeresgruppe Süd*!

Oberleutnant Warthmann issued orders: *"Panzer—Marsch!"* The *Kampfgruppe* rolled out, crossed a defile and fired at the Russians suddenly appearing out of the darkness, who scattered in shock. A creek blocked further progress. The vehicles looked for a crossing point. A bridge was seen. The *Panzer III* of the *Oberleutnant* approached. It was blown up. Gray figures sprang up. They were encrusted in dirt, had stubble beards. They waved and waved. It was men of the *2./Pionier-Bataillon 16* of the *16. Panzer-Division*! It was exactly 1820 hours.

The soldiers directed the *Kampfgruppe* to a fordable location. *Oberleutnant* Warthmann crossed in his vehicle and turned towards Lubny. A short while later, he reported to *Generalmajor* Hube. The fighting vehicles of the *3. Panzer-Division* with the large "G" (Guderian) on their steel walls were next to a tank with the letter "K" (von Kleist). The lead elements of the two field army groups had established contact! The Kiev Pocket was closed!

THE HISTORY OF *PANZER-REGIMENT 6*

The regimental history of *Panzer-Regiment 6* records the events of this chapter as follows:[4]

Towards morning, orders arrived at the regiment to put together a powerful combat patrol, have it advance south towards the city of Lubny and establish contact there with the *16. Panzer-Division*, coming from the south. The patrol, approximately forty-five men, was led by *Oberleutnant* Warthmann, the Commander of the 9th Company. The regimental command tank was placed at his disposal. *Oberleutnant* Müller-Hauff in a *Panzer III* and several personnel carriers accompanied him. Shortly after noon, the patrol moved out with Müller-Hauff in the lead, and started a memorable raid, which would result in the closing of the Kiev Pocket. Accompanied by nice weather, rapid progress was made through the rolling terrain of the Ukraine. Three hours later, the first Russian column was scattered. Immediately thereafter, the patrol advanced, guns blazing, through another column, consisting of batteries, trains elements,

---

4. Munzel, 93–94.

limbers, tractors, horse-mounted Cossacks and two tanks. The patrol then proceeded through defiles, across fields and over shaky bridges. At 1600 hours, it reached the locality of Titschi, where it crossed the Ssula River on an intact bridge once more, this time from the east. As it turned dark, the patrol recognized the silhouette of the city of Lubny from a plateau. It heard artillery firing and the rattling of machine guns; it saw haze and smoke clouds. The patrol was in the rear of the Russian defensive lines. When *Oberleutnant* Warthmann attempted to find a crossing point through a creek, dirt-encrusted soldiers with stubbly beards appeared in front of him. It was the lead elements of the *16. Panzer-Division.* They showed him a ford, and Warthmann found himself reporting to the commander of the division, *General* Hube, a short while later. The mission of the regiment's patrol—over a distance of more than fifty kilometers—had been fulfilled. Contact had been established with the southern group.

The days from 15 to 21 September were devoted to the closing of the numerous gaps that still existed in the eastern portion of the ring of the Kiev Pocket. At the same time, thrusts were made into the pocket from the west.

CHAPTER 4

Lead Army Elements Meet

OUR "POCKET FEST" WITH GUESTS FROM THE SOUTH

It was noon and a sunny day in September. German fighting vehicles and combat vehicles of the riflemen rattled on the country road that led southeast out of the friendly Ukrainian town of Lochwiza. Only a little bit of dust was churned up by the clanking tracks. The road was once again firm, fortunately. The occasional puddles and ponds and the clinging mud in certain spots demonstrated that it had poured the last few days. The thick sea of cotton had broken apart that morning; small lamb-like clouds had taken their place in the blue skies. The fall sun radiated a pleasant warmth; it was almost hot after the damp and chilly days of the previous week. The soldiers in the tanks found it doubly pleasant.

The combat outposts of the advance guard were positioned around the extended village[1] with the unpronounceable name of Iskowzy-Ssentschanskije. On the previous day, in an impetuous advance, the advance guard had taken the important wooden bridges at Lochwiza intact, thus creating the prerequisites for a rapid advance. Antitank elements and howitzers stuck their barrels over the edges of the high ground; engineers destroyed several creek crossing points. The rolling terrain beyond the village was still in the hands of the enemy, after all. Those were the last few kilometers that were left open out of a gigantic pocket being formed east of the mighty bend in the Dnjepr. Columns of defeated Soviet field armies were desperately seeking an escape there. It was imperative that the gap be closed.

Stuka squadrons were thundering back in disciplined flights of three, when the armored patrol headed out across the forward lines. Into the

---

1. German accounts referring to "extended" villages usually mean small villages that generally consisted of houses and other buildings located right in a row along the main road. These types of villages generally had no depth to them.

53

middle of the enemy. The main guns were loaded; the machine guns charged. Every passing second brought with it the possibility of an encounter with the enemy. The first round could decide the fate of the patrol and its handful of brave men. The certain expectation of combat and the natural excitement that such difficult reconnaissance patrols brought with them manifested themselves in the high morale in the hearts of the combat veterans. Each of them felt and perceived something of the greatness of their mission. On this day, they were not only the small, sharp point of their Brandenburg armored division, which had served as an unerring and tireless battering ram ever since the start of the campaign as it thrust through the Red flood . . . They were not only one of many thorns that their *Panzergruppe* had driven unrelentingly ever deeper into the sick body of the gut-shot and beaten Bolshevik enemy. This time, they were doing more than reconnoitering for enemy and routes. On that particular Sunday, 15 September, they were to symbolically represent the hand being extended from *Heeresgruppe Mitte* to *Heeresgruppe Süd*. What a proud mission! The soldiers of the patrol were also aware of it! The lead armored forces of the southern group had already fought their way into the city of Lubny, exactly fifty kilometers below Lochwiza. The historical moment of their establishing contact had to take place somewhere on the road connecting them.

The patrol leader was a young *Oberleutnant* and company commander. He intently observed the beautiful countryside of the Ukraine, looking as far as the distant wood lines, which rose above the swells in the ground like a blue-gray background. He had his flare gun next to him in order to fire a recognition signal to his comrades on the other side. Then, as expected, the first enemy convoys crossed their path. Trucks and horse-drawn vehicles. The crews, completely surprised and horrified, wanted to flee. But the gunners were faster. A few main-gun rounds, a few bursts of machine-gun fire were enough to scatter the surprised Bolsheviks. A few of them ran into the fields with the corn stalks and sunflowers as tall as a man. They looked like they were being pursued by the Furies. Before they could even recover from their panic, the tanks had moved on. They had no time to pursue. Their orders: "Push through!"

By means of the wonderful ether bridge created by the radio, the reports went from the command tank to the division command post. The division commander and his staff officers excitedly followed the route of

the patrol, which would complete the difficult work of the higher commands in a practical way. Every new location was received eagerly and
entered onto the map. Unknown burgs that suddenly became important.
The thoughts of the young comrades were flying kilometers ahead of their
actual location, which had to be wrested, meter-by-meter, on a dangerous,
difficult route. The route led down into the flood plains of the Sula, a
tributary of the Dnjepr. Water crossings needed to be forced; treacherous
routes mastered. Would the patrol be able to get over the bridge at Titschi?
An anxious question at the division staff. "As far as Luka at 1602 hours."
That meant that the natural obstacle was already behind the patrol.

The singing of an approaching engine. A solitary aircraft circled above
the extended column of the patrol. The tanks and riflemen were clearly
able to make out the *Balkenkreuz*.[2] A German reconnaissance aircraft that
wanted to bear witness to the great events from the air. It dove steeply to
greet the patrol. The messenger raced to the staff in the command post:
"Link-up of the two armor elements in five minutes!" The suspense rose
to its high point lightning fast. A short while earlier, contact had been lost
with the command vehicle of the patrol; the radio operators had strained
their ears in vain in the headphones. The minutes lapsed at a snail's pace;
they became a long quarter of an hour . . . then a half hour . . . finally
more than an hour. Aviators see things faster. Lubny was there for the
taking under him, but the tanks had to churn their way through steep
and narrow wooded defiles. They then arrived at a narrow tributary of
the Sula; off to the right, it spread out into a large lake. The bridge was
destroyed; not negotiable. But there were engineers on the other side.
The lead elements of an armored division from the southern group had
been reached! The city of Lubny could be seen in the background. A
handshake across the water, so to speak. Happy shouts back and forth.
Humorous questions and answers. The order had been carried out. The
radio message flew to the rear.

The clerk made the last entry on the map at the division headquarters:
"1820 hours." It was placed right next to the lake printed in blue. He
placed a happy face next to it. Then he entered bold letters on the special
map: "Link up *Heeresgruppe Mitte—Panzergruppe* with *Heeresgruppe Süd—*

---

2. Beamed cross. The standard recognition symbol for national identity on German vehicles. The aircraft is either a *Henschel Hs 126* or *Fiesler Fi 156 "Storch"*
(Stork).

Panzergruppe on 14 September 1941, 1820 hours." The *General* stepped quietly to the map table. The room was ghostly silent; you could hear individuals breath. It was a great moment in that campaign, perhaps in history . . . We were all happy to have experienced it.

The tanks forded at a suitable location to the far bank and rolled towards Lubny, where the sound of fighting could still be heard at the outskirts. The fighting vehicles of the two field army groups linked up. It was only then that the steely ring seemed to have been truly closed. In the midst of the hearty greetings and the happiness of the hour, the tankers almost forgot the dangers they had faced. The patrol had taken seven hours to cover fifty kilometers. The farther south they were, the more numerous the enemy columns approaching them. They had been fleeing Lubny and running almost straight into their weapons. More and more shot-up and burned-out vehicles lined the narrow route of the patrol through the enemy: Trucks with ammunition and rations, with engineer equipment and construction materials . . . artillery trains. The patrol itself suffered losses through engine failure. Vehicles had to be left behind, with the crews being distributed among the tanks. Almost all of the ammunition had been shot off, but they had done it, as they had always done heretofore. Lochwiza and Lubny—both names would remain in their memories.

Of course, an armored patrol alone does not close a large pocket like the ring of destruction east of Kiev in the greater Dnjepr bend. While the battalion fought its way through from Lochwiza to Lubny, a wedge from *Heeresgruppe Süd* pressed northward along the road to the east from the city of Mirgorod. It was the lead element of an armor division. Its objective was Lochwiza. Just as the arrows pushing south were entered on the map based on the situation reports, so to were the arrows heading up from down below. For them there was also a major obstacle in the form of a watercourse . . . once again, the Sula. The main focus of attention was the large bridge at Sentscha. It was needed for the quick closing of the trap. That succeeded as well! A radioed report arrived on Monday: "Sentscha Bridge taken at 0745 hours." The *General* made a few marks on the map and then the important words: "The pocket is now closed!" The remaining kilometers to Lochwiza were covered without difficulty. The men from Berlin and Brandenburg were already waiting for the men from Vienna.[3]

---

3. The "men from Vienna" were the *9. Panzer-Division.* Unfortunately, there is no text history of the division available to provide additional background material.

But the actual reception did not take place in the city proper. Instead, it was in the long village of Iskowzy-Ssentschanskije, where the commander of the advance guard still had his headquarters on that Monday. We were sitting in the schoolyard of the locality, under old, cozy trees, with a removed door serving as a table. In the small courtyard, it was swarming with khaki brown prisoners. There had been a small skirmish during the night. Columns that wanted to break out but which encountered our outposts everywhere. The usual picture of sneaking and running away. When it turned light, they surrendered. A lot of civilians among them . . . construction workers, who had been forced to dig fortifications. There were also a few female camp followers, with uniform blouses and skirts. They denied being civilians. They said they were soldiers, who could fire machine guns and revolvers. That meant they should march with the captured men . . . at the head of them. One woman in uniform, who had a strikingly attractive face, was interrogated separately. It was a doctor; her mother was a Baltic German. Then there was the second senior medical officer of the Soviet 21st Army, along with two of his staff physicians. One of them had personally seen Germany before.

Soon there were more prisoners in the village than German soldiers. None of them could comprehend how in a place 200 kilometers east of Kiev they could have fallen into the hands of the Germans, something they could have never imagined in their wildest dreams. Making big eyes, they then looked into the happy faces of the German soldiers, who were unable to conceal their great mood. They could not comprehend that we were celebrating our large "Pocket Fest" and that they belonged to the first catch. But one thing was clear to them: they no longer needed to construct and labor on the field fortifications, earthen bunkers and tank ditches, which we had found started but never completed.

Early in the morning, the *Kübelwagen* of the commander in chief of the *Panzergruppe* pulled in front of the command post. Accompanied by the division commander, he went to see the commander of the advance guard. On days like those, it goes without saying that *Generaloberst* Guderian was with his troops employed at the front, where they were marching, fighting and executing his bold will after a full night's work had entered lines and circles on the maps. The *Major* of the antitank battalion looked at the commander in chief expectantly; Guderian had been his teacher once as a *Major* and *Oberstleutnant*. The *Generaloberst* greeted the younger man heartily and with heartfelt appreciation, shaking his hand for a long time. "You've made me happy on two separate days!" Then, jokingly: "But then you attended a good school with me!" The commander in chief was in a great mood that day, just like everyone else. The warm sunshine made it even nicer.

The two events Guderian were referring to, those were the bold taking of the bridge at Lochwiza and at Romny, the important town ahead of Lochwiza on the avenue of advance. The last knots in the large net. It was a proud moment for the young *Major*. During the campaigns in Poland and France, he had had to work in the Army Armaments Office. This had been his first major front-line command. He had demonstrated that even "men with the red stripes"[4] know how to attack. But the contribution in the homeland was also of decisive importance. Good weapons create the prerequisites for victory, a fact that some easily forget. On the far side of the village green was the *Brummbär*,[5] a heavy self-propelled antitank gun. It was one of those impressive weapons, and its long thunder gun poked through the branch; it had seven white rings on it. Its tank rounds had torn apart the steel walls of seven tank monsters of the Bolsheviks. Like an antediluvian creature, it broke out of its concealed position and heaved its way thought he village on its powerful carriage. Soviet tanks had been reported at a nearby village.

Yes, the soldiers at the front know what thanks they owe to the homeland, especially the tirelessly working armaments industry worker. On days like those, the thoughts often drifted back to Germany, where the homeland would soon discover, how "the operations in the East were going according to plan." It was also an obvious topic of discussion that morning. But the Commander-in-Chief soon had to move on. He was headed for the riflemen in the forward trenches. He wanted to personally see how the track links were interconnected.

A short while later, a *Kübelwagen* hurried down the village road. It was the point rider of a tank division, a young *Leutnant* from Munich. He had reached the city of Lochwiza with his fighting vehicle and, together

---

4. This is a reference to the branch colors of the *Panzerjäger*, which the author mistakenly refers to as red. In fact, it was rose pink, since it was considered a part of the *Panzerwaffe*.

5. "Grizzly Bear." Most likely, this vehicle was the extremely rare *10.5-cm K18 auf Panzer Selbstfahrlafette IVa*. Only two of these vehicles that mounted a 10.5-cm high-velocity gun on a modified *Panzer IV* chassis were produced.

with a *Leutnant* of a rifle regiment, wanted to extend "greetings from the south" to our Division Commander. It was, so to speak, the counter visit from *Heeresgruppe Süd*. Soldiers like formalities. The mood was elevated even higher. *Generalleutnant* Model exclaimed, happily: "God knows, this is worthy of a nice round!" But where was that to be found? At that point, the commander of the advance guard came and, smiling, placed a bottle of champagne on the door table. He had dragged it around with him all through Russia, saving it for a special occasion. That was no time like the present! Even champagne flutes were produced! They were the pointed brass caps used to protect the sensitive igniters on Soviet heavy antiaircraft gun rounds. Just the right vessel for us! Rarely has a small sip of sparkling wine tasted so delicious as during that toast to victory in the cozy schoolyard at the command post in Iskowzy-Ssentschanskije.

We then talked about the perpetual topic of soldiers—the war. About the fighting that was behind us and what the future would bring. Also about the pocket that had just been sealed shut . . . two times over . . . three times over.

The battalion headed out on the village street. Riflemen followed. The battle in the east for the Dnjepr Bend was about to be completed!

THE DIVISIONAL HISTORY

The divisional history records the events of this chapter as follows:[6]

The *3. Panzer-Division* continued to close up in the area around Lochwiza on 15 September. *Generalleutnant* Model had his command post set up in a large private house in Lochwiza. That day, additional propaganda company personnel from *Heeresgruppe Mitte* arrived to capture the historical event—the linking up of the lead elements of two field armies—in words and pictures. Included among them were Bastanier, a cameraman who filmed for the weekly newsreel; Habedank, a photographer from the periodical *Die Wehrmacht*; and Fritz Lucke, a reported for the *Berliner Lokalanzeiger*. Lucke was the author of the only book that has appeared about the *3. Panzer-Division* to date: Panzerkeil im Osten. *Major Baron* von Behr, the commander of *Nachrichten-Abteilung 39*, was designated as the local area military administrative commander for Lochwiza, *Fürst* Mirski[7] was his translator. In addition to all of his military

6. *Traditionsverband*, 181.
7. Count.

and administrative duties, *Major* von Behr set up a restaurant, where the soldiers could eat for free. According to an extant menu, the following was already being served on 15 September: white cabbage soup with goulash and sliced tomatoes; stewed fruit and cake!

Major Frank screened the city to the southeast with his antitank elements and additional forces of his *Kampfgruppe*. He had established his command post in Iskowzy-Ssentschanskija. The antitank personnel and the riflemen had to be on their toes, sine Russian forces continuously tried to break in from the north and west. When one of those groups was caught, it contained the assistant senior medical officer of the (Soviet) 21st Army. Just before noon, dust clouds appeared to the east that were being churned up by tanks. The antitank elements were already taking aim when they white signal flares hissed skywards. The riflemen of the *1./ Schützen-Regiment 394* that were in position there got up and ran towards the approaching tanks. They were the lead vehicles of *Panzer-Regiment 33* of the Austrian *9. Panzer-Division* (*Generalleutnant Ritter*[8] von Hubicki). That division had taken the bridges over the Ssula at Ssentscha that morning at 0745 hours. When the young tank *Leutnant* reported to *Major* Frank, the pocket around Kiev was finally closed!

THE HISTORY OF *PANZER-REGIMENT 6*
The regimental history of *Panzer-Regiment 6* records the events of this chapter as follows:[9]

Towards noon, tanks approached the outposts of the division south of Lochwiza. Signal flares went up. It was the lead element of the *9. Panzer-Division, Panzer-Regiment 33*, which intended to seal off the pocket, coming from the south.

---

8. Knight.
9. Munzel, 94.

CHAPTER 5

Gold Stars and Torn Collar Tabs

BOLSHEVIK GENERALS IN THE WHIRLPOOL OF DEFEAT

This report is concerned with Bolshevik generals, dead and living, who went down with their field armies.

While writing, we frequently had to look out through the shattered windows of the carefully and meticulously maintained country home on the main street of the small Ukrainian city. An earth-brown flood of humanity had been streaming past for hours on end. The colors of clay and dirty gray, like the stirred-up waters of a reservoir after a storm and a glut of rain that were pouring through the cracks of a burst dam. We just looked up and down the straight improved road. No end and no beginning could be ascertained. Prisoners from the pocket battle of Kiev. Occasionally, you could hear the clopping of horse hooves. Those were the military police, who guided the unending armies of the defeated into the gigantic holding camp from high on their horses. Trying to imagine that sea of humanity in its entirety strained the limits of imagination.

Field armies, caught up in the torrents of a whirlpool and battered into pieces, which circle towards a certain demise, with no objective or goal in sight. They had been transformed into unarmed armies on a peaceful hike. All races and all age groups were represented—from child's faces to gray-bearded old men. They were tired from the long hunt and exhausted like driven game, which remains stationary with trembling flanks, awaiting its inescapable fate.

That was exactly what it was. They had attempted again and again to find a hole in the net that had suddenly been tossed over them. But the mesh was made out of steel and it held firm. And so they marched . . . day and night . . . back and forth; only hunger was their constant companion. Hopelessness crouched, grinning, on all roads.

The commanders, the political commissars, the *Politruks*, the special detachments of the NKVD—GPU—none of whom knew a way out themselves forced them at gunpoint to last desperate breakout attempts. Wherever they charged, they ran into the muzzles of German rifles and cannon. Panic broke out, completing the chaos. The defeated leadership no longer had any authority. The field armies, divisions, and regiments succumbed more and more to dissolution on a daily basis. The officers did the worst thing imaginable: they left their soldiers in the lurch. They only thought about their own safety. The enlisted were left to fend for themselves. They hope to fight their way through at someplace. They did it on foot; they had abandoned their vehicles. The only thing they knew for certain was that there were no roads leading out of the pocket. They believed they could sneak out unseen on hidden trails or by going cross country or through woods. The wild vortex sucked them all in.

Stalin's blood orders to the Red Army on 16 August left only two choices: break through or die. By name, the Moscow war criminal had listed commanders and commissars, who had laid down their arms in a hopeless situation and surrendered without dying. His hate was then directed against their guiltless families, their wives and their children. His slobber even vilified the dead, since he didn't know how many had fallen in the course of senseless resistance. According to Stalin, they were all nothing but cowards, deserters, and line crossers. Anyone was allowed to shoot them, as long as they found time in the race for their own lives.

Among those wandering around, who were only attempting to save their own skin at the last minute from the catastrophe, was a high-ranking Soviet field army commander, a Major General Popatow. Together with his artillery commander, who had no guns, he practically ran right into the arms of the advance guard of our division. He was taken prisoner like thousands of Red Army men, who had raised their hands in a timely fashion. He tried to flee one more time. But when the bullets whistled by and several 2-centimeter rounds from the antitank elements impacted,[1] he tossed himself to the ground and surrendered, along with the other officer. "I had no other choice," he said, shrugging his shoulders, to the first interpreter he identified himself to, "the Germans were everywhere." Certainly an important consideration—or so, at least, he had convinced himself. But would the slayer in Moscow believe him?

---

1. The division antitank battalion also had an antiaircraft battery among its elements.

The major general already knew the judgment that would condemn him, since he had spurned the final bullet. Stalin wanted his generals to die like Hannibal, who preferred suicide to captivity. This general was no Hannibal. We saw him again in the command post, where he waited to be interrogated by the German commander in chief. Captured generals generally placed the majority of the blame for their defeats, the destruction of their armies on themselves. That has always been the case in the history of war. It is understandable why the victor wants to look the vanquished in the eye. Why he wants to see the man, the "counterpart from the other side," who succumbed to German strategy and tactics. That's no cheap triumph over a beaten foe. It goes without saying that it was done with the tact of the German soldier, even if the defeated enemy was a Bolshevik general. It was a military gesture of politeness.

The Bolshevik general attempted to maintain his composure. You could see how he tried to keep a grip on himself. But the nervous puffing on a cigarette, the constant blowing of his nose . . . all that betrayed how agitated he was concerning the meeting. His khaki brown uniform could almost be called elegant. A vocal contrast to the many miserable creatures of his army, who filed past outside. On his collar tabs, he wore a small tank as the symbol of his branch above the two golden stars of his rank. An armor general, who was going to face a greater one, a master of the arm.

The Soviets had outdone the Germans with regard to young generals. The captured general was not yet forty. Alexander the Great was younger. But this general was no Alexander the Great. The *Generaloberst* asked him in amazement how he had come to be in such a responsible position as a troop leader. It was an impressive sight. The German commander in chief, with his youthful face under the gray hair and whose bright eyes inquiringly glanced at the black-haired, dark-skinned Bolshevik. He had greeted him with a slightly raised hand; the Soviet general did not know how he was to militarily greet him. He wanted to remain commander in chief and resorted to a slight bow.

His age? He had been in the Soviet-Japanese War[2] in a responsible position. He stated that with visible self-conviction.

As the commanding general of an armor corps, it went without saying that he had read the book of the German armored general. "So, was I

---

2. The Soviet-Japanese Border War of 1939, which remained undeclared and resulted in a humiliating defeat for the Japanese 6th Army. It also marked the first time that the future Soviet Marshall Zhukov would command forces in battle.

right with my theory?" He asked with a smile through the interpreter. The Bolshevik hesitated in answering the professional turn of the conversation. On our side, the generals are not asked, he finally said. They were only ordered. The major general did not reveal any secrets. No one had assumed he would. He was able to talk about the past, he said. That was part of history, after all. He said everything with the fatalism of the Russian, for whom even this defeat was inevitable fate.

It wasn't necessary for him to tell secrets either. The downfall of his army was recorded, step-by-step, in the situation reports that fell into our hands with all of their files and papers, when the headquarters of the Bolshevik Southwest Front scattered. The field army had been positioned northwest of the Ukrainian capital of Kiev, below the powerful natural obstacle of the pathless Pripet Marshes, intended as a threat to the flanks of *Heeresgruppe Süd.* In the face of the tidal wave of the raging German flood, it had had to pull back across the Dnjepr in the middle of August. It was then intended for it to hold the German offensive along the banks of the Dessna, the Dnjepr's large tributary. In his last situation report, the commander in chief of the Southwest Front, Colonel General Kirponos, reported reassuringly to the chief of staff of the Red Army and the Supreme Commander of the Field Army Group Southwest, his direct superior, Soviet Marshall Budjenny: "Army is pulling back and is engaging in stubborn fighting with the enemy, who is attempting to cut off the withdrawal route and take the crossings over the Dessna River."

On 8 and 9 September, the terrible knowledge became clear to the Bolshevik commanders in chief that they were also between the steel pincers. The general received orders to fight his way back. He left out who ordered him. It was also immaterial, whether it was Kirponos or Budjenny. His forces shattered into a thousand pieces against the wall that the lead armor elements of the two field army groups of *Generalfeldmarschall* von Bock and *Generalfeldmarschall* von Rundstedt had established between the Ukrainian cities of Lubny and Lochwiza. The grinding stones began to turn and, at the end, there was an iron law engraved once again in stone over the chaos in the pocket: *Mit Mann und Roß und Wagen hat sie der Herr geschlagen!*[3]

---

3. A line from a folk song about the defeat of Napoleon's armies in Russia. It has close parallels to biblical verse (Exodus) and the destruction of the Pharaoh's army. Literally: "God struck them down with their men and steeds and wagons."

The *Generaloberst* saluted when the Soviet general left. There was almost something forgiving and full of reconciliation in his hand movement for the so badly defeated opponent, in whom he only saw a soldier, who had been vanquished, like his superiors, Kirponos and Budjenny. Defeated by the better generals, the better soldiers and the better weapons.

But outside, the Soviet commander in chief became a Bolshevik again. That was when he was supposed to be photographed. He urgently requested the interpreter not to allow that to be done; he had to hold his hand in front of his face. He feared for the life of his wife and his children. He didn't need to say anything else. Fear spoke through every gesture, every expression . . . fear of the revenging arm of Stalin, who scrupulously sacrificed his generals for his crimes. The man who retaliated down to the youngest child! That was the most unsettling moment of that encounter. You could almost feel sorry for the man. But then you had to consider that he had also been a willing tool of Stalin, who had been prepared to bring the death and worldwide pestilence of Bolshevism to Germany, to women and to children. That man, the man who had risen to the top so quickly. Yes, victory was only possible when it was completely eliminated.

The victory at Kiev was one step towards that elimination. The portrait of destruction we had seen in some pockets was repeated here in large scale. Paths of death and perdition crossed through it. The fleeing men in the trap had tossed aside or abandoned everything that was a hindrance during the ceaseless pursuit: tanks, cannon, and rifles. There were antiaircraft batteries, from which barely a round had been fired. The dead were to be found in great numbers in the woods. They were the last victims of commanders and commissars driving the men against the iron ring. The attacking soldiers from Brandenburg also found officers under the mountains of bodies. Their rank could not be determined initially, but their striking uniforms made them stand out. The collar tabs had been ripped up, the stars missing. They had not been torn off, even though Stalin had condemned them as deserters. Four small holes were found in the tabs. At one time, there had been four stars there. A telegram, which the dead man held cramped in his hand, betrayed his name. It was the commander in chief of the Southwest Front, Colonel General Kirponos. There were two rounds to the head. He no longer had to be accountable to Stalin and tell him where his legions were. Next to him, the German soldiers found the body of the chief of staff of the 5th Army,

Major General Pissarewski, as the papers stated. His golden Soviet stars would also rust there under the moss and the leaves. He had not been as fortunate as his young commander in chief, Popatow.

The woods at Drukowschina, ten kilometers south of the city of Lochwiza, where the armored generals Guderian and von Kleist shook hands through their armored divisions, represented the dramatic conclusion to a Cannae, which reminded all of those woods at Tannenberg, where the Russian general Samsonow ended his life after the destruction of his Narew Army. No one could out run his fate. The destruction was complete and of scarcely imaginable proportions.

The endless stream continued marching along the road. The clay-gray waters from the pocket of Kiev continued to run off, hour-by-hour.

Comrades in fighting—and moving: our riflemen frequently climbed aboard the tanks to conduct an attack together. Once again, the infantry are seen riding *Panzer II's*, probably the most numerous tank in the German inventory in frontline service at the time.

Scrap iron was all that remained of these enemy tanks.

An antitank gun screens along a cut in the woods. This is the ubiquitous 3.7-cm *PaK 36.*

The rapid and deep advances of our armored division would not have been possible without timely supplies of fuel. Here reserve cans of fuel are filled up. Despite the rosy picture painted here, fuel supply was a constant headache for the forces in the field until the very end of the war.

The "milestones" of the Russian road network were measured in flats—and there was no shortage of them. This was probably a messenger for the tank regiment since *Panzer II's* and a *Panzer III* can be seen in the background.

The Soviet paradise in the Romny area. We would have preferred going to hell, since the roads leading there are at least known to be paved well.

Shot-up Soviet artillery position during the advance.

Soviet tanks that had been set ablaze bordered our "route." This is a BT-5, a light tank based on the Christie-type suspension. It was fast and maneuverable and armed with a 4.5-cm main gun. Its thin armor was its downfall.

Tossed-aside equipment marks the route of the Russians forced ever deeper into the pocket—they never had time to conduct a deliberate evacuation.

An important man in the front lines: the artillery forward observer.

Enemy positions are softened up by our heavy artillery in preparation for the attack. The *Sd.Kfz. 251* in front is an engineer version and would have belonged to the combat engineer battalion.

An antitank gun supports an attack by riflemen during the Pocket Battle of Kiev.

Panic at work: the aftermath of the Pocket Battle of Kiev.

One of the retreat routes in the Kiev Pocket. Enemy columns were overtaken by our armored division and completely destroyed.

The end of the major battle of attrition: the equipment of five Soviet field armies forms a single massive entanglement of debris.

Unparalleled victory: 665,000 prisoners from the Battle of Kiev march their way into German camps.

"Model Show": Following the victory at Kiev, our division continues its march in the direction of Moscow and new missions.

The advance guard moves rapidly. The tanks seen are the D model of the *Panzer IV*. It was the heaviest tank in service in the German Army at the time. Its short 7.5 cm main gun was no match for the 7.62 cm main gun of the T-34.

Tractors served as towing vehicles for heavy howitzers—but our tanks were faster.

The white-snowed rolling terrain stretches on endlessly. Riflemen jump down from their MTW's and move forward.

The latest edition of a military newspaper is distributed on the streets of Orel. Note the bewildering array of unit and formation signs behind the soldiers, as well as what appears to be a guard tower or observation post on the building in the background.

The mascot of our division, the Berlin bear, stands guard in front of the division headquarters.

Infantry watch observe the approach of the standard German light half-track—the *Sd.Kfz. 250*—which was frequently used as a command-and-control vehicle. In this case, it appears to belong to a motorized reconnaissance element.

Panzergrenadiere mount up at the conclusion of an operation. Their "ride" is an early version of the *Sd.Kfz. 251* medium half-track, the workhorse of German armored personnel carriers.

A *Panzer IV* and a *Panzer III* move down a village street in the Soviet Union. This image was probably taken about 1943, given certain uniform details and the fact that the *Panzer III* is a later model that was not in use during "Barbarossa."

An engineer *Sd.Kfz. 251* moves down the street in a larger Soviet city. The vehicle bears an identification flag to help keep it being engaged by friendly fire. The vehicle has racks for the mounting of rocket launchers on the sides.

A Horch staff car tows a 3.7-centimeter antitank gun through a morass of mud. By 1941, the light antitank gun was hopelessly obsolete, but it continued to be used until heavier, more effective antitank guns of larger calibers could be rushed to the front.

Another water obstacle negotiated. Staff cars and support vehicles cross a river on what appears to be a provisional bridge constructed by engineers.

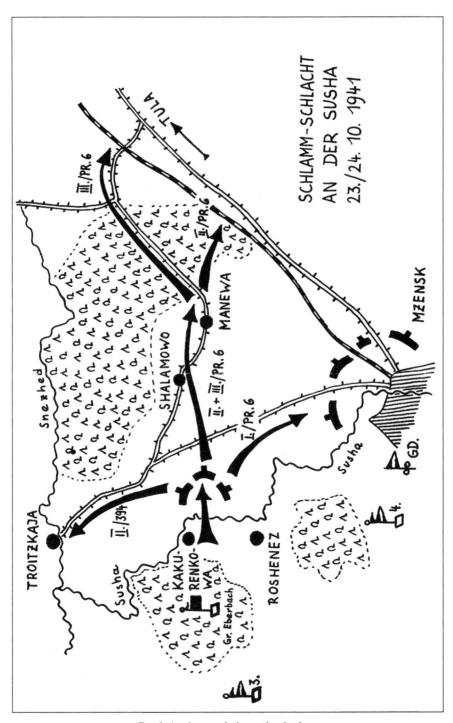

Battle in the mud along the Susha.
Legend: *Gr. Eberbach* = *Gruppe Eberbach* = Group Eberbach.

CHAPTER 6

The Great Tank Battle in the Autumn

FROM THE EDGE OF THE POCKET IN THE UKRAINE TO OREL

The tank destroyers of the advance guard rattled along on the broad, firm road that leads from Brjansk to Orel.[1]

The October day was inhospitably cold. The milky cloud cover was puffy and deep, like a poorly spanned stage sky. Watery mounds of snow were on the northern slopes of the terrain, rich in defiles. After a few sunny autumn days, an icy wind from the east suddenly whipped in the previous night and covered the landscape in a light blanket of snow. We were moving in the lead tank destroyer, shivering despite the heavy overcoats. We stared at the conveyor belt of a road through the optics for the machine gun at the radio operator's station. The voice of the company commander sounded through the headphones: "Eleven o'clock . . . Orel in sight!" Eleven o'clock—that was the direction. Off to the left in front of us, the towers, chimneys, and roofs of the large city of Orel grew larger out of the haze and cloudiness.

The first attack objective of our armor division had been reached. Once again, it had closed the final kilometers. They were the final kilometers of the main road, which ran around from Smolensk through Roslawl and Brjansk to Orel and then Moscow. A radius of 350 kilometers. The German armored wedges had advanced against that circle from different sides. As a result, a strategically important line was firmly in our hands on that October day.

A white signal flare arched skyward, then a second. We rolled through the combat outposts and into the city. The ringing echo sounded hollow

---

1. The original German is *Kanonenpanzer*, which means "cannon tank." These are most likely early versions of self-propelled antitank guns, which will be translated as "tank destroyers."

in the empty streets. Abandoned streetcars on their tracks. They were the first ones we had seen in Soviet Russia. From behind the windows of their homes, the inhabitants gazed at the tracks of the steel fighting vehicles, which were being passed by our motorcycle infantry.

The tanks disappeared on the high ground. For a few hours, we had an intact roof over our heads. The low structure at the edge of the city was impoverished and dilapidated, just as we had come to know all of the others in this country. But the family room was clean. The kindling in the oven radiated a pleasant warmth. Our involuntary hosts, an elderly couple, voluntarily placed a samovar on the table and offered us bread. Old, dark-brown bread. The only thing they had. We thanked them and unpacked our fresh army bread. But we were happy to have the hot tea. It quickly drove the cold from our limbs. While the tea bubbled just like home, we wrote down our accounts from the dairies of the last ten days. Ten days for an armored division in the large autumn battle: we were marching again! We were continuing to march!

From the summer, it had turned into fall. The German homeland, the entire world was still under the spellbinding impression of the overwhelming numbers coming from the *Führer* Headquarters, which soberly and factually recounted the unique military greatness of the battle of annihilation at Kiev, when the German Army lunged with a new and powerful blow of the sword.

The edge of the pocket in the Ukraine served as the staging area for a new attack to the northeast—back into the heart of the Soviet Union, central Russia. While Budjenny's field armies met their end in the pocket east of Kiev and while the entire headquarters of his Southwest Front, including its commander in chief, Colonel General Kirponos, was shot to bits offering hopeless resistance in the woods south of Lochwiza, the Soviet senior command had freshly called-up reserves charge the steely ring. Cavalry and rifle regiments, supported by tanks and bombers, attempted to blow open the chokehold, at a great cost in blood. The German armored corps had to fight on two lines for a while—interior and exterior. The hot spots of that difficult fighting, which extended over a length of 200 kilometers, were the localities of Nowogrod-Ssewersk,

Gluchow, Putiwl, Romny and Lochwiza. Those were the steel doors in the iron wall at which Moscow's reserve divisions were bled white, just as they had been previously.

During the last two days of September, the gates silently pivoted on their hinges. In the broad framework of the fall fighting, German armor corps moved out for a new assault. The tanks and guns, the vehicles of the riflemen, and the antitank and *Flak* elements of our division were rolling across the cobblestones of the rural Ukrainian community of Gluchow. That had been preceded by two days of rest. That meant two days of hard work on vehicles and engines, for the careful maintenance of weapons. In the end, it also meant washing clothes and mending socks. Those were two days of rest, where every minute was used to the utmost to get the divisions fully combat ready again.

Once again, there was a great mood prevailing along the long lines of vehicles and weapons, just as there was before every attack. But even the youngest riflemen felt that this German offensive before the complete onset of the Russian winter would once again demand the utmost and the complete commitment of every individual soldier. Proud and serious, imbued with the importance of the new mission—those were the clear words contained in the order-of-the-day of the commander in chief to his soldiers, whom he was leading into the fall battles.

Yes, the hardships would once again be significant. The soldiers only had to look at their boots, where the clay stuck in thick clumps. Or at the many puddles and pools of water, which the black earth was no longer able to swallow up. They knew what was ahead of them. But the fact that they would also have to work like dogs one more time was something that they knew only all too well.

It was to be a day of major fighting! That was always the case when the *Stukas* gave the signal to start the assault. Their gray silhouettes hung in a droning chorus under the low matt screen of the sky. The higher singing fighters danced around them. Just like at the Bug or along the Dnjepr, the squadrons attacked the field positions of the Bolsheviks, as well as the retreat routes on the far side of the small Klewonj River, which was the attack objective for the day, in waves. The terrain was broken up and rolling. The earth on the stubble fields and black-leaved potato fields was heavy with rain, clinging and goopy. The remnants of the Bolshevik rifle division, which had been rubbed out at Gluchow, was in position in the patches of woods on the high ground. The attacking German riflemen received bursts of machine-gun and small-arms fire. Rounds churned into the rubbery-soft ground with dull cracks. Black lumps of dreck sprayed around the ears of the assault soldiers; gray mists rose into the air. Smoke rounds! We saw that for the first time from the Bolsheviks.

The armored observation vehicle from the self-propelled artillery had pressed forward through the depression. The fire missions were radioed to the firing positions of the battery. The howitzers fired. The riflemen lay in concealed positions on the opposite slope and saw the red fiery balls jump over the crowns of the trees, followed by the black-gray lines of smoke. We had seen it so frequently before. But it was always a wonderful portrait of our strength, whenever we were cowering in a furrow in a field to be able to take one meter at a time under the protective cover of our artillery.

The *Stukas* were tireless. Yes, in the excitement of the fight, where hours shrink to minutes, we thought that their deep rumbling in the skies would never come to an end. They approached over and over again—as if on parade in their exacting formations. They then soared apart, circling and looking, only to dive like birds of prey on the woods on the horizon. Whenever they raced back to their home bases, flying low over us, their blows of destruction smoldered to the heavens for a long time.

The riflemen fought their way forward to the Klewonj, which snaked its way through the middle of small villages. They fought across marshy meadowlands, where a number of oxbows had been formed, either as lakes or ponds. The last remaining smoke rounds of the Bolsheviks had dissipated somewhere in the terrain. The machine-gun fire had stopped. Their resistance had been broken. When the assault detachments pressed into the villages, they had confirmed what they had feared after the last sound of explosions and a cloud of smoke from a detonation: All of the wooden bridges had been blown up. The terrain ahead of them was heavily mined, as expected. Engineer platoons were employed to clear them. The comrades with the black-piped insignia juggled with the dangerous yellowish-brown boxes as if they were harmless children's toys, while we kept ourselves at a respectful distance. It had become routine. The vehicles with the bridging equipment continued to roll into the village into the night.

✠

To the southeast of Gluchow on the Klewonj was the tiny village of Swarkoff. With its whitewashed houses and painted window frames, it differentiated itself on the outside from the rest of Russia. When the soldiers of our reconnaissance battalion worked there way forward there, they encountered the most unique enemy yet in a campaign that had no shortage of surprises. It was mine dogs that ran against them! Everyone knows the well-known joke about "pit dogs" which, in reality, are the small coal carts for underground work, with which the miner has duped the layman. This was dead serious. The mine dogs of Swarkoff were true four-legged creatures, which the devilish mind of a Bolshevik had attempted to train to run against German tanks with a demolition charge on its back!

The average German would initially shake his head. One comment should be allowed at the outset: The forward headquarters of the division didn't want to believe the report, either. It rang up the duty officer at an ungodly hour in his straw bed and asked him whether it was April Fool's Day all of a sudden. They could forgive the occasional soldier's joke, but this was an official report, after all.

The iniquitous report was true, word for word: All of a sudden, several dogs approached the lead vehicles on the narrow field path. A few meters out, they turned around and ran back with their tails wagging. They then came back. On their backs, they were carrying noticeable containers with carrying straps. It was a peculiar, suspicious occurrence; the soldiers could not put their fingers on it. The company commander decided to carry out his only option: the dogs were killed with submachine guns, carbines, and pistols. When the cadavers were searched—they were grey shepherd dogs and Dobermans—two demolition charges were in the containers. But the mines had not been armed, the lever had not been extended. Perhaps the dog handlers had not had the courage to arm them out of fear for their own lives; perhaps they had let the dogs run and sought their own safety. It was also possible that the animals had ripped loose themselves during the German artillery fire. We didn't know. The German soldiers provided the poor creatures with a last humane service: they buried the dogs, seven in all, along the side of the road. It was probably the strangest encounter they would ever experience. Too bad for the nice animals, the young *Leutnant* said. But he had no other choice.

Two dogs escaped and had to be running around somewhere. But they weren't captured. Instead, it was three dog handlers, who were cowering fearfully with their shepherd dogs, who didn't have any mines, under some trees. Their interrogation unfurled a tale of perfidious villainy, which only the bestial mind of a Jewish Bolshevik was possible:

There was no doubt: The Soviets believed they had found a weapon against the German tanks with their dressed-up dogs! They gave their dog units the highfalutin title of "destroyers." The prisoners had been drafted on 27 July at Wischnjaki, fifteen kilometers outside of Moscow. They were assigned to the 2nd Field Army Destroyer Detachment. Strength was around 235 men. Every man was issued a carbine and a dog. Two detachments were consolidated into a "Destroyer Battalion" of approximately 500 men.

The training started initially with tractors. The dogs were lured under the tractors with meat. In the next stage, the dogs were lured into crawling under a standing tractor from front to rear by holding out a piece of meat. The exercises lasted about five days. They were then repeated under a slowly moving tractor. In the course of the forty days of training, the tractor was replaced by a tank. To get the dogs used to the sounds of combat, firecrackers were tossed from the tank and carbines were fired with blank ammunition.

We could not hide a smile when we imagined the curious training efforts going on in the camp at Wischnjaki, where they were attempting to mortally wound the German armored force with such antics.

Towards the end of the training period, there were examinations. The rifleman squatted with his dog in a roadside ditch and released it about 100 meters in front of the slowly approaching tank. The destruction of the tank was supposed to take place by means of the demolition charge that had been attached to the dog's back. In the case of strong animals, it was up to 3.6 kilograms, a not inconsiderable amount. The explosion of the demolition charge was to be initiated by a wooden switch affixed atop the mine. When the dog was under the fighting vehicle, a jolt or contact would cause it to ignite.

Of course, the poor, starving pooches, who were only looking for a piece of meat under the tank, were to go up in the air as well. After "expenditure of the dog"—as it was referred to in the instructions given to the prisoners—the riflemen were to move back and be issued new dogs. Just try to actually imagine this scene on the battlefield: A company of German tank destroyers is moving along. The vehicle commanders observe the road and terrain attentively. Of course, they do not observe the fact that the "destroyers" are lurking in ambush for them in the roadside ditch. They boldly allow the lead tank to approach within 100 meters. All of a sudden, a pack of wild dogs runs towards the vehicles, at least one for every tank destroyer. Before they can comprehend what's going on, they can only hear the thunderclaps of the crashing explosions that tear appear the steel walls. In the background, however, the "destroyer riflemen" sneak away, grinning diabolically, in order to fetch more mine dogs.[2]

If it weren't such a base thing, it would almost be laughable. But there is nothing so dumb and tawdry, that it cannot be conjured up by a Bolshevik miscreant. But they had done their planning without taking into account the good soul of the dog, which wants to turn tail like any other animal while in front of a tank in combat. The mine dogs at Swarkoff proved it. The prisoners also confirmed it. Two of their three companies in the detachment were to be employed for the first time there along the Klewonj. Most of the dogs were not confident of their training; it was only in the rare case, if at all, that they crawled under the moving tank in the training camp. In addition, many of the dogs were fearful of the sounds of firing and took off whenever they heard the firecrackers. All types of dogs were used, which were involuntarily procured along the way. It was but one more sign of the desperate situation of the Soviets that they committed the dog companies in the hopeless fighting.

There were three nice examples of dogs that lay quietly at our feet and received each piece of bread with a wag of the tail. They had no idea what their "nice masters" had in store for them. We wanted to know which of the three was the most capable learner. A prisoner pointed to the middle shepherd, a light-gray male. He had crawled under the tank twice at the school. The general decided that he would be the one we took with us. If time permitted, we would conduct an experiment with him. We were eager to find out how it would turn out, even though we could imagine how it would go. In any event, we had a nice-looking division mascot.

---

2. Although plausible in theory, in actual battlefield situations the mine-dogs tended to run under the Russian tanks they had been trained with rather than those of the Germans.

The antitank elements of the reconnaissance battalion screened the village and the river line in a semicircle. The guards looked more for dogs that night than they did for Red Army men. But the night passed completely quietly. It was only in the village off to our right that there was still fighting. A Bolshevik reserve battalion attempted to cross the Klewonj again. It ran into our Brandenburg rifle regiment and suffered a bloody nose. The defeated remnants fled back, taking heavy losses in dead and leaving behind many prisoners.

On the morning of 1 October, the engineers placed their bridging equipment across the blown-up wooden bridge near the dilapidated water mill in the village of Studenok. Fighting vehicles, riflemen and antitank elements of the advance guard rolled across the Klewonj River. The "Berlin Bear" was marching.

After the morning dew had lifted and the new day dawned, the radio vehicle of the division commander moved forward. That was the routine, morning after morning. Ever since the radio operators had become the fastest messengers in the Armed Forces, most of the command posts had been orphaned. Conversations with the commanders on the ground, personal knowledge of the changing situation, personal contact with the fighting troops, taking a personal look at the supply situation— all that enabled the general to make fast decisions, render advise and provide assistance. That was especially necessary in the campaign in the East, where the terrain was not stingy with surprises and unimaginable obstacles. Especially if it had rained for several days.

There was a road from the Ukrainian town of Gluchow to Ssewsk, the first city in Central Russian on the other side of the frontier. The road was printed in red on the map; based on that, it had to be a road of the first order. But it was only that on paper. It became the avenue of advance for our sister division,[3] which was to jab through the Bolshevik front like a steel finger with its armor wedge. It was the southern flank of the Supreme Commander of the West Front, that is, Soviet Marshall Timoshenko, that we intended to break through. Those were the field armies of his so-called Brjansk Front.

The mission of our armor division was to screen the advance along its right flank and interdict counterattacks. For that reason, our march routes were not to be found on any large-scale maps. They went across field paths

_____

3. *4. Panzer-Division.*

and secondary roads from village to village, across fields and pastures, through woods and heath—all of which scarcely offered a difference.

From the very first day of the offensive, the roads were our enemy. In June and July, we churned through knee-deep sand. In August and September, the vehicles were occasionally stuck up to the axles in muck and mush. That first day of October presented us with another cross-country journey, which was full to the brim with natural obstacles.

The black earth was fruitful, and the countryside in autumn had a melancholy beauty. The yellow of the large stubble fields stretching across hill and valley and broken up by deep defiles mixed with the dark green of the meadows and the blue strips of forest to form a landscape that reminded us of our Harz lowlands. But the black earth had been softened and was as treacherous as a moor.

The young comrades of the *Reich* Labor Service[4] worked along the railway embankment beyond Gluchow in order to make the narrow roadway negotiable. The next generation of soldiers were eager helpers in every respect for the "old warriors." They had stacked their weapons in impressive pyramids, which could pass muster with any first sergeant.

The hard work started in the bottomland etched with the tracks of wheels in front of the first rise. A heavily laden engineer vehicle blocked the approach and forced the entire snake line of vehicles to halt. Its wheels were powerless whetstones that could find no grip in the smooth muck. The *General* had to be everywhere that day to help out with fatherly advice or a powerful thunderclap—in the end, it was all the same, wasn't it? He had his radio vehicle serve as a prime mover to tow a few trucks up the slope: "First gear . . . it'll make it!" While the radio operators received the reports from the neighboring division, which was moving rapidly on the road, of course, we bucked around with a field kitchen in tow so that the riflemen would get a gulp of hot coffee in a timely manner.

A few kilometers further on, everyone was bogged down in the muck. Trees were felled. "Get some wire netting here!" The *General* as an engineer. Birch branches and thick spruce limbs on top! Fortunately, wood was available in sufficient quantities everywhere. And even if we had

---

4. The *Reichsarbeitsdienst* was a paramilitary organization designed to reduce unemployment in the prewar years and, ultimately, prepare young Germans for the military, and a tour of duty—usually a year—was compulsory for all males prior to being eligible for the draft. As the war progressed, many RAD formations actually saw combat duty.

to cut down the entire forest—we would get through! As we always had up to that point. The howitzers had to get forward. The third prime mover to pass succeeded in pressing our entire efforts into the muck. Continue to build—the bridging column had to get through. The fuel trucks for the tanks were waiting. "Lend a hand, comrade! Pitch in! Right now!" The cautious ones had already put on snow chains.

We moved forward. It was the feverish picture of an advance; everyone pressed forward impatiently. A ceaseless pursuit of the enemy led to his destruction. That was a simple, but difficult law of war. The *Stukas* had to proxy for us initially. That morning, they once again placed their bomb loads on the retreat routes of the Bolsheviks. Then head back, flying low over us. Three squadrons. The squadron leaders wagged their wings in greeting, as if they wanted to report: No worries . . . we worked over everything thoroughly for you one more time!

The gray ribbon rolled again. Here's one of the reasons: Whenever the red collar tabs of a general appear, the work effort doubles. The division commander's betrayed it with a satisfied smile. "Those are the small things,"[5] he said, open to several interpretations.

The small things—those are the surprises that the umpires insert in planning exercises or maneuvers in order to test presence of mind and decision-making prowess. Their vivid imagination has been outdone in ways unimaginable in this campaign. And that was just in the approach to the village of Studenok, where the engineers were supposed to build a bridge over the Klewonj River!

This campaign in the East is not being won by the combat branches alone. Everyone is contributing an important part in winning it. The convoy drivers, who have to tirelessly bring up ammunition, fuel and rations and cover those terrible roads three and four times...the drivers of the field messes, who make it a point of pride to follow the companies and the batteries with their smoking "barrels."[6] A canteen full of hot tea or a steaming ladle of lentil soup at the right moment—that does a lot to make good for all of the hardships.

---

5. In this context, a more accurate translation for *Einlagen* would be "perks," but since the word can be interpreted differently and is used again in the next paragraph, it has been translated as given here.
6. A reference to the smoking chimney of the *Gulaschkanone*, the two-wheeled field oven that was towed by a prime mover or driven by a team of horses.

"Is the mess here . . . can the vehicles be refueled . . . can the tanks upload?"

"*Jawohl, Herr Hauptmann!*"

But that's not something that just happens by itself. It is a part of the quiet heroism of this war.

Also not to be forgotten are the non-stop, hard-working maintenance companies and the numerous maintenance contact teams and sections, which frequently get engines and vehicles running again, using only the simplest of means. They change pistons at the edge of the road, if that's what called for. It goes without saying that the wear and tear on the vehicles along those types of roads was no small matter. Victory is the sum total of the self-sacrifice and constant work of all soldiers. That was especially true for the fall campaigning in the East.

The Bolsheviks blew up all the bridges behind them. That meant heard work once again for the engineers, who had already erected several kilometers of bridge on our advance route. The Klewonj made a deep cut at Studenok, where it flowed in the village lake at the water mill. There had been two wooden bridges over one another; their beams were jumbled together in a crazy manner. But the bridging equipment was placed over it within an hour. There were no wasted motions. The engineer officer reported it would be ready for crossing in ten minutes. With encouragement from comrades, the final iron rods to hold the ramp in place were driven into the rocky earth with mighty hammer blows. Every strike was true; what had been learned was learned well. Humor and a good mood—that was the best supplemental ration for a soldier. No one could take that away from us, that was for sure!

The fighting vehicles rolled on. They were fully loaded with the assault detachments of the rifle elements. They had had to wait, since even the tanks would have bottomed out on the only available detour. Their objective was the next village, which was being placed under a hail of bombs from *Stukas. Schützenpanzerwagen*[7] and self-propelled antitank guns of the advance guard followed. The howitzers providing direct support rumbled along next. It was a strong lead element, which could knock out any resistance. But it appeared the enemy had fled again after the *Stuka*

---

7. This is the first time in the text that the author makes clear that he is talking about armored personnel carriers, as opposed to personnel carriers, which could also include trucks.

attack. That included the tanks, which the aerial observers had reported earlier.

Nothing distinguishes the difficulty of the terrain as the orders that were issued that morning. A patrol was dispatched in a personnel carrier. But its mission was not to search for the enemy. Instead, it was to look for possible detours. A rifle regiment was going to the field to fight the enemy "road." It received orders to fix the routes. For the time being, shovels and mattocks replaced carbines and machine guns. After all, an armor division consists primarily of wheeled vehicles. Getting them forward in time assures the advance of the entire division.

The advance route was well marked. That came from the bomb craters left by the *Stukas* that accompanied us to the next village, Kutschenowka. As expected, the Bolsheviks had fled head over heels. The last remaining tank was caught along the wall of the former rural estate. After the second round, it exploded. The turret flew off. The last round in the barrel only left a hole in the brittle wall. Once again, the *Stukas* had done a great job. Kutschenowka was also located on a tranquil lake, with ducks and geese peacefully swimming about. There was a short commander's conference along its banks. We had to continue along the original route; there were no usable detours. As we moved through the estate and past the grain tower of the collective farm, an uncontrolled herd of horses galloped through the column of tanks. We took a moment to enjoy the long-legged and still somewhat wobbly foals, before the tracks started moving again. Rifle companies screened in the neighboring villages to the flanks. Groups of prisoners were escorted to the rear to the collection points.

We crossed through new villages; names were spelled on the maps and then promptly forgotten. Only the *Stuka* craters were the permanent milestones. The "small servings" were forced. At that point, we were in the middle of the so-called central Russian black-earth zone. The villages marked the border. The wooden houses were much more impoverished than those in the Ukraine.

The walls weather-beaten. The straw roofs poorly thatched and worn. The locals wear ragged footgear, their legs wrapped in cloth rags. In the roadside ditch were more than a hundred pitiful creatures, who had given up every attempt to flee: Agricultural workers, whom the Soviets had driven together for the construction of roads and fortifications. They rolled their own cigarettes out of newspaper and an indefinable plant leaf. For anyone else, it would rip your lungs apart. But all of those people savaged by the Soviets had a common quality: They were happy that the Germans had shown up. We've been expecting you for a long time, they told the interpreter. Then you should have built better roads, he grumbled.

That evening the report arrived that our neighboring division had taken the city of Ssewsk. We stopped on some high ground. It was like a hill for generals—it permitted observation over the countryside for miles on end. The outposts went into post, just as they did every night. The soldiers fetched the padding for their foxholes from the haystacks. The nights were already very cold.

The division headquarters bivouacked in the village before it. The last prisoners were interrogated. And what kind of a parade of the Soviet Union did we see filing past! This time, an alert-looking youth of nineteen years stood out. It turned out that he had been one of the engineers, who had emplaced mines along the Klewonj. He stared attentively at the parade of tanks and guns rolling past and said to the interpreter: "The *Politruk* had told us that you bound the soldiers with chains to the guns and machine guns." He had also believed it, although he was laughing at himself at that point. Take a closer look, the interpreter told him ironically. It was only during the march that the chains were removed! After that, the cannoneers were chained back up again! As we started to take pictures of that rare exemplary specimen, the belles of the village then showed up in order to get their pictures taken as well. But only down to the skirt! Thank God they were aware of what type of crazy rags they had wrapped around their legs.

All that just to provide a few small vignettes on the periphery of the war in order to round out the picture.

We remembered a scene to the south of Lochwiza, where officers of the Southwest Headquarters, who had no desire to meet their end in the woods near the village of Drukowschina, were taken prisoner. One of them was a commissar, a big "Senior *Politruk*." The riflemen naturally shouted out what a big catch they had made. The comrade realized he was causing quite a stir. He addressed the interpreter, who replied, casually: "The activities of the commissars have slowly made the rounds among our forces . . . for example, you *Politruks* and commanders have an itchy trigger finger on your pistols to force your people to fight."

For someone who was a leading Bolshevik in captivity, the answer that came out of his mouth was completely surprising: "Well then, that's what your officers do as well!" Even the interpreter, who had already heard just about everything imaginable, was speechless for a moment. But the gentleman was completely serious—you could see it in him. So, those were our enemies! They even believed their criminal lies. They would suffocate on them. What kind of unimaginable fruit had this Bolshevism cultivated?

The next day, the heavens had descended to the earth. Thick, white fog. An hour later, the sun broke through for the first time. But it could not magically transform the land into being dry. We had to advance along the route of the neighboring division to get to Ssewsk faster. It is the advantage of a motorized division in that it is highly mobile. We would be back on the old road in a few hours. The main thing—we were moving forward. How we did it, we didn't care.

The prisoners that we took with us ever since the Ukrainian village of Swarkoff were the rifleman and the dog from the 2nd Army Destroyer Detachment from Wischnjaki. The prisoner, who was forced to move in our steely band, was living a fairy tale. Just the fact that he was eating on a regular basis seemed like a miracle to him. As long as that was kept up, he was happy. The gray male shepherd was one of the mine dogs that had been trained to crawl under German tanks with a demolition charge in order to send it skyward. His name was not something that made sense like Ivan or Stalin the Terrible, but simply Rex. He received the name at the training camp in Wischnjaki. Perhaps it was intended to be a quiet honor for King George. The dog handler was unable to fathom what Rex meant. He didn't even know what "king" meant. But Rex had certainly won his way into the hearts of the soldiers who took care of him. He immediately came when called. He was always hungry.

The armored division integrated itself into the advance route of the neighboring division. That gave us a half hour's time to do the planned experiment with Rex. We wanted to test whether he would actually run up to a German tank and perhaps even crawl under it. Every one wanted to see that unique demonstration. We had drilled into the prisoner, who had trained the dog, that he was to do everything the way he had learned it in the camp. He said he would and asserted that Rex had crawled under a slowly moving tank twice. He was all agitated with what he had to do, as if six *Politruks* were breathing down his neck.

The sudden appearance of the autumn sun was warm, a gift from heaven after the rainy, wet days. The "destroyer rifleman" squatted in the roadside ditch with the shepherd dog, just as he had learned and in accordance with the doctrinal manual. The road was empty! Rex and the eight-wheeled armored car were to carry out their duel undisturbed. We hid behind some concealment in order to be able to photograph the unusual presentation,

The armored car rolled slowly closer. The dog had all of the advantages. No horrible pyrotechnics were being tossed; nobody was firing practice rounds into the air. The Bolshevik released the choke chain. At that point, the distance was about the prescribed 100 meters.

"Go!" The dog jumped right out into the middle of the road and moved towards the armored car! The radio operators were already wide eyed. Would he actually crawl under it? But then he only ran to within ten meters of it. Then he came under the spell of the black monster. As dogs do, he tucked his tail between his legs and ran back at a full gallop. His master sent him out again, only to get the same result, of course. Rex was satisfied with a vicious bark at a respectful distance. During the third attempt, he immediately ran across a field.

The Bolshevik was very disappointed. Like a breeder who wants to sell a trained purebred at a hefty price but only takes a fall during the demonstration. Completely nonplussed, he raised two fingers in the air. The dog had crawled under a tank twice. Perhaps after a piece of *Wurst*— but that was more than was available in military rations.

Perhaps he needed to have the shepherd dog crawl under a stationary tank and repeat the first five days of training. But Rex was too ornery, or perhaps too clever—take your pick. The Bolshevik beckoned and pulled and pushed, but the dog whimpered terribly and could not even be forced to crawl under that terrible steel crate by means of a collar. We indicated he could stop. Everyone around us was laughing, staff officers and soldiers. That's basically how we thought the experiment would turn out. You can train a good dog with an individual, but to have him go out against a heaving steel colossus that was approaching was to overestimate the bravery of a dog and underestimate its cleverness. Only someone like a Bolshevik could have come up with that; they were always wide of the mark. In the end, that was not of decisive importance. For us, it was really a matter of establishing once again the limitless baseness that was behind those "destroyer detachments."

The dog handler became another digit in the millions of prisoners. Rex was allowed to ride along as the division mascot. He was a loyal pooch. It was only around the armored vehicles that he cut a wide circle…

We integrated ourselves into the march column of our armored division.

The red line that went from Gluchow to Ssewsk on the 1:300,000 map led across the usual worn-out sandy roads. Why would it be any different that time? But with the exception of a few bridge bottlenecks, it was broad and firm. After the last few cross-country trips, it looked like an *Autobahn* to us. Bomb craters marked the route at regular intervals. Once again, the *Stukas* had been guides in this sector as well.

It was nice that on that 3 October, the red fireball of the warming autumn sun climbed above the white clouds. Even the war had put on a friendlier face.

The tank regiment had established its command post for a short while next to the road in front of a windmill with idle arms. The city of Ssewsk was in front of us with a few light-colored houses and high onion-domed towers. The neighboring division had already moved through it. Our mission was to protect its back and flanks. To the left of us, another armored division was pushing its way forward.

At that moment, a few clouds climbed high from explosions around the outskirts of the city. That meant Bolshevik bombers. But nothing could be seen of the machines. Whenever the Soviets showed up in broad daylight, they dropped bombs from such high altitudes that they could barely be made out with the naked eye, not to mention you couldn't hear their engines. You then heard the bombs rushing, hissing and hurtling down from the high heavens. But it was an infrequent occurrence.

Far in the distance, a small cloud floated down to earth, as if it were composed of thousands of flapping white birds. Soviet leaflets. The wind carried them somewhere out into the countryside. We never did find one of those scraps of paper, but it didn't take much to imagine what was in there. Without a doubt, the worst weapon the Bolsheviks employed.

By contrast, our *Stukas* could be heard a lot better. They were roaring in, making a victory run low over our windmill and escorted by our Messerschmitts. It was two *Stuka* squadrons. They were flying towards one another right in front of our eyes, only to then fly above and below one another, as if it were child's play. A nice spectacle by the gray birds. They showed the black tankers that they dominated the skies like hawks. We watched them disappear into the horizon.

Perhaps they were hunting Bolshevik tanks. That was also the main mission of our armored regiment, which was approaching along the road. The regimental commander issued his orders to the commander of the 3rd Battalion. The commander of the lead company, who was summoned over the radio, would have to be appearing shortly.

The division headquarters had been alerted early that morning. It was said that Bolshevik tanks had been seen in a neighboring village. Fighting vehicles and antitank elements of the screening force positioned themselves in expectation. The radio armored car checked its 2-centimeter cannon and machine guns and rolled forward to the next fork in the road. But we waited and searched in vain. Only a few *panje* carts from a regiment's scattered trains were snapped up; they had been sauntering through the area, completely unaware of the over-all situation. The usual scenes you see when a "front" has been overrun and broken through. During their odyssey, the prisoners believed they had seen tanks stuck in some marsh somewhere. They thought there were around twenty of them. There had also been a gun and tractor there. Of course, they didn't know where, the one believable part of their story. Perhaps they had run out of oil. Without fuel, even the best of tanks doesn't accomplish much . . . We had frequently found some like that along the way.

The reports had arrived. Thirty to thirty-five enemy tanks were said to be wandering around out there somewhere. Observation posts in a tower in the city of Ssewsk saw those tanks heading north in the vicinity of the village of Gapanowo. That could mean a temporary endangerment of the supply lines. The regiment received the mission to find and destroy the Soviet tanks.

The march serials of the division had to halt. The tanks moved past them. The led company arrived. The maps were spread out on the hoods of the staff cars of the commanders. The commanders of the howitzer battalion and the antitank battalion reported in. The prospects of a tank engagement shot through the ranks like an electric spark.

The lead company rattled on. A large combat patrol was directed to sneak through the terrain. But the greatest of caution was necessary. The area was large, broken up with deep defiles and full of marsh and quagmire.

Everyone was to report every half hour to the Battalion Commander. We wished the young *Leutnant* good hunting. And that's what we wished for all of us.

"Panzer marsch!" The commander moved to the head of the column with his *Kübelwagen.* We rolled towards Ssewsk at twenty kilometers an hour. It was only a small likeness of an armor avenue of approach. The wrecks of individual trucks edged the road. The Soviets no longer had so many spoils of war to lose as they did during the first few weeks. The construction battalions that had been pressed into fortification work at the edge of the city had labored in vain on the broad tank ditch. In their hurried flight, they did not have any time to blow up the road. A water-filled tank trap does damn little by itself. Two medium tanks, which had been employed to defend there, were shot up and burned out along the route.

The city showed few traces of the previous fighting. The long wooden bridge was also intact—that's how quickly and surprisingly the advance came. The area beyond the bridge represented our extended "hunting preserve." The earth was broken up with deep defiles in places; chasms with steep banks encroaching on the road. The village locals had fled into some of them with bag and baggage, sheep and goats. They would be able to return to their cottages in the morning. The war was racing past them there with gigantic steps.

No matter how hard the tank commanders searched the terrain through their binoculars, no hidden tank turret allowed itself to be discovered. The localities were empty, including the village where enemy vehicles had been sighted earlier that morning. The radio reports from the lead company and the patrol came in at regular intervals to the command vehicle of the commander. Our hopes began to sink.

In the next village was the command post of a rifle battalion. A short halt there and greeting of the commanders. They had already had a few engagements fought together behind them. The entire division had become a large family over the last few weeks and months. Yes, it was true that a big Soviet tank had showed up on the opposite ridgeline early that morning, but it had disappeared again. The *Major* had put the *Flak* on it, but it still had not returned from the hunt. Perhaps there were still prospects for a good catch . . . a couple of heartfelt questions concerning the state of the convalescence of our armored commander . . . a quick couple of fare-thee-wells . . . then we rolled on again.

The commander of the 3rd Battalion, *Hauptmann* Schneider-Kostalski, a Knight's Cross recipient, had his right arm in a sling. Antitank-gun shrapnel in the hand. He walked around without wearing a cap. A grazing wound had placed a royal scratch on his forehead. That was a recent souvenir from the woods at Drukowschina, south of Lochwiza, where the headquarters of the Bolshevik Southwest Front was wiped out in a hail of German artillery fire. The tanks were unable to penetrate into the deep defile in the thick woods. When the *Hauptmann* approached the wood-line on foot along with a few soldiers, the surviving Soviet officers fired from pointblank range. The bullet went through the oak wreath around the cockade of the field cap. "With this Austrian skull," the commander laughed, "I can put up with a lot." He had served earlier on in one of the Austrian tank companies.[8] After the *Anschluß*, he was transferred to the Brandenburg tank regiment. That's a terrific combination, he said. Humor and a natural wit, an even temperament and a good heart—that equaled good soldiers.

The field cap, which was dangling from the windshield as a trophy, still had two previous holes in it. A French bullet had passed through the top and a piece of British antitank-gun shrapnel had found a home there. Whoever was looking for the 3rd Battalion only had to keep an eye out for a completely perforated command pennant, whose tin backing had been turned into a sieve by shrapnel. Probably not necessary to explain that the front side of the command tank was also covered with scars. But the Bolshevik round had slammed into the spare track links in front of the turret, which then served to double the armor.

But we had no hunter's luck that day. The powerful column of fighting vehicles, howitzers and antitank elements had been rolling along for hours without getting even one of those yellowish green monsters in front of the muzzle. We talked about the first week of the campaign, when the battalion was the armored wedge of the division and the corps. During the victory march from the Bug to the Beresina, it had knocked out a total of sixty-four tanks, sixty-five cannon, and twelve antitank guns. On this day, we only saw the many trucks of a munitions convoy, which had been

---

8. The author is referring to his service in the Austrian *Bundesheer*, prior to its annexation into Germany in 1937. The pre-*Anschluß* Austrian Army had a tank battalion and several motorized battalions—all of which were eventually incorporated into formations of the German Army.

destroyed while fleeing Ssewsk by our sister division, which had broken through. Large crates with silvery glittering, almost meter-long rounds with wing nuts. Perhaps they were the new Soviet rockets for the launchers . . . perhaps some sort of aerial bomb.[9] We could not determine while moving past them. Then there was a column of almost new tractors, some of which had trailers. All along one long village road were field cannon, new and with rubber-tired wheels. Based on Bolshevik organization, almost the entire weaponry of an artillery regiment. The bomb craters that were as deep as a house showed who had found their victims there with uncanny precision.

The *Hauptmann* had worn the Knight's Cross ever since the Beresina. But there were laurels to be won for us that day. The report came from the regiment that the hunt was over. The "tanks" had been found! But they were no tanks at all. We had already basically guessed the solution to the puzzle: A large column of tractors, which used up its last remaining fuel while driving around aimlessly, in order to find a place to sneak out in an area where barriers and obstacles had long since been emplaced. The patrol reintegrated with its company. One thing had been determined: The hay barns and outbuildings that were seen in the barren fields were not always as harmless as they appeared to be. When the *Leutnant* wanted to climb up on one of the hay piles during his stalking trip, he discovered a camouflaged column of trucks that had run out of fuel just in time to be discovered by us. All of them were captured; they had hoped to get away behind the penetrated front. Sooner or later.

Everything that's being reported here is but small potatoes within the over-all scheme of things—we all agree on that. But that's what makes up the daily activities of a soldier! That, which we understand under the collective term of the everyday fulfilling one's duty. Night after night, the outposts are at their machine guns and antitank guns, wet from the dew or the rain, or as was then the case, frost or the first snows, in every type of wind and weather, without having to experience anything other than an icy fall wind or a romantic moon, the latter of which is rarely the case. The soldier has to be able to wait for weeks on end for that decisive moment— perhaps the decisive moment of his life—to be armed and ready. That's

---

9. Almost certainly, these were rockets for the Soviet multiple rocket launchers called "Stalin organs" by the Germans.

what it's all about. That's why the many small things out there are so important. They help contribute to the great victory!

✠

The motorcycle battalion advanced with the tanks. Kilometer after kilometer . . . after reaching the 2,000th one we would fire a celebratory round! We already had an idea where that might be. It had become afternoon. For the first time since that morning, a Bolshevik bomber squadron allowed itself to be seen, this time, with four Ratas as escort. They flew past us. The bombs fell far out to the front; they left behind large fires. One more impoverished village would have a few less weathered wooden shacks. Soviet aircraft and tanks were growing fewer and farther in between; we experienced the sinking curve on a daily level. Of course, there were still enough to eliminate in that country, where a criminal class of men without scruples raised militarism to an idol!

All of a sudden, the road had asphalt. Factory facilities and large outbuildings. Rows of trucks were parked in front of them. We had reached the important Smolensk–Kharkov rail line at the station in Komaritschi. A large portion of the embankment had been blown away. There was still fighting for it going on. As a platoon of motorcycle infantry advanced, it encountered a Soviet patrol, which had been brought forward from the other side on trucks. In a short, sharp fight, the Bolsheviks were beaten and scattered. A portion of them was taken prisoner. One truck was able to flee. Unfortunately, the *Leutnant* with the motorcycle infantry was wounded.

The platoon went into position along the gravel of the embankment. The motorcycle infantry screened the broken terrain of the railway station outside the locality with machine guns and carbines. The fighting vehicles would relieve them. It was said that two Bolshevik regiments had unloaded twenty-five kilometers farther north of the railway line. The prisoners had stated that. Perhaps it had been a *Politruk* fairy tale to pour some courage into the patrol. If it were really true, then so much the better. The regiments would march right into the arms of the neighboring division to the left.

A platoon of tank destroyers rattled and droned into the dead locality. Perhaps a couple of the fleeing Bolsheviks had hidden themselves there.

But there were only a few miserable creatures flitting around the houses. Probably those miserable hyenas, who exploited the few minutes when the speck on the ground was still being contested and no-man's-land to plunder it. A powerful double blow shook the air. A gigantic mushroom cloud climbed skyward above the railway line. The high-shooting flames indicated the Bolsheviks had set off an ammunition depot that had been prepared for demolition. Probably the work of the patrol that had been surprised.

All of the fighting vehicles and howitzers of the advance guard had closed on the locality. Initially, they spread out in the broad terrain. The railway line had been the day's objective. The field kitchens and fuel trucks arrived punctually. Tanks and tummies were filled. Hot tea and rice with beef chunks—a feast for the gods after the morning bread with honey. In the blink of an eye, the fuel trucks were empty. Tanks have a thirst reminiscent of Störtebeker![10]

We sat next to one another in the roadside ditch and spooned down our soup with relish. Then our gaze settled upon a couple of white pieces of paper. The small radio operator from the platoon leader's vehicle noticed them first. They were some of the Soviet leaflets that had been printed for us to undermine our morale. Anyone was free to read them who felt like laughing his guts out. We hadn't had that much fun for a quarter of an hour in a long time.

The scrap of paper was entitled: "Announcement of the Information Office of the Soviet Union for 22 August 1941." Apparently, nothing more had occurred to the pulp writers in Moscow since that date, since the paper showed that it could only have been dropped on today's date. It would have been hard to top that strange spawn of stupidity. To our amusement, we read that all of us had long since been wiped out—at least three weeks before the August date of the publication. Our armored division right at the front; in addition, our sister division, which was breaking apart the Brjansk Front. Of course, that also applied to the division to our left and many others. There was "nothing left by numbers." Yes, indeed, the entire German Army practically ceased to exist, while Soviet Russia was only missing 110,000 men, presumably prisoners. Each one of us had personally seen more than that back then. Only a hopeless

---

10. Klaus Störtebeker was a privateer of the fourteenth century who was alleged to have been able to drink four liters of beer in a single gulp.

madman could come up with the crazy idea of immediately killing his own lie through ludicrousness.

Suddenly, the word went around that the *Führer* was speaking that night. One man passed it on to the next. The command and radio vehicles had it easy; they simply had to put on their headphones. The rest of us had to press around a receiver like grapes, so that not a single word was lost. At that point, we heard that the other field armies had moved out starting yesterday evening. We tried to imagine the huge quantities of spoils-of-war in terms of prisoners, aircraft, tanks and guns. We thought about the man, who clearly and soberly saw that danger grow and who drew the sword at the right moment to save Germany and Europe. The man, who bore the heavy burden of responsibility on his shoulders.

We only needed to march! There was a lot to be talked about that evening. We saw where this road was leading us. Our comrades were marching everywhere, doing what the law demanded. The law—that was our homeland of Germany!

The moon was radiant and had turned full. The attack time was the usual one.

Fire lit up the horizon in red. The guards at the tanks, the guns and the machine guns stared into the night.

Tomorrow we continue. To victory!

THE DIVISIONAL HISTORY

The divisional history records the events of this chapter as follows:[11]

On 26 September 1941, *Heeresgruppe Mitte* issued an operations plan for the continuation of the offensive. Its contents, inasmuch as they regarded the forces of *Panzergruppe 2*, contained the following:

"6) *Panzergruppe 2* advances—most likely two days before the [remaining] field armies move out—across a line running Orel–Brjansk. The right wing is to abut the Swop and Oka River lines. Its left wing rolls up the Dessna from the south and holds the enemy in the southeast Dessna bend, in conjunction with the *2. Armee*. The city and industrial areas of Brjansk are to be cut off initially by a mobile force and then taken later by the *XXIV. Armee-Korps* in conjunction with the *Luftwaffe*."

---

11. *Traditionsverband*, 181.

The plan established the date for the start of operations for the field army group as 2 October. Guderian requested his forces start two days earlier so as to receive the bulk of the initial support from the *Luftwaffe.*

The *XXIV. Armee-Korps,* to which the *3. Panzer-Division* continued to be attached, was put in the main effort outside of Gluchow. The formations of the division, which had pulled out of the line in the Lochwiza–Pirjatin area, occupied bivouac and battlefield reconstitution areas around Krowelez. Although there were only a few days available, they were used to conduct a battlefield reconstitution as much as possible. The division headquarters was located in Krowelez. Since its quartering area was constantly being subjected to Soviet air attack, the battle staff moved to Pogrebki on 26 September. The terrain in the area was beautiful; less exciting, however, was the fact that there were already signs of lively partisan activity in the area. During the day, however, the area was spared the appearance of that attendant phenomenon. The regimental and divisional bands played in the village marketplaces and the chaplains held services. Replacements came form the homeland and had to get quickly integrated into the framework of the forces.

It was intended to reorganize *Panzer-Regiment 6* after its receipt of new tanks. Once received, the regiment would again have three full line battalions. The regiment's organization on 27 September: each battalion had a headquarters and headquarters company; a light company consisting of approximately seventeen *Panzer III's* and two *Panzer II's;* a medium company consisting of approximately five to seven *Panzer IV's* and two to three *Panzer II's;* and a company attached from *Panzerjäger-Abteilung 521.* The battalion headquarters of the antitank battalion remained intact to process personnel and administrative matters, while the commander, *Major* Frank, assumed acting command of the *I./Panzer-Regiment 6* for *Oberstleutnant* Schmidt-Ott, who was on leave. To be able to engage heavy tanks, *Panzer-Regiment 6* had the *5./Artillerie-Regiment 75* and a battery of 8.8-centimeter *Flak* from the *II./Flak-Regiment 11* attached to it, with each tank battalion receiving one light field howitzer and one 8.8-centimeter *Flak.* The attachment of the individual guns later proved to be ineffective. Given the poor weather conditions of the fall and the fact that they were unarmored, the guns proved to be more of a hindrance than a help. Finally, *Panzer-Regiment 6* formed a company under *Hauptmann* Staesche, which was charged with monitoring movements and regulating traffic.

The division issued orders to occupy staging areas. *Generalleutnant* Model held a commander's conference oat 1030 hours on 28 September to discuss the upcoming attack. The division issued supplemental orders as well. In one of the orders, the units were directed to take 3.5 basic loads of fuel with them. The division logistics officer was responsible for bringing that amount of fuel forward. On that day, the *3. Panzer-Division* had 15,050 men assigned to it.

Panzergruppe 2, on the right wing of *Heeresgruppe Mitte*, had the initial mission during the offensive of preventing any type of Russian impact on the wings of the *4. Armee* and *Panzergruppe 4*, which were attacking in the direction of Moscow from Rosslawl. Allocated to *Panzergruppe 2* on 29 September:

• *XXIV. Armee-Korps (mot.)* with the *3, Panzer-Division, 4. Panzer-Division,* and *10. Infanterie-Division (mot.)*

• *XXXXVII. Armee-Korps (mot.)* with the *17. Panzer-Division, 18. Panzer-Division,* and *29. Infanterie-Division (mot.)*

• *XXXXVIII. Armee-Korps (mot.)* with the *9. Panzer-Division, 16. Infanterie-Division (mot.),* and *25. Infanterie-Division (mot.)*

• *XXXIV. Armee-Korps* with the *95. Infanterie-Division* and *134. Infanterie-Division*

• *XXXV Armee-Korps* with the *262. Infanterie-Division, 293. Infanterie-Division,* and *296. Infanterie-Division.*

Two motorized corps (the XXIV and the XXXXVII) staged to break through the positions of the Soviet 13th Army, while the other corps were still closing in. It was intended for the two infantry corps to be echeloned right and left, following the motorized corps. The main effort of *Panzergruppe 2* was at Gluchow. The *XXIV. Armee-Korps (mot.)* placed both of its armored divisions in the front lines, while the *10. Infanterie-Division (mot.)* initially remained in the second wave. The first attack objective of the corps was the Orel–Brjansk road.

The weather on 29 September was anything but promising. It had rained the entire night and the routes and pathways were a single mass of mud. Starting on 27 September, *Pionier-Bataillon 39* was under its new commander, *Major* Petsch, who replaced *Major* Beigel, who had been transferred to the Engineer School at Dessau-Roßlau. Together with a battalion of *RAD* personnel (*5./313*), the engineers were given the mission of constructing corduroy roads. The division took up its positions south and southwest of Gluchow, six kilometers east of Jareslawez. The main body of the *3. Panzer-Division* was placed under the command of *Oberst* Kleemann. The *II./Panzer-Regiment 6, Kradschützen-Bataillon 3* and the *3./Pionier-Bataillon 39* were attached to the *4. Panzer-Division*, which had been directed to attack to the left of the *3. Panzer-Division*. Detached to the corps, as its reserve, were the *II./Schützen-Regiment 3*, one battery from *Artillerie-Regiment 42* and one company from *Panzerjäger-Abteilung 521*. To screen the staging area, *Kampfgruppe von Manteuffel* with the *I./Schützen-Regiment 3* and the *II./Artillerie-Regiment 42* was employed along the Klewenj from Wjasenka to Ljachow, eight kilometers east of Gluchow.

The night passed quietly. Visibility was extremely limited, since the heavens were completely blanketed by clouds. Right at the designated minute—0530 hours—all of the batteries of *Artillerie-Regiment 75* opened the new offensive with a barrage on the lead Russian positions. The men of the two rifle regiments then jumped out of their trenches and worked their way in bounds towards the enemy lines, which were still being covered by friendly artillery fire.

Kampfgruppe von Manteuffel was employed along the right wing to protect the flank of the division through offensive operations and maintain contact with the *XXVIII. Armee-Korps (mot.)* on the right. In executing that mission, the *I./Schützen-Regiment 3*, supported by the *II./Artillerie-Regiment 42*, attacked Sawarkow. In the lead were the remaining armored personnel carriers of the 1st Company (*Leutnant* Lohse), on which the riflemen of the 3rd Company (*Hauptmann* Peschke) were riding. The attack took place across an open field. There were Russian positions in front of the village outskirts, which were quickly overrun. The riflemen were then among the wooden cottages, which were stubbornly defended by individual Russians. The lead elements of the *1./Schützen-Regiment 3* made it to the center of the village, where it stopped at a church with a dilapidated cemetery.

All of a sudden, a few dogs sprang out of the second line of the enemy's defenses, about forty meters away. The animals ran quickly towards the *SPW's* and were not distracted by the machine-gun firing. *Obergefreiter* Müller cried out: "It's got something on its back!" His comrades identified a wooden lever, about twenty-five centimeters long. It rose vertically from a rack on the dog's body. A few of the Russians had jumped up from their positions in the trenches, encouraging the dogs. Instinctively, the machine gunner on the first vehicle, *Obergefreiter* Ostarek, took the animals under aimed fire. The lead dog continued racing. *Oberfeldwebel* brought his submachine gun into firing position and fired until the animal collapsed. At the same time, *Hauptmann* Peschke had finished off a dog with a carbine, and the third animal was shot by *Feldwebel* Hoffmann's machine gun. Another four dogs followed with attached two-kilogram charges, but they were also killed. *Leutnant* Lohse radioed out the new danger: "Mine dogs!"

When the Russians saw that their dogs were unable to deliver their deadly charges anywhere, they evacuated their positions behind the church and pulled completely out of Sawarkow. But as soon as our riflemen reached the edges of the village, Soviet artillery fire slammed into the wooden houses. In between were unknown rounds, which rained down all at once by the dozens and had a tremendous shrapnel effect. Those were the first "Stalin organs" the soldiers of the *3. Panzer-Division* had encountered!

Friendly losses mounted considerably. *Leutnant* Vetter from the *3./ Schützen-Regiment 3* was badly wounded. All of a sudden, the fires stopped around noon. An immediately launched patrol under the command of *Unteroffizier* Buggert brought in an additional forty-eight prisoners. While the 3rd Company remained in Sawarkow, the 1st Company was ordered back, with the squads of *Unteroffizier* Dreger and *Unteroffizier* Hesse then moved to screen in the direction of Cholopkowo.

Schützen-Regiment 394, which was employed as the division's main effort, quickly broke through the enemy resistance and advanced fairly rapidly. It was just that the roads and trials were a problem that could barely be solved. One was amazed that the armored personnel carriers and other vehicles were able to hold up to the demands placed on them. Since the terrain was not suited for tanks, the tank battalions remained behind for the time being. *Oberstleutnant* Audörsch believed he would be able to accomplish his mission with the support of the fighting vehicles.

By 0830 hours, the *I./Schützen-Regiment 394* had reached the high ground east of Frigoltowo, hardly encountering the enemy. The advance was then halted due to an extensive and barely identifiable mine obstacle. The engineers had to go forward to clear a lane. The situation was made even more difficult by the fact that the Russians had occupied Studenok to the east and causing further delays through artillery fire.

In the meantime, the *II./Schützen-Regiment 394* reached the area two kilometers west of Klewenj. It was there that the first fighting vehicles of the *III./Panzer-Regiment 6* arrived. Both formations joined together and continued the march form Klewenj. The first obstacle appeared after four kilometers: Destroyed bridges. Shortly thereafter came the second obstacle: The minefield at Studenok. The clearing of the mines took a long time, since they were almost all wood-encased mines, which could not be detected by electric mine detectors. The *II./Schützen-Regiment 394* lost a lot of time and was only able to continue its attack at the onset of darkness. It eventually established all-round defensive positions in the Naumowka area.

The *I./Schützen-Regiment 394* got through Studenok in the afternoon and occupied the high ground to the east at Chinel. That meant that the day's objective had been reached! A patrol advanced as far as Kutscherowka, which was reported as being clear of the enemy. In any event, the railway line to the southwest was not to be crossed.

Shortly after first light on 1 October, all of the divisional elements continued their forward advance. *Kampfgruppe Oberst Kleemann* assembled around Studenok by noon and reached Kutscherowka with *Schützen-Regiment 394* and the *II./Panzer-Regiment 6*. The completely softened ground did not allow for any rapid advance. The supply routes coming in from Gluchow were already completely ruined. Every vehicle got stuck in the mud and could only be guided out with assistance from a prime mover.

Patrols were sent out from Kutscherowka and determined that the road from Esmanj appeared more-or-less trafficable. In the meantime, the *I./Panzer-Regiment 6* had advanced to the northeast and reached the village of Ulanow, moving through Suchodol. The tank regiment could advance no further that day, since the thirty-five new fighting vehicles had arrived and had to be distributed among the battalions, with the 3rd Battalion receiving ten *Panzer III's* and *Panzer IV's*.

Kampfgruppe Oberst Kleemann was reinforced during the day by *Kampfgruppe von Manteuffel*. This group had remained in its old positions in the morning and had turned back several Russian counterattacks, in the course of which *Leutnant* Thomas was killed and *Leutnant* Doll was badly wounded (both from the *I./Schützen-Regiment 3*). The *2./Schützen-Regiment 3* also suffered casualties, since the Soviets succeeded in breaking up Bachert's platoon. Two of the squads encircled by the enemy were able to fight their way through and make it back to the battalion. *Aufklärungs-Abteilung 1* cleared the area around Tschernewa. By noon, the *3./Schützen-Regiment 3* had to be detached to return to Studenok to take over the security there. The remaining companies followed a few hours later, after *Maschinen-Gewehr-Bataillon 5*[12] had relieved the *Kampfgruppe* in the positions it had taken the previous day. In Studenok, *Pionier-Bataillon 39* was in the process of erecting a sixteen-ton bridge over the Klewenj. The 1st Bridging Column provided three span and two surface trucks.

By the evening of 1 October, the lead elements of the division reached the area twenty kilometers northeast of Kutscherowka. The enemy was pulling back. *Generalleutnant* Model reported to his superior headquarters that a rapid advance could not be continued due to the bad condition of the road network. At that point, the corps decided to pull the *3. Panzer-Division* out of its previous sector and have it march on the better roads to Ssewsk.

The regrouping took place at night. The division turned to the north behind the *4. Panzer-Division*. On the morning of 2 October, which finally brought with it nice weather again, the division disengaged the bulk of its forces and marched through Suchodol and Polkownitschja in the direction of Ssewsk. On that day, the division command post was moved from Suchodol to Prilepy, off the side of the road. The march was frequently interrupted, since the road was completely jammed with vehicles of all types. For the first time, Russian aircraft dropped phosphorous bombs on the columns.

During the day, *Schützen-Regiment 3*, elements of *Panzerjäger-Abteilung 521* and the *1./Pionier-Bataillon 39* provided security for those movements. In the process, the riflemen were unable to cross the railway line. During the night, the enemy had emplaced additional minefields. As a result, only reconnaissance and combat raids could be conducted. The enemy remained on the defensive and only disturbed friendly movements by means of artillery fire. Some casualties were taken. For instance, *Leutnant* Dr. Sieverling of the *4./Artillerie-Regiment 75* was killed.

As the sunny second day of October came to an end, the *XXIV. Armee-Korps (mot.)* had achieved important initial success. After the *4. Panzer-*

---

12. This was a general headquarters element that was not assigned to any division or corps.

Division had taken Ssewsk on 1 October, it not only penetrated the enemy front 130 kilometers deep, it also ripped the Soviet 13th Army apart. The Soviet 21st and 55th Cavalry Divisions, the 121st and 150th Tank Brigades and the 183rd Rifle Division were separated from the rest of the field army and were pulling back to the north.

The *3. Panzer-Division* did not undergo any major combat activity on that day with the bulk of its forces, since it was moving behind the *4. Panzer-Division*. On the same day, the new major effort on the part of the army got underway. At first light on 2 October, *Unternehmen "Taifun"*[13] had started. Its end objective was the capture of Moscow!

THE HISTORY OF *PANZER-REGIMENT 6*

The regimental history of *Panzer-Regiment 6* records the events of this chapter as follows:[14]

Valuable weeks were lost due to the participation in the Battle of Kiev. It was imperative at that point to reach the major objective of Moscow before the onset of winter, as *Generaloberst* Guderian had insisted up from the very beginning.

On 28 September, a commander's conference was held, in which orders were issued for staging on 29 September and attacking on 30 September. But the new tanks had not arrived yet. Since the *4. Panzer-Division* was directed to move out first, the 2nd Battalion was attached to it.

The two other battalions moved as part of their march serials on 29 September in order to reach Gluchow (1st Battalion) and Jaroslawez (3rd Battalion). There were already major difficulties at the start of the march, since the route were very muddy as a result of heavy downpours. For example, every truck had to be towed by tanks out of a deep defile. Before moving out, there was a warning about Russian dog sections with the Russian light infantry battalions. Those dogs carried demolition charges with antennae and were trained to go after vehicles. Nonetheless, no tanks were damaged by them. A few dogs were shot by a rifle battalion.

During the attack on 30 September, the 3rd Battalion initially followed *Schützen-Regiment 394*. The 1st Battalion also reached its intermediate objective without enemy contact, with the exception of the clearing of mine obstacles. In the process, the battalion's engineer platoon removed

---

13. Operation "Typhoon."
14. Munzel, 96.

seventy-eight mines which had been cased in wood so as to avoid detection by electric mine detectors.

The new tanks finally arrived and were quickly integrated into the battalions. Attached to the *4. Panzer-Division*, which was in the front, the 2nd Battalion reached Ssewsk. The other battalions were only able to move forward slowly, since the routes were a morass and a destroyed bridge slowed down the advance considerably. When the Lujkoff–Briansk rail line was reached, a sugar factory flew into the air with a mighty explosion. The enemy aerial attacks resumed with a vengeance. During the first two days of the attack, friendly power was concentrated in support of *Panzergruppe Guderian*, since it had moved out two days in advance of the other formations. It was a very necessary measure.

The routes were extremely bad. For example, a requested fuel column took six hours to cover seven kilometers. The regiment was reduced to one basic load of fuel.[15] Nevertheless, the 2nd Battalion, which was able to receive a basic load of fuel, was able to advance as far as Schablykino. In the vicinity of Ssewsk, a number of trucks were discovered that had rockets on board for the so-called "Stalin organ." Since the routes for the division were so bad, it was moved forward behind the *4. Panzer-Division* on the latter's avenue of advance.

---

15. In essence, a basic load of fuel was enough fuel to allow the unit or formation to operate for 100 kilometers.

CHAPTER 7

In the Lead Tank to Orel

The Brandenburg motorcycle infantry battalion of our armor division had reached the major road and railway line. It was the first Sunday on October. *Erntedanktag.*[1] In a fiery and colorful exchange, a full moon relieved the red disk of the sun. In the trenches and along the edges of the villages, the riflemen shoveled their dugouts for the cold night.

This road is the fruit of the difficult exertions of the last few days. The first important attack objective of our armored formation. After all, this improved road—indeed, even asphalted in some places—ran parallel to the railway line, which led from Smolensk and through Roslawl, Brjansk, and Orel and, like the arc of a circle, was some 350 kilometers from Moscow. Like rams, the armor divisions had broken through the southern flank of the Supreme Commander, Timoshenko. They had chipped away at the so-called Brjansk Front and fought their way forward along the last 150 kilometers of that double strand. The large industrial and armaments centers that ran along it had been stormed. They were Brjansk along the high banks of the Dessna, the largest tributary of the Dnjepr, and the city of Orel on the Oka, the main river of central Russia that flows into the Volga.

The small village, which we reached by going through a deep defile, was between those cities. The road still had to be cleared. There were still scattered companies and battalions in the woods and localities; the remnants of battered and overrun Bolshevik rifle regiments. In the last remaining villages before the road, they had surrendered in groups after offering short resistance.

Anyone who still doubted that motorized forces could cross any terrain should have spent the last two march days of our armor division. Once again, it was a cross-country journey full of small surprises. After all, the

---

1. Thanksgiving.

117

deceptive autumn sun did not stay loyal to us. We moved once again across narrow field paths, across stubble fields and potato fields, through woods and heath. The journey under the shining moon only stopped for a few hours because a tank broke through a rotten bridge. In the morning, the rushing rain transformed the famous black earth of central Russia into soft soap. On a slight incline, which normally would hardly even be noticed, the tachometer showed three kilometers for a distance of only 100 meters. A thanks to the tank that pulled us up that slippery slide as if we had been on asphalt. When the young motorcycle messenger in front of us tipped his machine into the soft muck for the third time, he called out: "Whoever invented the motorcycle must be the enemy of all mankind!" It was that type of route! But he did say it with gallows humor. We didn't allow ourselves to become irritated. First of all, the prime movers helped. Then, at noon, the heavenly hosts arrived with sun and wind and blew the road surface dry. We stiffened old bridges and constructed footpaths over ditches and creeks. Everyone pitched in, whether general, staff officer, rifleman or radio operator. The medical company competed with the engineers, who could not be omnipresent in that terrain. And so we did it once again! The forested defile was the last test before the road.

The routes, which generally led from south to north towards Brjansk, Orel and Karatschew, which was in between the two, had been taken by the lead armored elements. It was imperative at that point to secure the cross roads. The motorcycle infantry mounted up: March objective—Orel. It was 6 October.

But it was only a few kilometers farther down the road—behind the next village—that the Bolsheviks were defending the road with strong forces. Heavy fire was received by the lead company from the patch of woods off to the right and from a vegetated area along the railway embankment, which offered a lot of concealment, off to the left and in front of another patch of woods. Rifles firing and bursts of machine-gun fire. Off to the right, there was the *bupp-bupp* of a light antiaircraft gun. In the blink of an eye, the motorcycle infantry had left their bikes and vehicles and disappeared in the roadside ditch. It was not the first ambush of a treacherous enemy that they had to eliminate, after all. The empty row of motorcycles looked eerie along the slightly rising road, over which the bullets were whistling. There was a clicking and a clattering, whenever metal was struck. Fuel was dripping out of a few gas tanks; the ricochets twittered.

The battalion attacked and advanced in an effort to envelop. One company received orders to work its way along the railway embankment and hit the Bolsheviks in the rear. A second company felt its way toward the woods to the right. An antitank gun went into position along the road to rule out any surprises. The platoon leaders placed the pouches for the extra magazines for the submachine guns on their belts as well as a couple of hand grenades for good measure. The riflemen checked their weapons one more time, the carbines and the machine guns. They cinched the chinstraps on their helmets tighter. They automatically performed the many movements necessary before a soldier assaults and gets ready for a new fight. The squad leaders were briefed. The soldiers then disappeared into the terrain on both sides.

The provisional bridge to the rear in front of the wooded defile had collapsed for the second time. Finally, the heavy prime movers could cross it again. The battery attached to the advance guard rolled forward. The howitzers pushed their barrels through the hedges and vegetation along the edge of the village. From there, they could hammer the woods off to the left with direct fire. A second battery remained behind the shaky bridge so as to take the woods on the right under fire. The forward observer had his scissors scope and radio equipment set up in the roadside ditch. The light infantry guns were also pulled into position. All of that took place with the quiet certainty of practiced leaders and combat-experienced soldiers. It always looked like they were on maneuvers. Only the determined faces and the sound of fighting reminded one of the actual seriousness of the situation.

We looked through the scissors scope to the distant wood-line from the forward position of the battery commander in front of the village. The *Oberleutnant* had been wounded in his right lower arm the previous day. It had been from one of those shrapnel bombs dropped from great altitude by the Soviets; you usually only heard them as they were hurtling through the air. They usually caused little damage, but sometimes the shrapnel hit a comrade. He should have gone to the hospital immediately. But with the help of the battalion surgeon, he was patched up enough that he could remain forward with his battery. That type of example of military duty was taken as a matter of course. He wasn't the only one during those weeks of constant combat. A number of officers in the tank and rifle companies had white bandages. It was a small part of their living by example.

Of course, on this day, he wasn't allowed to go forward with the armored observation vehicle. That was his greatest worry. The battery officer had to assume those duties. Through the scope, we saw him move forward through the field next to the road and through the skirmish line of riflemen. Most likely, the bullets from the rifles and machine guns were pelting the steel walls. He issued fire commands to the battery by radio.

There were numerous mounds of dirt—not unlike molehills—that could be identified in front of the band of vegetation in front of the left-hand woods. They were the dugouts of the Bolsheviks. You could see the muzzle flashes . . . individual soldiers crawling forward . . . others running back, bent over. The armored vehicle in front of them that was not firing appeared unnatural to them. Occasionally, camouflaged helmets popped up fro behind the railway embankment. Squads crawled forward in front of us. They disappeared for minutes at a time, covered and concealed. They were probably still receiving machine-gun fire over there.

The attached battery then let its weighty voice be heard with two claps of thunder. The first rounds slammed into the holes in front of the vegetation; they exploded as fireballs. Round after round was then placed there. The Bolsheviks became terrified. They clambered out of their holes everywhere and ran to the edge of the woods. They were then caught up in the next batch of rounds that swept through the running groups. They remained where they were. Only a few groups disappeared into the thick woods. The guns immediately followed them. There was the appearance of fire twitching between the trees. Clouds of smoke rose above the crowns; shrapnel and broken-off branches came crashing down below them.

But is was also difficult shooting for the battery, since the assault detachments pushed their way ever closer to the woods under the protective fires. Two signal flares shot up. The impacts were probably too close for the riflemen in front of us. Not to worry. The armored observation vehicle and the forward observation post had them in their sights. We were waiting for the next signal that had been arranged to announce that the left-hand company was in the enemy's rear.

At that point, the higher-pitched sounds of the infantry guns mixed into the chorus. The second battery reported it was ready to fire. As a precautionary measure, the observer had a combination fuse fired into the sky. Too short . . . it was almost right over our heads! A second round. That one was just right . . . right above the right-hand patch of woods. The rounds then hammered over there on the dugouts and trenches of the Bolsheviks.

The first prisoners were brought back along the railway embankment. It was a lieutenant, who suddenly saw himself and his platoon surrounded and who probably didn't mind putting his hands up. He was immediately interrogated by an interpreter so as to find out who was facing us. It was a battalion from a rifle regiment. With the exception of their officer, all of the soldiers were Tatars from the Volga region. They had no artillery . . . only carbines and machine guns. There were approximately 500 men in the woods. They would probably all surrender. But when they were asked who wanted to volunteer to return to their comrades to ask them to desert, all of them shook their heads, horrified, and defensively raised their hands. No, no one wanted to return to those woods. They were visibly happy to have escaped the clutches of the *Politruks.* They did not know how strong the forces were in the other patch of woods. They did not belong to their regiment. The commander had only told them that they had to fight their way through from Orel to Brjansk.

The assault against an enemy toughly defending in a patch of woods takes hours, if unnecessary casualties want to be avoided. It became afternoon. The skies suddenly clouded over. The wind whipped hail into our faces. White vortices danced on the road. For a quarter of an hour, the woods disappeared behind a gray wall of haze. The veil then lifted again. It was the harbinger of an early winter.

Individual groups then attempted to press forward from out of the woods. But the rounds kept forcing them back. At the outermost corner, small groups waved something white in the direction of the riflemen. They had already discarded their weapons and moved out with large steps towards the railway embankment in order to surrender. Behind the woods, the anticipated white signal flare climbed above the trees. The Tatars were sitting in a trap. The forward observer scaled back the fires a bit.

But the other rifle company had bogged down. The Soviets in the right-hand patch of woods were desperately defending from their well-camouflaged holes. It was barely possible to advance in the hail of fire from their automatic weapons. The 2-centimeter rounds of the light antiaircraft gun sprayed as far as the positions of the howitzer battery. Without exact targets, the guns could only put grazing fires on the woods.

The armored observation vehicle was ordered back to the edge of the village. The battalion commander rode in it to the company commander in order to form a picture of the situation for himself. Time was pressing. The days had become hellishly short. When our watches showed 5, evening started to fall.

When the battalion commander returned, he said that the open terrain in front of the woods could only be crossed by taking heavy casualties. The Bolsheviks had established one of their usual cleverly laid-out ambush positions behind the trees, in the crowns, under the thick vegetation and in dugout field positions. But there was no point in gaining a "prestige" success when positions were being cleared. That was intuitively obvious. It was just a matter of a few hours before those pockets of resistance would be obliterated.

Tanks were needed to assist! They were the loyal helpers of the motorcycle infantry. The field-gray soldiers carefully made their way from their concealed positions to the woods. They waited for the fighting vehicles. The artillery rounds howled above their heads, singing their comforting song. The heavens were full of snow. We didn't like it at all.

A couple of short orders rode through the ether on the radio frequencies. The tank company, which had been attached to the rifle regiment advancing on the right flank of the division, turned off. It raced head over heels across the wobbly provisional bridge and churned through the defile to the road. Of course, that took its own sweet time. The tanks were greeted in the village with friendly shouts. They would clear the route to Orel—that much was certain.

The young company commander was briefed by the *Major* commanding the motorcycle infantry. When he walked, one of his legs lagged a bit. There was a piece of shrapnel in it. Not a whole lot needed to be said. The two woods with the Bolsheviks in them could clearly be seen. The commander moved his finger along the map. His companies had advanced that far. Their attack was no longer able to advance due to the enemy's fire. They had to be freed up again. That was the mission.

"Platoon leaders up front!" The familiar order. Everything was explained telegraphically. The platoons received their missions. It was directed for the tanks to move along the road to the patches of woods and then comb them in convoy fashion. A "land convoy" in tanker terms was the fighting conducted when the steel cruisers moved ahead of riflemen as "obstacle breakers." They paralyzed the enemy just by their appearance or at least reduced the effectiveness of his resistance. The company commander would stay in the middle so as to keep an eye on all three platoons at once.

The heavy tank with the turret number of 731 was the lead tank that day. Once again, it was to be a hunt that appealed to the hearts of the "black hussars"! They had not fired a round since engaging the armored train in the Ukraine. "Fire up!" We could only faintly hear the whoosh of the powerful engine. *"Panzer marsch!"*

The world we saw was round and had a aiming post in the middle. It was the scope on the machine gun, which we used to search along the road. To the left, the row of telegraph poles passed by; to the right, it was the string of motorcycles that were still waiting to move on. The world had grown small. We were only connected to the events around us through the radio and the headphones and the vehicle commander—the only thing we could see of him were his legs and the edge of his overcoat—and the voice of the company commander, who we knew was watching carefully behind us.

Somehow, these war wagons reminded us of a submarine on land. In that regard, the term "convoy" was the right one. Here or there, it was a small team of men who had turned cohesive in battle and knew what his counterpart would do. Everyone knew the strengths of the others. Everyone knew he could blindly trust the others. In the turret was the powerful, compact figure of the *Oberfeldwebel*, who scoured the terrain to the edge of the woods with his binoculars. He personified the quality of composure. In front of him was the gunner, who was aiming towards the woods, ready to fire. Next to him was the loader, who readied the rounds for firing. In the front was the driver, had to steer the heavy colossus through the most difficult of terrain with strong hands. A lot depended o his nerves; he had to be an artist behind the wheel. He smoked his cigarette, the soul of composure, as the woods grew larger in front of him. To his right was the small radio operator, the mobile ether switchboard. With his quick wit, he was the funniest of all of them.

The deep voice of the company commander rang out clearly: "We are riding with the motorcyclists to Orel!" At that point, everyone in the company knew what was up. "The motorcyclists' attack has bogged down in front of the vegetation in front of us. We're moving up to them. But be careful and slow, the motorcyclists are supposed to follow us." Every word had to be emphasized.

We rolled on. The woods were palpably close in the binoculars. The gunner was ready to pounce.

"Enemy rifle fire from the woods to the left. Move along the edge of the woods and engage the riflemen!"

The 1st Platoon attacked.

"Be careful, our riflemen are lying there!"

They were starting to get some breathing room!

Nothing could be heard of the sound of fighting through the rush in the headphones and above the clatter of the tracks. The steely battle animals calmly pushed their way forward to the edge of the woods from all sides. "Traverse the turret!" The voice of our tank commander to the gunner. "Faster . . . there you go!" There were fleeing Bolsheviks in front of us. "Fire at will!" A stream of fire but only a muffled bang in the fighting compartment. The thunderclap could only be heard outside. "Another one . . . that's it!" The high-explosive rounds sprayed into the Bolsheviks. That was followed by a few bursts of machine-gun fire. The tracer rounds were right on target. "Halt! . . . Move out slowly . . . A walking pace so the riflemen can follow." A few more impacts sent the dirt flying at the edge of the woods. The other fighting vehicles thoroughly raked the enemy positions with main guns and machine guns. The Soviet resistance was quickly and rigorously destroyed. Motorcycle infantry jumped behind our vehicles and followed us under cover of the armored walls.

The company dealt rather unceremoniously with the Soviets and shot their positions to bits. The first mission had been accomplished. The motorcycle infantry were mobile again.

"Motorcycle infantry are here to fetch prisoners out of their holes!"

The 2nd Platoon reported: "There're Bolsheviks everywhere here."

"Be careful!"

But in the blink of an eye, the tanks had broken all resistance. The prisoners were led off in large groups. Only the numerous dead remained behind in the woods.

The field fortifications along the edge of the woods had been overrun. We then moved along the road through the middle of the woods. The main guns were alternately pointed left and right.

"Transmit!" the tank commander said to the radio operator.

The radio operator moved the switch: "Go ahead!"

"Foxholes everywhere to the left of the road. Dead in them. Over!"

That was the effect of the artillery, whose impact craters could be seen. The motorcycle infantry following us would check to see whether some were only playing dead.

We wanted to get to Orel quickly. The motorcycle infantry were told to get back on their bikes. The battalion commander radioed that some of the motorcycles had been shot up.

"One platoon of motorcycle infantry up front to reconnoiter."

We soon heard their motorcycles rattling and rumbling through our headphones. The tanker knew in advance who was near them. The radio operator fine-tuned his set.

Silence in the woods. The road was empty. The deep-hanging gray-white cloud cover allowed the evening to come early, too early. The first small bridge site appeared in the round optics. Wildly tossed-around beams showed us while approaching that the Bolsheviks had found enough time to blow it in the air during their flight.

"Bridge blown. Reconnoitering detour."

Mines had not been emplaced. The *Oberfeldwebel* was able to determine that quickly. The heavy tank felt its way forward like a careful elephant across the road ditch towards the edge of the woods. The tracks sank deeply, but the ground held.

"Pull left . . . gas . . . it's going . . ."

The nose of the tank edge higher on the other side.

"Detour negotiable!"

That was heard by the entire column.

"Can motorcycles and wheeled vehicles cross?"

"*Jawohl*, they can make it as well!"

"Move slowly until everyone catches up!"

There was hardly any light left. The woods, the road and the skies were practically one in the snow=shrouded dimness. But in front of us were the flames of a large fire, almost like a beacon.

"What's that burning ahead?"

"The fire ahead is the rail station at Larischbylow . . . La . . . risch . . . by . . . low. Out!"

The snow was already dancing with tiny flakes, as we approached the next small wooden bridge. We were still in the woods. It was also a pile of wood. The tank commander intended to check for a detour. At the same time, the calm voice of the driver sounded: "*Achtung!* Vehicle ahead!"

"Already in!" That was the sober response of the gunner, who already had the target in the optics—no, better yet, his aiming point.

Another few seconds of observation. It would be impossible for a German vehicle to approach from that side. It could only be made out like a faint shadow. No tank. Just a Soviet truck with soldiers on it. It probably wanted to "break through" to Brjansk.

A short fire command: "200 meters! Fire at will!"

The round had already left the tube. Fire and dirt sprayed high next to the vehicle.

"Right . . . over," the tank commander said.

Scarcely anything could be seen. Dark figures sprang with large strides towards the woods. The second round was a direct hit to the engine and the front wheel. The vehicle was whipped around and remained hanging on the left embankment. A couple of bursts of machine-gun fire whipped into the small pack of fleeing men.

"Bridge destroyed. Truck destroyed. Some of those on board escaped into the woods. Looking for a bypass."

"Wait!"

We waited in front of the destroyed bridge. We had a feeling why we were waiting. Our radio traffic had given us away. Night had suddenly fallen. Based on our watches, it was just before six. It was possible to go around at that location as well. But it had to be assumed that the next few bridges would also be destroyed. The terrain beyond the woods would be no less broken up than this was. In the dark woods, the tanks were also blind at night. The expected order came.

"We're turning around!"

A fighting vehicle from our platoon took up security from the rear. We then moved back through the woods that the tanks had just cleared.

"I'm towing a motorcycle," the trail tank reported.

From that point forward, there was only humorous radio traffic. The tankers and the company commander were happy about the quick engagement that was won without any losses to the motorcycle infantry. That naturally brought about high spirits.

"We need to cancel the reservations for the hotel rooms in Orel!"

All well and good that the advance on Orel would continue the next day. Another day no longer mattered to us in this campaign. Then the battalion commander of the motorcycle infantry was asked whether he could find quarters for the tankers in the village.

The tankers were already eagerly anticipating that. They wanted to fire up the old ovens so much that they would crack. It was cool in our steel fortress. An icy wind was whistling outside. The night was as dark as a raven. The tank commander and driver steered in the wake of the vehicle in front. The "convoy" was pulling into port.

The tank was parked next to the old log cabin along the road. A light coat of snow lay upon it, camouflaging it at the same time.

The tea was hot. The slices of bread had been covered with a terrific canned *Wurst* and captured honey. The straw was spread out thickly. The kindling crackled in the oven. We sat around as if around a chimney. It was easier to talk when you looked into the playing flames.

✠

It was back in Unetscha, the large transportation hub on the Gomel–Brjansk railway. A railway line from Smolensk to Kharkov also went through it. It was the time of the armor thrust in the Ukraine; the wedge was working its way south at surprising speed. The platoon leader's vehicle was no longer there. Its engine had rebelled and the main gun no longer ejected the shell casings. The crew wanted to have the vehicle repaired in Unetscha; it had already prepared everything for the maintenance company. That happened to also be on the day that the Soviets broke through. That type of surprise was part and parcel of a bold advance through the Bolshevik front lines. The Bolsheviks attempted to reduce the long flank of the armor formation with heavy tanks. But with the cold-bloodedness of the German soldier, who never loses his composure and quick thinking even in situations that appear difficult, the combat outposts and all available reserves—antitank elements, *Flak*, signals and maintenance companies, in short, anyone with a carbine or a pistol—were committed against the Soviets.

Instead of going to the maintenance company, the tank instead limped off to battle. It encountered a thirty-two-ton tank. With its 7.62-centimeter main gun and ten centimeters of armor around the mantlet, it was certainly a difficult nut to crack.[2] The monster intended to roll into the city of Unetscha. The German tank blocked its way. Like two battleships,

---

2. The tank was probably a T-34; the heavier KV-1 is usually described as a fifty-ton tank.

the steel fortresses circled around and hunted one another. The thirty-two-ton tank fired poorly. Its rounds usually were way off the mark. The German rounds hit, but they ricocheted off. It was a unique feeling for the tankers to see their rounds hit dead center, only to bounce off. Their main gun was not sufficient for armor that heavy. And every round was difficult.

After each round was fired, the small radio operator scampered out of his hatch. With a gun-cleaning rod in his hand, he pushed the casing out from the front. Fire . . . raise the hatch . . . get out . . . in with the rod . . . out with the casing . . . load . . . back into the hatch . . . take aim again. Take aim on the turret race . . . on the tracks . . . there had to be a vulnerable spot somewhere! Fire and another ricochet. Once more, the radio operator had to race to the front of the gun tube. That evening, in the retelling, the light-hearted side of the tale predominated, the farcical aspects of the strange duel between two tanks. Back then, the bullets and shrapnel had whistled around his ears. He almost had to take his heart in his hands in order to jump up all over again.

In the end, the radio operator ran next to the fighting vehicle and, after it fired, ran forward again. Probably thirty times, perhaps more—time flies in combat, after all—he enabled the main gun to fire again. But the colossus was not interested in the mosquito bites. It kept on approaching the city. They weren't going to be able to do it with their rounds, they realized. Moving along a parallel route, they attempted to divert him. Of course, a tank engagement usually takes place at more substantial distances—not at hand-grenade range. The radio operator trotted along next to the tank, ready to jump forward again with his barrel rod.

A *Leutnant*, the engineer platoon leader of a rifle regiment, joined them. They discussed how they might be able to finish off the steel monster. Bundled grenades would do the trick! The tank rolled into the city, with the *Leutnant* and the radio operator trotting fast behind it. They turned on the first side street. At that moment, all of them were no more than 15 meters in front of the Soviet tank! That was a damn ticklish situation, the tankers freely admitted. But their fighting instincts guided them correctly. The driver approached the thirty-two-ton tank, which had to be even more surprised than they were, and rammed it at full throttle. The yellowish green vehicle turned on its axis and then skidded backwards against a house wall.

That must have been an impressive picture: the two steel monsters wrestling in the swept-empty streets of Unetscha and then getting ensnarled! The house wall held. The Soviet tank was unable to back up. It tried to push the German fighting vehicle away, but the driver pulled the brakes with all of his strength and the prisoner was unable to move the dead weight. It was trapped. It couldn't do anything with its main gun. It was only able to fire past the German tank. It had to elevate its long main gun above the German turret. But the Bolsheviks did not surrender. No hatch was opened. They probably sat in horrified panic in their steel crate and thought their last minute on earth had arrived.

The *Leutnant* and the radio operator placed the first bundled charge on the tracks and jumped under cover. Although there had been a powerful explosion, no track had been broken. That wasn't going to work. A second charge was bundled, but where was it going to go? The radio operator ran along the house wall to the rear deck—the engine access cover had to be opened from the outside somewhere! That was the ticket. He excitedly ripped the cover open, while the *Leutnant* initiated the charge. He threw the hand grenades into the engine compartment, slammed the cover down and then they made like the devil to get out of there!

That time, it worked. A flame shot out of the engine compartment. As expected, the hatches were then unbuttoned and the wax-pale Bolsheviks bailed out. Their overcoats and uniforms were already burning: One lieutenant and three men. For his actions, the radio operator received the Iron Cross, Second Class. God knows, he could wear it with pride. But the tankers explained the story with the humility that is unique to all experienced front-line fighters. It was all actually told while remembering their dear, old fighting vehicle; the memory of it at the warm oven let them chat.

"Another bread with honey!" The small, clever radio operator always had the appetite of a giant. A few more wood logs and then off to sleep.

"When are we getting up tomorrow?"

"Five!"

The eastern wind, mixed with snow, howled around the house. The motorcycle infantry were outside. Screening, just like almost every night.

It was an unpleasant and unfriendly Tuesday morning, that 7 October. A light blanket of snow covered the countryside. The cutting east wind was howling over it with a raw wildness. The Russian winter started in the fall. The tankers swept the snow from their vehicles. The humming and growling of the engines, which were being warmed up, could be heard along the roadway. We were doing the same thing.

Right at 0600 hours, the company rolled to the outskirts of the village. Once again, our tank was point for the advance guard, which had been directed to close the final part of the Brjansk–Orel road. We clanked up the slight rise once again towards the patch of woods that had been cleared for the motorcycle infantry by our tank company. It was only the many foxholes and toppled trees that gave away the fact that a Bolshevik ambush had been throttled there yesterday. We moved as a "convoy" once again. The motorcycle infantry followed us, and then the prime movers with the howitzers.

But we didn't see them. Our world was once again reduced to the circle of the optics for the machine gun. It was cold. You could see your breath. The red headphone cushions were good ear warmers.

"Radio ready!"

The weapons were prepared. The landscape was dead and bleak. If there had been still a Bolshevik who wanted to escape from that patch of woods, the whistling snow wind would have driven him out a long time ago.

The engineer platoon from the motorcycle infantry battalion had already been up long before us. An improved detour had been constructed at the first destroyed bridge for the motorcycles and the other wheeled vehicles. They were still working at the second destroyed bridge. The tank pushed its way past them through the roadside ditch.

"Halt!"

The company commander spoke with the engineer officer. No, the engineers had not seen any Bolsheviks this morning. Not a shot had been fired. Most likely, the rest of them scattered to the four winds when the tank showed up, as had always been the case in the past.

Nevertheless, it was prudent to be cautious! There could be more lying in ambush in the next village or woods. Almost gently, the driver gave power to the tracks. For a moment, the truck was in our field of vision . . . the last one the tank had dispatched yesterday. There were a few high spots in the snow, most likely the dead that had not reached the safety of the woods. The last thirty kilometers of the road were ahead of us. We all intently looked for the next bridge. Would it also be blown up? The tank commander observed attentively with his binoculars from his cupola.

The tracks chewed meter after meter of the long ribbon. The next village was quiet and empty. The night had also extinguished the fire at the railway station. Not a single human soul showed itself. No Soviet soldiers, either. In the case of the tanks, however, they usually hid themselves.

"Nothing to be seen of the enemy far and wide!"

A prompt answer: "He's freezing!"

The company commander was in a good mood. The tankers laughed. The sun even broke through; it would be a nice day. Our observers could hurry ahead faster. The next patch of woods was suspicious. That's right . . . a couple of figures were sneaking back with rifles. Probably stragglers. They could have made it this far. The turret had traversed within seconds. *Rat-tat-tat . . . rat-tat-tat.* The deadly tracer birds flew over towards the enemy. They weren't worth a main-gun round. It was intended more as an orientation for the following motorcycle infantry. Over there were more lost elements that didn't quite yet know how to be captured.

Keep going! At that point, a large wooden bridge was in the sights. We could tell by the railing that it had not been destroyed. Also not mined. Go over it! It didn't wobble; it had been built recently and was stable.

"Good bridge along the road; easily crossed."

"Well, then, that makes me happy, too!" was the humorous reply.

That went without saying, since the beams crossed a considerable hole in the ground. That would have cost the engineers a lot of sweat.

What was that over there walking in front of us, looking like stalking hunters with slung rifles? They were taking a stroll along the side of the road in front of our muzzles. It was a bunch of Bolsheviks, who by then had turned, frozen with fear, towards the approaching tank. The tank commander indicated to them that they should toss down their arms. They flew towards the ground and into the snow in a high arc. They could care less. The snow and the storm of the previous night had visibly battered them. We dismounted and transferred the miserable creatures to the approaching motorcycle infantry.

"*Marsch!*"

The scenes changed quickly in a war. Today, it was like a Sunday drive in the country in order to pick the ripe fruit. There were more and more bridges. The road crossed numerous defiles in the broken terrain. Everything was well maintained. We moved along without any worries. At the point where the road went under the railway, we saw that the tracks had been blown out for some distance. The underpass wasn't mined, either. It was good that only the railway had been blown up. That allowed us to move at a fast pace. The company commander issued his orders: "Faster! The warm ovens are waiting for us in Orel!"

We stopped a couple of times outside of individual villages in order to observe. But there were only civilians on the road. The hunt was over. The screening forces sent out form Orel had to link up with us soon. Two white signal flares had been arranged. The blurry silhouette of the city was already in view.

"Eleven o'clock . . . Orel in sight!"

What would have been a strain in the night turned out to be a nice ride for everyone in the long snake of vehicles of the advance guard. The tank commanders waved in a satisfied manner to the friendly outposts. The company commander placed himself at the front of his proud war wagons, which rattled noisily through the streets, as if they knew that yet another important chunk of roadway in Soviet Russia had been conquered. The German divisions were marching and fighting on numerous roads. Every one of them was important. Because all of them were leading to the same objective: Victory!

Every day brought its own fighting and every division had its own missions in the big plan of the *Führer* and his army commanders. It was only when the flanks and the rear were secure that the assault divisions could attack. The city of Orel on the Oka had been stormed by the neighboring division, whose advance we were protecting. Its armor spearhead had already moved beyond the city and was involved in heavy fighting.

The Bolsheviks had attempted to penetrate back into Orel with heavy tanks. They had advanced as far as the city outskirts. They were shot to pieces there in the defensive fires of the heavy *Flak* and the antitank elements. The burned-out wrecks and the annealed monsters were scattered along the road to Tula, a testament to German aiming. Whoever moved across the bridge over the Oka saw the five fifty-two-ton tanks right behind the train station on the main road. The German antitank rounds penetrated the ten-centimeter-thick side armor and the eight-centimeter turrets like steel bits though iron. The forces of the exploding ammunition in the interior had flung off a turret and its main gun like a child's toy.

With its population of 120,000, Orel, located along a tributary of the Volga, is a major city in Central Russia. Almost all types of industry could be found there. It was a center of the black-earth region. This advance had also come to the Soviets so surprisingly and so unexpectedly, that they were unable to fully finish their work of destruction. But in the interior of the city, there were a lot of ruins—destroyed by fire. Almost all the work of arsonists and GPU agents. There had been a headquarters for the "People's Commissariat for Inner Affairs" in Orel. Military police patrols had to act sternly, but that also brought a sense of security to the peaceful populace. Bilingual posters were placed on the house walls and fences, which reminded the civilians to go about their daily business for their own benefit.

In the armor school housed in the former Tsarist cadet academy we discovered a stuffed bear, two meters tall, which was the spitting image of the animal on our coat of arms for Berlin. It was designated the divisional bear and was allowed to carry the battle pennant of the Berlin-Brandenburg armor division. All of the soldiers enjoyed it. A little bit of happiness was always necessary in that bleak and soulless country and in that weather, which announced the arrival of winter, snowy and wet.

The advance guard rolled out of the city in the direction of new fighting. The Bolsheviks were putting up fierce resistance to the north of Orel with strong reserves. It had to be broken.

The weapons and vehicles with the Berlin bear as an insignia moved out!

Every new day brought with it new fighting.

THE DIVISIONAL HISTORY
The divisional history records the events of this chapter as follows:[3]

At 1145 hours on 4 October, the division advanced from Dmitrowsk to the north with an advance guard that had been reinforced with the *II./Panzer-Regiment 6*. After five hours, it reached Robja in dank and chilly weather, continuously held up by bad roads and missing bridges. The lead elements of the division were then thirty kilometers north of Dmitrowsk. The three *Kampfgruppe* of Kleemann, von Lewinski, and von Manteuffel followed slowly. Very poor, sandy routes, and stretches of sand on both sides of the bridge at Nerussa caused difficulties for the wheeled vehicles. For example, the fuel columns of *Panzer-Regiment 6* needed six hours to cover a stretch of seven kilometers that day!

---

3. *Traditionsverband*, 189–91.

The division used the day to pull its own forces closer to Dmitrowsk, replenish supplies of fuel and ammunition, erect bridges and improve roads. The division command post initially moved to Robja and then on to the schoolhouse in Molodewoje.

Soviet aircraft were very active that day and disrupted friendly movements. Some casualties were taken. The escorting *Flak* batteries could not complain about a lack of work. Just over Dmitrowsk alone, they were able to shoot down nine bombers. By evening, the elements of *Schützen-Regiment 1* and *Aufklärungs-Abteilung 1*, which had transitioned to security duties in that area, were relieved by formations of the *10. Infanterie-Division (mot.)*. They then moved on to catch up with the division. The rifle regiments cleared the villages of Schablikino and Molodewoje along the road.

On 5 October, the corps again placed its main effort in the sector of the *4. Panzer-Division*. The *II./Panzer-Regiment 6*, the *5./Artillerie-Regiment 75*, and the *2./Panzerjäger-Abteilung 521* were attached to that division. They left Robja at 1000 hours and advanced through Schablikono as far as Bunina along the Orel–Karatschew road.

The sixth of October 1941 was an event-filled day in the history of the German Army in the East. Rain showers pelted down all morning long from the low cloud cover, driven along by the strong northwest wind. In between were the first snow falls! Those were the signs of the onset of the mud period, which would make any further advance appreciably more difficult and cause delays. On that 6 October, Hitler also issued instructions that the *Panzergruppen* were to be re-designated *Panzer-Armeen* from that point forward. Likewise, the motorized corps were to be redesignated as *Panzer-Korps*.

The *3. Panzer-Division* was so held up by the rain and mushy snow on its march routes that none of its daily objectives was reached. *Panzer-Regiment 6* was stuck in the mud for three and one half hours. *Schützen-regiment 394* was turned off in the direction of Orel to provide security for the flank of the *XXIV. Panzer-Korps* to the east.

On that day, the *17. Panzer-Division* took Brjansk, while the *18. Panzer-Division* reached Karatschew and the *10. Infanterie-Division (mot.)* fought it out with scattered enemy elements in the area west of Ssewsk. It was directed that the *XXIV. Panzer-Korps* screen the encirclement around Brjansk from the east. The *Panzer-Armee* crossed its first attack objective, the Orel–Brjansk road, and was headed for the crossings over the Ssusha at Mzensk, so as to later be able to advance from there in the direction of Tula or along the Oka. On that day, the *4. Panzer-Division*, with the attached *II./Panzer-Regiment 6*, advanced northeast of Orel in the direction of Mzensk. It was there that the fighting vehicles encountered T-34's for the first time! The *4. Panzer-Division* succeeded in bypassing those enemy formations, reaching Mzensk on 7 October and taking it. It was not possible to establish a bridgehead over the Ssusha, however, since the Soviets held the high ground on the far side. The *III./Panzer-Regiment 6*, along with *Kradschützen-Bataillon 3*, were able to advance as far as the area around Bogdanowka as the lead elements of the *3. Panzer-Division*. The attached platoon from the *1./Pionier-Bataillon 39* was able to blow up a section of the Orel–Brjansk rail line in the vicinity of Bogdanowka during the night. The engineers then found themselves surrounded by the Russians a short while later, but they were able to fight their way through to *Kradschützen-Bataillon 3*.

Right at midnight during the night of 6–7 October, a violet snowstorm commenced, which quickly transformed the entire area into a winter landscape. Unfortunately, the snow did not remain on the ground, and the expected frost did not arrive. By first light, the snow had mixed with rain, and it transformed all of the roads within a short time into a morass. Driving was an unbelievable effort on men and materiel. Every truck had to be towed at the destroyed Zon Bridge. A member of *Schützen-Regiment 394* described the situation that day with the following lines:

"We could advance no further. There was no more fuel. Nothing came forward. The way was long and the roads even worse than the last few days. The snow had melted again and, as a result, the mess even bigger. Rations didn't come forward, either. We sat in the muck the entire day."

The *3. Panzer-Division* reached the area around Orel and set up security. Most of the vehicles—more than 1,000!—were stuck in the mud between Dmitrowsk and Kromy. Almost without exception, all of the fuel and rations vehicles were among them, as well as the entire maintenance company of *Panzer-Regiment 6*. It could not be determined with certainty when the entire column could get moving again.

After it appeared that the operations around Wjasma and Brjansk would turn out well, the *2. Panzer-Armee* received orders on 7 October to advance on Tula and take the crossings over the Oka there for further advance in either the direction of Kolomna or Kashira. Since the other corps were still hanging considerably back, only the *XXIV. Panzer-Korps* was available for that thrust.

THE HISTORY OF *PANZER-REGIMENT 6*

The regimental history of *Panzer-Regiment 6* records the events of this chapter as follows:[4]

On 4 October, Dimitrowsk was reached, but the division had to turn off to the north again and once again encountered horrible routes. On the same day, the 2nd Battalion left Dimitrowsk and reached Robje at 1800 hours.

Due to the bad road conditions, the 3rd Battalion was once again returned to the main avenue of advance. The battalion moved out behind *Marschgruppe von Manteuffel* at 1100 hours on 6 October and reached Lubniza. The 1st Battalion remained in the Ssewsk area. The 2nd Battalion, returned to the division once more, had its lead companies at Goroditsche.

On 7 October, the first violent snowstorm appeared, which transformed the entire area into a winter landscape. After a march lasting twenty-two hours, the regimental headquarters and the 3rd Battalion reached Orel with their last drops of fuel. Towards evening, the 2nd Battalion also arrived. The 1st Battalion was along the miserable advance route, held further back as the corps reserve. In the area between Dimitrowsk and Kromy, there were countless vehicles that had bogged down. Of vital importance to the regiment was the fact that those included important elements of the maintenance company. In some cases, it was not possible to recover the vehicles until weeks later.

The 2nd Battalion was reattached to the *4. Panzer-Division* on 9 October. That division was the first one to move out again in the direction of Tula.

---

4. Munzel, 96–97.

Street fighting in Bolochowka

Legend: *russ. Gefechtsstand* = Russian command post; *russ. Batteriestellung* = Russian battery position; *russ. Panzer* = Russian tanks; *Fluchtweg…* = Flight of the tanks until their destruction.

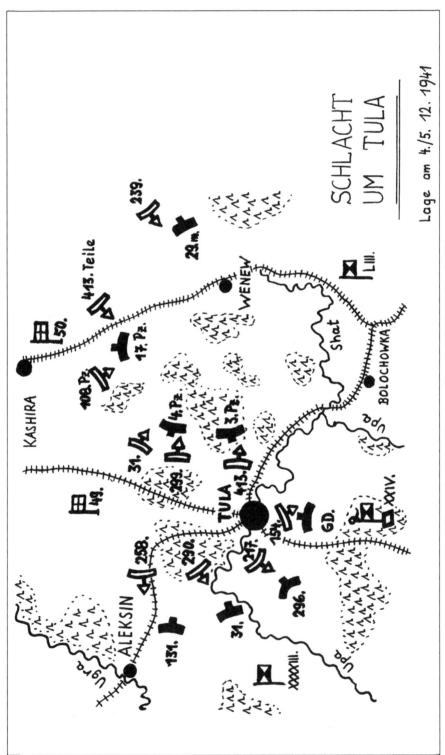

SCHLACHT
UM TULA

Lage am 4./5. 12. 1941

Battle for Tula: The situation on 4–5 December 1941.

CHAPTER 8

Assaulting the Area around Tula

**FORTIFIED MINING TOWN CAPTURED—SIBERIAN DIVISION
DEFEATED**

The crossing over the Upa had been forced. Bolochowka had been
assaulted in heroic attacks, in an exemplary combination of all weapons. A
Siberian rifle division, freshly committed to the fighting by the Soviets, was
wiped out and eliminated with its three regiments. The flames were still
blazing in the ruins. The last few Soviet personnel, distraught and halfway
out of their minds, came crawling out of the pile of rubble that used to be
a two-story residence. They were the few who survived the destruction. The
commander of a rifle regiment was lying in the roadside ditch in front of
the building. He was shot as he attempted to flee from his headquarters
in the building.

The Upa and Bolochowka don't mean much to those in the German
homeland. But for the armored division that fought there they represent
a new laurel in its history. The Upa is a river to the east of our avenue
of advance that snakes its way up in many tributaries on its way to Tula,
the armaments center south of Moscow. Bolochowka, on the other hand,
is a small industrial town, surrounded by mining pits, which, located on
a commanding piece of high ground, had been transformed into an
important bastion, like a fort.

The armored formation had advanced some 200 kilometers in the
black-earth region from Orel during those rain-filled days of October.
It had moved along the major road that leads from Kharkov to Moscow,
via Kursk and Tula. Numerous rifle divisions, the remnants of formations
from the Brjansk Front, reserves from the huge army of men of the Soviet
Union, already battered and brand-new tank brigades, cavalry regiments,
and elements of an airborne corps—all those attempted in vain to hold
up the advance. The black earth, softened into a single desert of slickness,

created difficulties that required superhuman efforts. But the strong Soviet fronts were always broken through or hit in the rear by means of bold flanking maneuvers—defeated in days of fierce fighting.

The frost of November turned the mud bone hard like ossified lava. An ice-cold wind swept across the barren fields, across which the attack continued. The area around Tula was reached. As had been expected by the German command, the Bolsheviks defended that arsenal, from which a large portion of their immense armaments came, with all the means at their disposal. Once again, it was terrain that looked like it had been created by nature for the defense. The extended coal and industrial area, which delivered the raw materials to the numerous factories and blast furnaces, was packed with pockets of resistance. The high ground, which was only sparsely covered with patches of woods, allowed observation of the depressions and valleys of the rolling terrain for kilometers on end. Deeply echeloned field positions, covered by artillery, antitank guns, mortars, and numerous machine guns, created the same picture outside of Tula as the one offered outside of Moscow on a larger scale.

The latest natural barrier for the German assault divisions was the Upa, which flowed through the area in a large arch. Its middle point was formed by Tula, with its population of 300,000. For the first time, Siberian regiments showed up as part of the enemy forces. They had been brought in from the Far East in an expedited fashion. They attempted to break through the long flank of our armored division, but they were hit in their flank instead. They were defeated and, leaving behind many dead and numerous prisoners, they were hunted back across the Upa. The commanding general immediately ordered a pursuit with all means available.

On the morning of 18 November, two powerful *Kampfgruppen* of our armored division advanced across the river. The riflemen assaulted across the ice while it was still dark and surprised the clueless Bolsheviks in the houses in the villages on the other side. An important railway bridge was taken intact by the aggressive *coup de main* of a *Leutnant;* the guards were overrun and the charges cut. But the Bolsheviks defended desperately in the next few villages. The deep foxholes and dugouts, built while the ground was still soft, had become firm bunkers as a result of the frost, greeting the assaulting soldiers with devastating fires. It was another assault, filled with casualties, since the rock-hard earth offered little concealment to the riflemen. It was impossible to dig in. The artillery and mortar rounds did not penetrate into the ground, thus scattering their shrapnel twice as far. The antitank elements and the tanks were able to move through a ford that had been discovered. Under their protection, the riflemen worked their way towards the ambush positions and cleared them. The main body of tanks and artillery rolled across the railway bridge to the far bank of the Upa and continued the attack. By that evening, the road southeast of Tula had been crossed.

But every ridgeline had to be wrested from the enemy; every village and every house assaulted. The early darkness, which descended by four o'clock our time, forces us to wait for the next day. A portion of the tanks and the riflemen had to camp out in the open that ice-cold night. Whenever the fighting vehicles ran their engines occasionally, the soldiers were able to warm up their stiff limbs somewhat on the exhaust stacks. As one commander stated, it was the worst night of the campaign for some companies. But the riflemen attacked again the next morning with steely determination and unshakeable wills. The terrain, which was as flat as a plate with high edges, had to be wrested from the enemy, meter-by-meter.

The assault on the mining town of Bolochowka started on 20 November. The main resistance of the Siberian regiment was concentrated there. There was 800 meters of clear fields all the way around that had to be crossed. Three rifle battalions, supported by fighting vehicles, fought their way towards the extended village from three sides. High-explosive rounds from the tank main guns beat down on the enemy foxholes. Trench after trench, foxhole after foxhole had to be taken. The Siberian riflemen were in battle at Tula for the first time. Their commissars and commanders had convinced them that the Germans first cut off their ears in captivity, before executing them. They believed it, as prisoners later confirmed. They figured their lives were lost no matter how you looked at it, so they preferred to get killed in the trenches and foxholes to surrendering.

The edge of the village was taken. Houses and a large factory were already burning brightly. Intense street fighting followed. The Bolsheviks fired from behind any opportunity that presented itself to push a rifle barrel through: windows, cellar shutters, fences made of board wood, fence posts, narrow, camouflaged dugouts—in short, from everywhere. The riflemen bounded from house to house, from one piece of cover to the next. The antitank elements advanced. The infantry guns followed. The machine guns hammered away without interruption. There was a park at the end of the main road. The Bolshevik guns had gone into position there. They were eliminated by the fighting vehicles and the infantry guns. The Soviet tanks then attacked—fifty-two-ton KV's and T-34's, which were twenty-six tons and had a 7.62-centimeter main gun. A tough fight in the middle of the road at a distance of 150 meters. Round after round left the barrels of the German antitank guns. One Soviet colossus was hit and pulled back into the park.

The heavy *Flak* was alerted. As it was unlimbering, a second 52-ton tank approached. After the fourth round, it went up in flames. At the same moment, a T-34, a twenty-six-ton tank, stormed against the *Flak*. It tried to ram the gun. It was within thirty meters—extremely dangerous! Then it suddenly disappeared, as if swallowed up by the earth. It had collapsed into an excavation, presumably for the construction of a new house. Only the top of the turret could still be seen. The hunt for the third tank continued. The *Flak* went into position at the edge of the park, just as a fifty-two-ton tank broke out into the open depression. By then, it had turned twilight. But on the opposite rise, the ninth round slammed right into its rear deck as a direct hit. It exploded and the turret with its main gun was dislodged. A fourth tank, another fifty-two-ton KV, was taken care of on the far side of the woods by the antitank elements.

Dead Bolsheviks, torn-apart horse cadavers, destroyed guns, mortars and machine guns and ammunition littered the battlefield. The remaining Bolsheviks had barricaded themselves in a two-story brick building at the end of the street. It was probably the command post of the Siberian division. Rifle companies had encircled the building. The rounds from the infantry guns, the tanks, and the howitzers crashed into the walls and windows. There was no getting out for the surrounded men. But they did not give up. In the evening, which was lit up by the burning houses, combat engineers went forward with demolition charges, Covered by friendly weapons, they jumped into the dead zone below the house. Piece after piece was blown out of the building. The only one who attempted to escape was a single officer. He fell after a few steps. Papers showed he was the commander of a rifle regiment. The engineers worked their way forward, climbing over the rubble and bringing up new demolition charges, until the large building was a single heap of rubble. One *Feldwebel* boldly pressed into the collapsed entrance of what had been the garage. He found seventeen dead Soviet officers in that one area.

The battle had been decided. It was deep in the night. Only the large fires crackled. The armor division had assaulted the famous Dyle Position once. According to all of the commanders, the line of resistance encountered at Bolochowka was no less difficult. But the heroic bravado of the German soldier, his unconditional willingness to risk his life, his determined will to succeed—all those are greater than the animalistic apathy of the Bolsheviks with regard to life and death.

One day later, sixty-nine soldiers dug themselves out like moles from the collapsed cellars. The next day, it was another twendy-five. Those were the last ones remaining from the destroyed rifle regiment. On that day, a few kilometers further on, the fifth heavy Soviet tank, the second T-34, was discovered. It had become immobilized with broken track while fleeing. The entire Siberian division, on which Moscow had placed such high hopes when it committed it into battle on the Upa, only had a few scattered elements left.

The rapid victory at Bolochowka was the result of excellent cooperation among all of the combat arms, which supported one another in a comradely fashion in extremely difficult house and street fighting. It couldn't have been done better at a training area: The riflemen, their heavy weapons, the engineers, the fighting vehicles, howitzers, antitank elements, and the armor-defeating *Flak*. It was the fruit of decisive leadership and the bravery of soldiers. The signature event at Bolochowka was the employment of those heavy weapons in close combat at pointblank range. Fighting vehicles, *Flak*, and infantry guns fired at 150 meters and less! The dramatic highpoint: the blowing up of the enemy command post! A brilliant flash of lightning with a powerful detonation!

THE DIVISIONAL HISTORY

The divisional history records the events of this chapter as follows:[1]

The *XXIV. Panzer-Korps* reorganized over the next two days for an attack to the east. *Infanterie-Regiment "Großdeutschland"*[2] was employed to screen

---

1. *Traditionsverband*, 209–13.
2. *"Großdeutschland"* was an elite army formation and one of the few that was authorized the wearing of a sleeve band, much like *Waffen-SS* formations. Within a year, it would be expanded to a motorized infantry division.

the road south of Tula, where it relieved the elements of the *3. Panzer-Division* that were positioned there. The corps employed the *4. Panzer-Division* on the right and the *3. Panzer-Division* on the left. The main effort was directed to be along the inner flanks, with the object of breaking through the enemy between Dedilowo and Tula and then, later on, advancing to the northeast across the Schat with the objective of Wenew. The corps had the following tank forces at its disposal: *Panzer-Regiment 6* with fifty-two vehicles (three *Panzer II's*, thirty-seven *Panzer III's*, nine *Panzer IV's*, and three command tanks), *Panzer-Regiment 35* [*4. Panzer-Division*] with thirty-five vehicles, and *Panzer-Regiment 39* (*17. Panzer-Division*) with fifteen vehicles. The fighting vehicles received whitewash. The attack was scheduled for 0500 hours on 18 November.

The division formed two *Kampfgruppen*. The righthand battle group, forming the main effort, was *Kampfgruppe Oberst Kleemann*, consisting of *Schützen-Regiment 3*, *Panzer-Regiment 6*, the *1./Panzerjäger-Abteilung 521*, the *1./Schützen-Regiment 394*, the *2.* and *3./Pionier-Bataillon 39*, the *6./Flak-Regiment 59*, and the *I./Artillerie-Regiment 75*. The lefthand *Kampfgruppe* of *Oberstleutnant* Audörsch consisted of *Schützen-Regiment 394*, *Kradschützen-Bataillon 3*, the *2.* and *3./Panzerjäger-Abteilung 521*, the *1./Pionier-Bataillon 39*, and the *III./Artillerie-Regiment 75*.

The Upa was a small river that snaked in twists and turns east of the road to Tula. It was the first objective of the *3. Panzer-Division*. It was still dark, when the batteries of *Artillerie-Regiment 75*, as well as *Artillerie-Regiment 69* and *Mörser-Abteilung 818*,[3] sent their fiery greetings over to the positions of the new Siberian regiments opposite them. Our riflemen raised themselves out of their trenches and foxholes, assaulted in the direction of the river and hastened across the ten-centimeter-thick ice to the opposite bank. The engineers placed boards and beams on the ice so that the motorcycles and personnel carries did not break through.

With the exception of the large railway bridge, all of the other bridges along the Upa had been blown up. It was the division's intent to take that bridge intact, if possible, since it was of great importance for the execution of the attack as well as future supplies. The commander of *Schützen-*

---

3. Both of these were separate artillery formation allocated to field armies and equipped with heavy howitzers of at least 15-centimeter caliber or, more likely, 21-centimeter caliber.

Regiment 394, Oberstleutnant Audörsch, used his engineers, commanded by the Knight's Cross recipient *Leutnant* Störck, for that mission. The brave officer made use of a ruse. Störck took off with four men—*Unteroffizier* Strucken, *Obergefreiter* Beyle, and two Ukrainians of ethnic German descent in Russian uniforms. The rest of the engineer platoon, fourteen men under the command of the assistant platoon leader, *Feldwebel* Heyeres, followed within earshot.

The engineer platoon snuck through the thinly held Russian lines in pitch darkness, and the men reached the bridge without incident. Right in front of it, along the embankment, the men discovered foxholes on both sides, each with two men in them! The guards were sleeping! "Calmed down with a pistol butt," they continued to sleep. The two machine guns emplaced there were taken along. While Störck walked upright with his four men across the approximately eighty-meter-long bridge, the engineer platoon moved up and took the "sedated" guards under control.

The men had crossed two-thirds of the bridge, when a Russian guard approached them. They had to then use the ruse that had been discussed earlier, so that things did not go wrong. The Ukrainians then acted as though they had prisoners with them and spoke Russian to one another along the lines of: "Well, it looks like we're in a neighboring sector, but we need to get rid of these prisoners shortly." The guard was deceived by the measure and could be taken prisoner himself without a sound being uttered. Despite the darkness, things did not seem quite right to another guard, who was standing at the end of the bridge. He ran before Störck could reach him. He sounded the alarm and sought cover along the embankment.

By then, however, the rest of the platoon was across the bridge, and the machine guns could be quickly emplaced where ordered. In the blink of an eye, there were wild fireworks with machine guns and hand grenades. Most of the sleep-drunk Russians of the bridge guard force, who had been rendered panic stricken by the fires, surrendered. The bridge was taken. Signal flares arced skyward, the signal to the regimental commander, who had collocated his command post with the point of departure for the engineer platoon, that the operation had succeeded and that support needed to be sent to the engineer platoon. As it turned light, an immediate counterattack by the enemy lasting some thirty minutes was beaten back, since the regimental attack had also commenced by then.

In all, the Russians took losses of eighty-seven men in captured, killed, and wounded. The engineer platoon was able to capture five machine guns, two antitank guns and three mortars. In the course of that risky mission, it lost one man dead and one wounded.

A similar ruse was employed by the *II./Schützen-Regiment 3*. As a result of the fluent Russian of *Unteroffizier* Roemer (6th Company), the guards were overrun and his company was able to cross the Upa without a fight.

Schützen-Regiment 3 rapidly crossed its 1st Battalion across the river and took Demidowka. *Leutnant* Heurich, the acting commander of the 3rd Company, was killed. *Leutnant* Schuppius took his place, combed through the locality with his riflemen and drove the enemy from his closest trenches. The battalion was unable to advance further, however, since the Soviets held their main field positions. The 2nd Company of the battalion screened the right flank in the direction of Malaja Sujewa, since there was a constant stream of fire coming from there. When a patrol from the company felt its way forward toward the village around noon, it surprisingly entered the village, only to suddenly be engaged from all sides. The friendly riflemen had to pull back quickly; four dead and two wounded remained in the hands of the Soviets.

By early morning, the *II./Schützen-Regiment 3* had taken Dubowka. In the process, it spent its strength. The 7th Company advanced as far as Kamenka, but it was unable to move any further, despite support from the 10th and 11th Companies. It was not until *Schützen-Regiment 394* had crossed at Truschkino and Oserki that the general advance started making progress again.

Although a *Stuka* attack late in the morning had demolished considerable portions of the enemy field fortifications, it had not broken the enemy's will to resist. The riflemen were subjected to the full fury of the Russian fire the entire time. *Panzer-Regiment 6* did not join the fray until noon, since there was still no crossing point for tanks at Truschkino. *Oberstleutnant* Munzel decided to pull his 1st and 3rd Companies back and send them over the railway bridge that had been taken by the engineer platoon of *Schützen-Regiment 394*. While the two companies rolled north, the *I./Schützen-Regiment 394* succeeded in taking Truschkino after heavy fighting. Fortunately, the Upa in the vicinity of Kamenka was not too deep, with the result that the 2nd Company of *Panzer-Regiment 6* was able to immediately start fording the ice-cold water.

The friendly advance then turned fluid again. The fighting vehicles of *Oberleutnant* Markowski and the men of *Hauptmann* Peschke attacked east. Contrary to expectations, the heavily fortified Hill 292.2 could be taken. The tanks started advancing along the road between Wjewka-Staraja and Wjewka-Nowaje. The *7./Schützen-Regiment 3* had to conduct a fierce fight for the houses in Wjewka-Staraja, however, since numerically superior enemy forces had barricaded themselves there. Since it had turned dark in the meantime, the company was stuck outside the village.

Hauptmann Schneider-Kostalski arrived on the battlefield with his two companies. His 1st Company was immediately inserted into the line on the right wing of *Schützen-Regiment 3*, while the 3rd Company prepared for operations outside of Wjewka-Staraja. Since it had turned completely dark, the advance was halted for the day. Success was great. *Schützen-Regiment 3* took in 280 prisoners, but it also lost 16 dead and 51 wounded.

As soon as morning dawned, the attack was continued. The terrain was fairly flat; there was only high ground at the edges. Chimneys and mine works were seen everywhere, a reminder of the industrial area south of Tula. The men suffered terribly under the cold, since they still did not have any winter uniforms. Moreover, they offered good targets to the enemy in their field-gray coats in the snowy landscape.

Shortly after 0700 hours on 19 November, both *Kampfgruppen* moved out. On the right wing, the *I./Schützen-Regiment 3* (*Major* Wellmann), along with the attached *1./Panzer-Regiment 6* (*Oberleutnant* Vopel), succeeded in occupying Malaja-Sujewa. By doing so, it eliminated the threat to the flank there. *Oberleutnant* Vopel and the *2./Schützen-Regiment 3* advanced further to the east and established contact with the *3./Schützen-Regiment 3* (*Leutnant* Oesten) at Ssalassowka. An attack by the 3rd Company to the south was unable to develop, since the enemy opened heavy fire from the flank.

The *II./Schützen-Regiment 3*, neighboring its sister 1st Battalion on the left, had also moved out to the southeast and advanced just to the east of the main road. When contact was established with the 1st Battalion, the Russians pulled back. By noon, both battalions had reached Kalmyky-Mal. While *Major* Wellmann's riflemen screened to the south and west, *Hauptmann* Peschke's men continued advancing. His companies were able to occupy Kalmyky-Bolsch. That battalion then pushed its screening forces east as far as Markaschowa.

The main effort of the attack was with *Schützen-Regiment 394* and the two tank companies of *Hauptmann* Schneider-Kostalski. The objective was Bolochowka, which was entered on the Russian general staff map with a total of four houses. Imagine how surprised the German soldiers were when they fought their way forward, kilometer after kilometer and found out that they were dealing with an extensive industrial town! Bolochowka was no village—it was a defended industrial city!

As a result, *Schützen-Regiment 394* (*Oberstleutnant* Audörsch) was unable to take the locality in a frontal attack. Instead, his men pulled back slowly to the south in an effort to penetrate from there. Although the riflemen succeeded in getting over the high ground and literally work their way into the town meter-by-meter, the regiment suffered considerable losses on the first day. The 1st Battalion alone lost twelve dead and fifty-eight wounded. The losses were that large because the Siberians, who were facing our units there for the first time, did not open fire until practically pointblank range. The Soviets defended stubbornly from well-concealed positions, firing at the riflemen that appeared right in front of them. An example should suffice: The *II./Schützen-Regiment 394* was bounding its way forward into the town. Its lead company encountered a wooden fence. The fence suddenly collapsed upon itself. Behind it were Siberians. They opened fire on the 7th Company at fifty meters, cutting it down. The commander, *Oberleutnant* Multhaupt, was killed, along with two other officers and many enlisted personnel. By then, it was 1600 hours and night. The *3. Panzer-Division* transitioned to a security posture at Bolochowka and just to its south.

After Stalin was certain that Japan would not march against Russia, he withdrew the Siberian forces from the Far East and committed them to the fighting in front of Moscow.

Kampfgruppe Oberst Kleemann, consisting of *Schützen-regiment 3*, *Panzer-Regiment 6*, the *I./Schützen-Regiment 394*, , the *I./Artillerie-Regiment 75*, the *9./Artillerie-Regiment 75*, the *6./Artillerie-Regiment 69*, *Pionier-Bataillon 39*, elements of *Panzerjäger-Abteilung 521* and elements of *Panzerjäger-Abteilung 543*, was given the mission of taking Bolochowka.

The brigade staged around Ulanowka and started its attack at 1000 hours on 20 November. The artillery preparation proved ineffective in places, since it landed too short and, as a consequence of the morning fog and the smoldering mining facilities, observation was barely possible.

The *I./Schützen-Regiment 3* moved out with its 2nd Company on the right and its 3rd on the left. The 1st Company of *Leutnant* Lohse was used to reconnoiter and also screen the flank, oriented to the east. The *SPW* company advanced from Pagassowa, which was clear of the enemy, to the north. In doing so, it encountered two Russian tanks at a large mine. The Soviets from the 413th Rifle Division pulled back in the direction of Bolochowka. The *SPW* company then swung west to reinforce the attack of the battalion. *Leutnant* Braun, moving in the lead vehicle, was able to effectively support the 2nd Company, which was struggling for some mine facilities on the east edge of Bolochowka, with his 3.7-centimeter cannon. The Soviets had set up defensively there and in the wood line to the north. They were firing with mortars and heavy antitank guns. For the time being, the battalion had to call off its attack and set up all-round security. Contact with the 2nd Battalion of the regiment was maintained by a patrol led by *Unteroffizier* Ronneberg of the 3rd Company.

The *II./Schützen-Regiment 3* of *Hauptmann* Peschke, along with the *3./ Panzer-Regiment 6* of *Oberleutnant* Müller-Hauff, advanced on Bolochowka from the south. The 8th Company was able to assault the collective farm quickly and take the residential areas arrayed in front of the town from there. The 6th Company moved up alongside the 8th. The movements of both companies then bogged down, since they were receiving heavy fire from the nearby woods and the industrial facilities. The battalion brought up its infantry guns and the antitank platoon that had been attached to it. For the time being, however, they were still unable to advance, since Russian tanks had rolled up in the meantime.

Major Haas's reinforced *I./Schützen-Regiment 394* had crossed the 800 meters of open ground in the southwest in the meantime and was positioned at the edge of Bolochowka. A lot of houses and factories were burning in the town proper. The Siberians put up a brave defense and could only be driven out in tough house-to-house fighting. Since heavy Soviet tanks appeared, the rifle companies were unable to advance.

The regiment ordered the 8.8-centimeter *Flak* forward. The gun was able to take out the first fighting vehicle within a few minutes, but a second one approached. After four rounds, it was also eliminated. Then a T-34 appeared in front of the *I./Schützen-Regiment 3*. It drove into an excavation pit for construction and got stuck there.

The fighting for Bolochowka continued. House after house was taken in close combat. The fiercest resistance was being offered to the attacking riflemen from a two-story brick house. The headquarters of the Siberian 2nd Rifle Regiment, along with about seventy Red Army men, had barricaded itself inside. The infantry guns and a howitzer that had been brought forward fired sixty rounds into the building. A platoon from the *6./Schützen-Regiment 3* then moved out to assault. Russian rifle rounds started whistling around the ears of the German soldiers. *Hauptmann* Peschke thereupon ordered the attack called off.

The *I./Schützen-Regiment 394* had cleared the remaining houses of Bolochowka, although a few Russian tanks continued to cause unrest within the town. When the *8./Schützen-Regiment 3* combed through a nearby park, *Oberleutnant* Brandt and *Leutnant* Pauckstadt noticed an apparently abandoned KV-I. Just as the officers approached it, the heavy fighting vehicle rolled away with a howling engine and switched-on headlights. Fortunately, the 8.8-centimeter *Flak* was nearby. The cannoneers immediately took up a sight picture and, after the third round, they knocked out the tank. A fifth Russian fighting vehicle was set alight later on by antitank elements.

Darkness had descended. The Soviets continued to defend from the high brick house. *Leutnant* Weigel's engineers from the *2./Pionier-Bataillon 39* were brought forward. They penetrated into the house with 350 kilograms of demolitions and blew it up. Seventeen dead Russian officers remained behind; only a single First Lieutenant escaped with his life. The fighting for Bolochowka was over!

The *II./Schützen-Regiment 3* lost nine dead and thirty-seven wounded, including *Leutnant* Zimmermann and *Leutnant* Stegemann. Victory also cost the *I./Schützen-Regiment 394* dearly. In the last two days, *Schützen-Regiment 394* had suffered 125 wounded; since the start of the attack, 63 had been killed. *Leutnant* Dr. Lotze assumed command of the wiped-out *7./Schützen-Regiment 394*, with *Leutnant* Dürrholz taking over the regiment's 2nd Company.

The *I./Schützen-Regiment 3*, supported by the *3./Panzer-Regiment 6*, had continued to remain on the right flank. That afternoon, *Oberst* Kleemann had directed it to reconnoiter the wooded terrain to the northeast of Bolochowka. The 3rd Company took Hill 243.3, initially screening to the west and then to the north. The 2nd Company and the tank company turned towards the woods after a short artillery preparation. Despite the onset of darkness, the fighting vehicles and the riflemen entered the woods and combed through them. Around 1700 hours, the northern and eastern sides were reached. The riflemen spent the night there, after contact was established with the 3rd Company. The battalion took ninety prisoners; it lost two dead and fifteen wounded.

The night passed without any serious incident.

THE HISTORY OF *PANZER-REGIMENT 6*

The regimental history of *Panzer-Regiment 6* records the events of this chapter as follows:[4]

On 17 November, there was an orders conference concerning the attack scheduled for the next day. It was intended for the corps to break through the enemy forces on the Schiworona and the Upa with its two armor divisions and initially advance on Wenew, while screening in the direction of Tula. That meant, an envelopment of Tula from the right. Prior to the attack, the tanks received a coat of whitewash, which greatly diminished their visibility in the snow-covered terrain.

On 18 November, the tanks of *Major* Schneider-Kostalski headed out. Due to the black ice, progress was slow. It was not until 1200 hours that the locality of Trushkino could be taken by the riflemen. The 2nd Company forded the Upa. The men rested in a few small villages after the onset of darkness and did not advance on Bolochowka until the following morning. In contrast to the old Russian maps, which showed the locality as only having four houses, it turned out that the village had extensive industry. It was defended by heavy Russian tanks.

Bolochowka could not be taken by that evening. The tank companies and the regimental staff remained in a small village right below the ridgeline of the enemy-occupied town. It was not until 20 November that Bolochowka could be taken by *Schützen-Regiment 3* and *Panzergruppe Schneider-Kostalski*. Following that, the 2nd Company was attached to the *17. Panzer-Division*. On the following day, the 1st Company went to the *4. Panzer-Division*. The 3rd Company was then detached as well, a sign of the depleted numbers of tanks within those two divisions. During that time, the weather remained hazy, with frost conditions predominating. Over the next two days, there were no serious incidents.

---

4. Munzel, 104.

CHAPTER 9

Attack at Thirty Below

THE HEROISM OF THE GERMAN SOLDIER IN THE WINTER FIGHTING

We moved into the village last night, so that we could get a few hours of sleep. That pile of dirt had some name, no doubt. But no human could remember all those crazy names, which don't say a single thing to a soldier. Even the commander had to look at the map each time. Usually, he just said, "Whatchamacallit." Everyone knew what he meant. There was always an —owka, —owa, —awa, —ewa, —enka, or —inka involved. Who knew? With a few poverty-stricken wooden houses. The armored division had taken a number of villages in those frosty November weeks. In every case involving a "Whatchamacallit," one thing was in common: the quarters were limited, small, and damned uncomfortable—not to mention the bugs.

In the summer, we were thrown back by the unbearable stench that emanated from those dirty cabins. Not even a downpour forced us inside. Ten horses couldn't do it . . . or so we thought. Terrible thoughts about the itchy roommates: Bugs, fleas, and lice. Back then in the summer and then into the fall. Today, however, we were happy to be in any hole with a somewhat intact roof over our heads, where we could squash ourselves together on the straw like sardines in a can.

The straw provided limited warmth in those windy shacks. The German concept of a stall would be too lofty for these. Those ovens! They must have been invented by the mythological daughters of Danaus! They crackled and roared like chimneys in feudal lodges. But that was all they did. The heat shot out the chimney, with embers spraying across the roofs. If you put your body in front of it, the backside froze. Or the opposite. Under the blankets, the warm stink was thick enough to cut. Hammocks—that's what was needed. Since the floor maintained the temperature of an icebox. The cold rushed mightily in through the cracks, fissures and mouse holes in the frail floorboards, which had probably never seen a wet cleaning rag. The only thing that helped you was to be as healthy as a horse!

MARCHING AND FIGHTING!

Yes, it had become December. In the East!

War year 1941, the year of unparalleled victories, was coming to a close. We are fighting!

Marching and fighting! That was the ongoing slogan for the German warrior. Marching and fighting so the German homeland could live. The laws of the fathers are the orders for the sons.

Immortal was the luster of heroism that our victorious field armies had written in the incorruptible book of history during the difficult winter fighting during the World War in the East. It radiates over into our martial times. The murderous battles of attrition diverted our gaze more to the West. But the army in the East now knows what the last generation accomplished here. Like our fathers, so too do the youth march and fight on the side of comrades, who once also had the same youthful faces under their helmets.

It is the same raw winter of the eastern land. Only twenty-seven years later.

One powerful difference: the young army is fighting deep in the heart of the Soviet Union.

Bitterly hard winter fighting followed the battles of the fall with their endlessly streaming rainfall and tenacious muck. The hardships have become enormous. No fight demands more in superhuman effort than warfare in the hellish blaze of the wasteland or the ice storm of the East!

We march and march and march! Yesterday, today and tomorrow. Step-by-step, the miles grow. Kilometers that number by the hundreds, by the thousands on the long road.

But what does the soldier at the front know of heroism? What does he know of the laurels that are added to the flags and standards? He only knows the iron requirement of fulfilling one's duty to the utmost. That is always more than the individual person believes he can do: The highest measure of strength; courage that comes from the entire heart; self-sacrificing bravery; hardness to the point of exhaustion; deprivation to the point of collapse; unbending defiance; and, finally, putting your life on the line, day-by-day. That German fulfillment of duty, which only inquires about the virtues of a man, which only judges by that and which dares anew each day. That is a lot!

NIGHTS WITHOUT SLEEP

Around here, the heroes are marching by the thousands, and they do not know it. After all, the true warrior only perceives everything in his subconscious without rending an account of it. It is good that it is that way. Perhaps that is the reason, one of the secret sources of why the frontline soldier finds the strength to conduct his unimaginable performance. You shouldn't think about things . . . but, then, the winter storm pelted the shaky house with a thousand whipping furies. We could not sleep on the cold straw. The long hours bring about pondering all by themselves.

The life of a soldier takes place soberly and factually in the routine changes of his difficult duty. At some point, the snow and the frost will cause the fronts to solidify; we don't know when and don't ask. We will march. Yesterday evening, the liaison officer brought new orders for the Brandenburg rifle regiment. A couple of villages had to be taken, a couple of "Whatchamacallits" with —ki and —ka at the end. And so the day began one more time in the middle of the night with the darting light of a flashlight and the abrupt morning greeting of "Get up!" We get goose bumps when we peel out from under the blankets.

The time available before moving out is always short, even if you get up fully dressed. The flickering flames from the open oven door help the miserable stump of a candle to at least illuminate some of the narrow quarters. The riflemen look for their personal items. Not quite so simple, when one person is always standing in the way. You also have to scratch at the same time, since the bugs and the lice have been horribly intrusive once more. How can people vegetate year in and year out in this disgusting squalor? We've asked ourselves this question numerous times over the last few days, without ever being able to find an answer. It remains a puzzle. "Don't scratch!" one person warns. That's quite a trick when your throat is full of bite marks. I hope we didn't get any lice, someone else chimes in, while carefully wrapping newspaper around his woolen socks. That was our main worry. The *Obergefreiter* swore that straw was the best. He said he was smart stuffing his boots full.

WHEN THE TIP OF YOUR NOSE TURNS WHITE

"Dress . . . warm . . . ly," the *Unteroffizier* crooned. That was his daily greeting. Properly pull the head protection over the ears so that only eyes, nose and mouth appear as little moons on the face. "Watch out for the tips of your noses! If they turn white . . ." The *Unteroffizier* didn't need to say anything else. The squad knew what was what. You had to pay damned close attention to yourself, so that you did not get frostbite on your feet, hands, cheeks or nose. The motorcycle infantry and the motorcycle messengers had to take special precautions. The riflemen promised to pay attention to one another and to massage faces lovingly, if only the smallest white fleck showed up.

Belt on . . . a couple of hand grenades in it . . . carbine or submachine gun in your hand. The cold steel bit icily through the woolen gloves and into the tips of the fingers. "It'll soon get warm enough," Gunner One said, reflectively. That was the first sentence spoken about the upcoming attack. A sip of tea—the canteen was a solid block of ice. The carefully preserved contents from yesterday were frozen all the way up to the neck. That happened whenever you placed the canteen on the floor next to the sleeping area.

The snow-covered landscape appeared eerily like a distant moonscape. The moon, which had hung in the night blue heavens like a large lamp yesterday evening, had disappeared. The outlines and shapes of houses and trees, pathways and ditches became indistinguishable and flowed into one another as a foggy haze. The wind blew the snow dust across the fields. The funeral shroud of nature still barely reached the height of the stubble. The days of heavy snowfall were yet to come.

WASTELAND IN ICE AND SNOW

The path was slick and bumpy. All of a sudden, someone was up to his knees in snow. He roared out some curse words. You could not see the sides of the road. The toes had been icy cold for a long time, no matter what you did. Occasionally, some one would breathe into his gloves in order to loosen up the stiff fingers. Where was the north? The directions of the compass circle on a turntable—it was no different in the African desert. Again and again, the compass needed to come to the rescue. No route, no pathway was marked; one settlement was the same as the next. The battalions of the motorized rifle regiments marched on foot. They were infantry, just like grenadiers and musketeers. The vehicles could only be brought up later. The supply route was marked for them. A tiresome, slow march. It went across frozen-over creeks and across the ice cover of a pond. The hours crept by; morning did not want to arrive. But the *coup de main* could not be conducted without light and sight.

Finally, in the background, the blue-shimmering wall of an extended patch of woods was distinguishable. The assault soldiers prepared to attack in front of it. The villages and patches of woods, which were like islands and islets in front of the dark and threatening belt of woods, were the first objectives. A broad cut in the woods went right through the middle, just as indicated on the map. The area to the right was fully contaminated by mines. The patrols had determined that already. Woodland fighting places the highest of demands on the individual soldier. It demands complete mastery of close-combat weapons and the highest of bravery from the individual. The terrain rolled slightly in the approach to the village with its two long rows of houses. The depressions were the only concealed spots. The earth had turned into a mass of stone. It was frozen solidly a good thirty centimeters deep. No shovel would work there. Even with a mattock, you needed hours. That meant you needed to exploit every hollow fully.

THE ASSAULT DETACHMENT ATTACKS

The riflemen worked their way forward in a wide arc. The machine guns went into position. It was the same as it always was, except that the stiff limbs didn't want to cooperate. On the inside, however, the natural excitement ran hot through the veins. For some young soldiers, newly arrived as replacements, their hearts were beating out of their chests. Only the "old hands" looked at the wood line with narrow eyes. That was the place where all hell could break out at any moment. They had the confidence of the experienced veteran, the warrior, who had turned hard against fate in many an assault. The fireball of the sun pushed its first ring, glowing red, above the horizon. The machine guns hammered out their familiar *rat-tat-tat-tat*, which made one's heart settle down. The mortars banged away at the edge of the village. The assault force surged forward all at once. Before the Bolshevik guards could recover from the shock, they had been overrun. Individual firing from the houses. Hand grenades blew open doors . . . rounds were fired through windows. A house on the right side of the street caught fire and machine-gun bullets whipped down the long village street. The Bolsheviks fled to the other side of the creek bottomland and then further into the woods. By the time the disk of the sun hung deeply in the azure skies like a red-glowing iron disk, the village had been conquered.

Behind every hill was a toughly defended strongpoint of the enemy. The signals platoon raced forward with its drums of wire and field telephones. The regimental commander came down the road at a rapid clip. For a second, the icy legs thawed out. The house that bore witness to the lively activities of a command post for a short while had been nicely tiled by the Bolsheviks. The prisoners were already being given a quick interrogation. Approximately 300 Soviet personnel had escaped into the woods. There had been 386 soldiers positioned in the village. The rations count of the mess sergeant, who had also been taken prisoner, proved that beyond the shadow of a doubt. The sound of fighting echoed ever stronger over from the wood line.

The sunny winter days are nice! Like sleepy alpine villages, the small localities sought their protection in the depressions. To have a set of skis under you right now! From a distance, one could imagine sugarcoated gingerbread houses—but only from a distance, as already stated. At that point, the Soviet artillery turned lively. Their shells and heavy mortar rounds were already sweeping into the creek bottomland. It was right at the spot that the prime movers and trucks had to cross. The Bolsheviks had dammed the waters and then released them. Because of that, the first prime mover broke through the ice blanket. The ice wasn't thick enough for the tanks yet, either.

DIFFICULT OBSTACLES

The hardships take no end! First the mud soup, in which the tracked vehicles were outclassed, and now the slick black ice, on which the tracked vehicles cannot get a grip. An embankment or a slightly rising riverbank, over which cross-country wheeled vehicles roll without any particular problems, are a terrible obstacle for the tracks of the combat vehicles, assault guns and prime movers. The crossing had to be forced in a hail of enemy artillery fire. Contact up front could not afford to be lost. Those were some bitter moments at the iced-over creek! The slope was made "tractable" by the use of pick mattocks, and a ramp was created with beams and tree trunks. The close-by impacts forced people under cover again and again. On the rock-hard earth, the shrapnel was projected with triple force. The rushing and gurgling of the German artillery then answered back into the identified enemy battery positions. The Bolshevik mortars fell silent; the artillery rounds started to be scattered. Round after round impacted into the edge of the woods until the flanking fire had been eliminated. At that point, the sled run was the only opponent that had to be overcome...for the time being.

At the edge of the woods was a long column of antitank vehicles, fighting vehicles and motorcycles. It was a tried-and-true and powerful ready reserve that was waiting for orders. The white-camouflaged vehicles barely stood out from the gleaming snow. The wind had fallen asleep. During the noontime hours, the temperature had climbed to 12 below [10.4 Fahrenheit]. But fingers and toes did not want to get warm. The drivers continued to hammer on the tracks of the tanks. They tightened up the ice cleats. Otherwise, the heavy steel vehicles would slide down steep slopes like sleds or spin their tracks, powerless, on the opposite slope, not budging from the spot. This winter warfare brought difficulties and unimagined obstacles, wherever you looked. The soldier had to cope with it somehow. In the woods, there was a deep-cut defile over a creek bed that had to be crossed. No one could say in advance whether the tracked vehicles could force it. It was impossible to go around, as route reconnaissance had determined.

HARD FIGHTING FROM VILLAGE TO VILLAGE

The Commander pulled out his watch again and again. But we had to wait. Every once in a while a couple of endurance runs to warm up. According to the radio reports, the rifle regiment was making good progress in the woods. The village in the woods, located along the long cut, was assaulted after a short firefight. The Bolsheviks, who had fled from the first village, got tangled up with the ones there. The time and the sun were pressing— but this is how it is: The soldier looks at the clock face on which the hands turn, slowly or fast, depending on fate. The leadership looks at the delicate clockwork behind the face. It looks at the finely machined teeth on the cogs that move the hands. The main effort of this attack was with a neighboring division, whose advance we were protecting along its flanks. In the creation of the world, this flank is but a shrunken piece of the earth's crust, like a dead sea struck by a high wave. The eye only scans for a new ridgeline that has to be taken. Peaks and valleys, like an entire life. It was a landscape created for the defense. The Soviets had therefore transformed the many villages and clusters of houses into innumerable strong-points, in which their reserves, most of them fighting for the first time, struck hard and fiercely. Their main point of resistance was located in the left-hand portion of the woods that stretched out broadly in front of us.

Along its southern edge, a hard fight raged from village to village. A rifle regiment employed there was only able to advance slowly. The tank company was alerted. We rolled towards the Brandenburg rifle regiment with the antitank elements and the motorcycles. The rifle regiment had already fought its way to the northern edge of the woods. The cut in the woods, packed with tree trucks, was difficult to negotiate. The tracked vehicles had to go back and forth in order to make it through at all. The village in the woods showed signs of a successful *coup de main.* One gun with its tractor was suddenly in the middle of German assault forces; a complete column of supplies was caught on its way to the front—forty *panje* carts fully loaded with ammunition, machine guns, and rations. A couple of trucks completed the picture.

THE IMPOSSIBLE MADE POSSIBLE

But that valley with the creek—a veritable "Wolf's Gorge" from the *Freischütz! Kübelwagen* and trucks were able to make it through with aplomb. For the antitank elements, however, the ice cover over the creek—or was it a river?—had to be reinforced with beams. Every vehicle had to be guided through individually. It seemed impossible to scale the steep serpentine on the other side. The company commander yelled himself hoarse, but that didn't matter. By evening, the watercourse had been forced. That was the main thing! The wild decision to make the impossible possible had also triumphed over that natural obstacle. No one would have ever thought of such a thing on maneuvers—yes, we did those at one time! Even the most experienced of generals would have shaken his head.

In the first village beyond the woods, the regiment set up its command post for the night. The regimental commander, *Oberstleutnant* Z.[1] a

---

1. Hermann Zimmermann, who received his Knight's Cross on 4 September 1940 while still a *Major* and the commander of the *II./Schützen-Regiment 3.* He went on to command the same regiment. He was also a recipient of the German Cross in Gold (28 July 1943). He survived the war, passing away in Lensahn/Eutin on 11 January 1978.

Knight's Cross recipient known throughout the armor division for his pluck and dash, sat next to the oven and thawed out his ice-stiffened limbs. He had marched the entire day, just like his riflemen. As always, in an effervescent mood. His soldier's humor could not be shaken by anything. "It went well!" He said to the commander of our *Kampfgruppe*. A supply headquarters had been surprised in this village. There was also a large spotlight set-up with film projectors and a printing truck. One battalion reported the taking of a large communications center. Another battalion had reached the main road north of the woods. It still had to be secured. By surprise, the division commander, Knight's Cross recipient *Generalmajor* B.,[2] appeared with his aide-de-camp in the packed room. He blew into his hands, knocked his feet against one another and cursed the damned cold just like everyone else. He was an icicle, just like everyone else who came in from outside. The *Oberstleutnant* cheerfully offered his warm oven. The *Generalmajor* waved it off, with a laugh: "No need, Z[immermann], I'm training to be a sled driver at the North Pole." The brigade commander then arrived, *Oberst* K.,[3] big and lanky.

The commanders then looked at the map with the *Generalmajor*. The area for the combat outposts was established. It was anticipated that the Bolsheviks would launch counterattacks the next day.

OUTPOSTS IN THE NIGHT—DEFENDING AT ALL COSTS

The small village that our *Kampfgruppe* with the antitank elements had to screen was located between the woods and the road. It had become a clear, frosty night filled with stars when we pulled in. The full moon had a gigantic halo. How cold was it? Our thermostat only went to 20 below [-4 Fahrenheit]—that wasn't low enough! The edges of the woods were dark and secretive, like stage backdrops. The soldiers of the rifle company were happy to see us, their reinforcements. Engineers hacked out foxholes at the edge of the depression. The antitank elements rattled up to the high ground in front of the village. The howitzers occupied firing positions in front of the last few houses. Their tubes were pointed towards the road, which could be made out with its telegraph poles 1,500 meters to the right. There was a rifle regiment there; it would most likely be the one that would initially have to fend off the counterattack of the Soviets. We walked

2. Hermann Breith.
3. Ulrich Kleemann.

the line of outposts with the commander one more time. The village was located deep within a depression. It was relatively safe against artillery fire, but no edge of the large pot could afford to be lost, otherwise we would be sitting there like cornered rabbits. Three houses along the village street were ablaze. They served as guideposts from afar for the Soviets as to where the German lines were. The Bolsheviks had not been able to set more on fire during their flight—fortunately.

Most of the houses were unfit for humans. An infernal stink made even a short stay impossible, worse than some dilapidated Negro kraal. To a certain extent, the cold allowed us to bear most anything, but the crap had a limit! The commander designated a wooden house as his command post. Believe it or not, the hole had a living room of two by three meters! That was being generous. Next to it was a portioned area next to the oven, where the family stayed: a man emaciated by illness; his wife; a toothless hag, probably the grandmother; and children of both sexes, arrayed in size like organ pipes, six in number. They lay on the oven, on the bench in front of it and on rags next to it. Two skinny dogs played with three young cats—they were terrible quarters, but the others were no better. Those nights—no one in the homeland could imagine what they were like!

NO THOUGHT OF SLEEP

There were no hay barns far and wide. We had to take the bushels of straw that had been mounted all along the walls to protect against the frost in order to create a sleeping area. The engines had to be kept warm as well. Despite that, the machines had to be run every hour to keep them immediately available. Together with the commander, the five of us slept "on edge." Turning was impossible. We were just happy to be able to stretch out a bit; sleep was impossible, anyway. Whenever tiredness overpowered us, the ring of a telephone jarred us awake. After midnight, the situation was clear. We would not attack the next morning. The village had to be held under all circumstances.

The rockets of the Bolshevik launchers rattled over our positions several times in a wild whirlwind of a barrage. There were flames shooting up on the right flank in the village. The Soviets had fired incendiary rockets again. Machine guns rattled with warning bursts of fire. Then fifty, maybe sixty rounds howled over the village. Get out! The fiery flowers shot up in the snow on the opposite slope like dancing will-o-the-wisps. There was no doubt about it: The Bolsheviks were going to launch their counterattack while it was still dark. But we were ready. Once again, the shower of rockets hissed over the roofs and into the opposite slope. Mortar, dreck and dust trickled down on us. Then the antitank elements up front let loose with the high-pitched bark that was typical of them. The howitzer battery sounded its loud alarm thunderously. It was 0600 hours. The heavens were covered over with clouds; visibility was poor. The Soviets had initiated the expected attack on the village along the road on the right flank.

It was the opening act of a fierce struggle against a manifold numerical superiority and against tanks and artillery that was to last days and nights for two miserable villages, two "whatchamacallits," whose name no one knew and hardly anyone cared to know. They had to be held, since the advance of the other *Kampfgruppen* was dependent on their possession. It was immaterial why! They had to be held and held they were. Their names were burned into our memories.

Our eyes were filled with tears, when we trotted out to the battery position. The east wind was as sharp as a knife.

SIBERIAN RIFLEMEN OVER THERE

The division order for that day was two pages of narrow-spaced type. For our small *Kampfgruppe*, there was a sentence: "holds the line reached and secures the area until the arrival of *Infanterie-Regiment 'Großdeutschland'*" This meant defending against an enemy attacking with strong forces, who wanted to retake the lost ground with all the means at his disposal! It had been determined that the remnants of a Siberian rifle division were in the woods arrayed around our village in the depression like an open hand. The division had been pushed back at this spot—the widest portion of the belt of woods, some eight kilometers deep—in the weeks of fighting. The forward Soviet outposts were located at the point where the woods started off to the right of the main road.

Attack and defense! Those were the two polar extremes in the world of the warrior.

Attack! Short and cutting, like a rousing clarion call. Defense! Heavy and weighty like three muffled drum beats. That the way it sounds in the soul. An idle question to ask which a soldier prefers. Does he prefer the exhilarating rush of the wild charge, during which the charging soldier chases after his own racing heart until he breaks into the positions of the enemy? Or does he prefer biting onto a piece of foreign ground that is being swept by a fiery hurricane from the enemy and has to be held to the last drop of blood? The frontline soldier takes the lots that fate dispenses from the horn of plenty. Yesterday attack, today defense. One order as difficult as the next. There is no difference.

If there is one thing that burns itself deep into your heart from the experience of war, then it is the truly deeply stirring image of the self-sacrificing assault soldier, who goes into battle with confident equanimity and manly composure—both the young and the old, regardless of whether infantryman, rifleman, engineer, cannoneer, tanker, antitank man or *Flak* cannoneer. For weeks . . . for months . . . for years. It is heroism that is taken as a matter of course. It the bridge between the generations of two world wars.

This observation—the fallout of our nightly conversations on the unfriendly straw mattress—is placed here ahead of the account of the defense of the two localities, our village in the depression and the neighboring village along the road. Caught up in the swells of the martial happenings, the eyes can only register with professional objectivity the external events of the fighting.

AN ENEMY COUNTERATTACK IS TURNED BACK

The village on the road was under Bolshevik artillery fire. We heard the rolling impacts reverberate and saw the flames of the bursting rounds between the houses, as we crawled up the high ground behind the last of the log cabins. It jutted out there a bit, perhaps two kilometers distant. For that reason, the first counterattack of the Soviets took place along the road. The outposts of the rifle battalion had to pull back, fighting, from the outskirts of the village into the village proper. At that point, our howitzer battery placed a barrier of fire on the road in front of the village. The guns were located at the edge of our village in the portion that sloped downhill. The battery commander, one of the most dashing artillerymen of the regiment, personally directed the fire by radio from the flank. The radio section sat in a wood shed. The icy wind whistled through the cracks. The battery officer called out his commands from there. "Distance same . . . fire!" *Rumms!* The rounds thundered out of the barrels.

The dawning day slowly allowed more visibility. They were in dire straits over at the edge of the next village. The Bolsheviks had worked their way forward dangerously close to the edge. In the short breaks between the firing of the guns and the impacts of their rounds, the rapid hammering of the German machine guns firing extended bursts echoed our way, as well as the slower tack-tack-tack of the Soviet machine guns. The Bolsheviks made small bounds in groups of twenty or thirty men. Whenever the German rounds hit among them with whirlwind fury, they hit the deck. At that point, they were barely identifiable in their white snow shirts. But their ranks grew thinner with each bound. Only one figure always remained standing, his armed stretched out in front of him. That was probably an officer or a commissar. Eventually a direct hit devoured him. At that point, the others attempted to run back.

The rounds were right on their heels. The lightning flashed in short intervals from the howitzers. The cannoneers trotted about in their thick overcoats. Their breath surrounded them like smoke from a beekeeper's apiary. At the edge of the depression, it might have been a bit colder. Whenever you spend a moment on the ground observing, you fear you might freeze to the earth as a clump of ice. The enemy attack was turned back. The Bolshevik artillery continued to fire round after round into the village, however. The riflemen had to hold out in the hail of shrapnel and rock, next to collapsing house walls and in front of burning houses and stalls. Would the Bolsheviks be forced into another attack?

ANTITANK GUNNERS TO THE FRONT!

Of course, the command post of the commander of our *Kampfgruppe* was connected by wire with the command post of the battalion commander in the neighboring village and with the regiment. Soviet tanks had approached ever closer to the village next to the road through the extended fold in the ground. Antitank elements were requested. One platoon was ready to move with running engines. The tank destroyers rolled through the valley at the entrance to the village and towards the rear of the contested village. The valley crossed the depression like a tub. The company commander had instructed the young *Leutnant* to "be careful while approaching...the terrain can be observed from some distance." The advice was the same for the second platoon, which was directed to patrol from our village in the direction of the edge of the woods.

"Don't take your eyes off the woods . . . there's got to be AT guns there!"

In their thick shrouds, the platoon leaders were only able to nod. Despite their youth, they were old hands, who had been on successful hunts before. But the location of the village turned out to be even less favorable in daylight than we had assumed when we pulled in during darkness the previous day. The superstructures of the tank destroyers grew like masts on the horizon whenever they crossed the high portions of the rolling terrain. They were more likely to come into the enemy's view before they could see anything themselves.

In the west, there was a patch of woods located in front of the large forest. Next to it was a suspicious haystack. That was the objective of the patrol. Under cover of the antitank elements, a platoon of riflemen had been directed to establish an outpost in that patch of woods. On the map, the small green fleck marked with the map symbols of coniferous trees looked like a brush. The commander christened it the "brush woods."

"Come back when it turns dusk!"

In case of a night attack, the patch of woods could not be held by a platoon. The *Leutnant* placed his hand to his helmet, on which he had mounted some white linen as a field expedient. He was still very young, but you could tell he was all man and a warrior by the way he shouldered his submachine gun, straightened out his hand grenades and tramped through the snow at the head of his platoon, as it moved in column. The "brush woods" were in good hands!

THE CAPTURED VILLAGES BECOMES AN ISLAND

"This is 'lamp,' over!"

The codenames for the units were inventive, whenever a composed voice reported in the middle of hot combat action and "zebra," "toothpick," "Indian," "linseed oil," or someone else said something striking. This time, "nuisance," the regiment, reported back. The commander's forehead narrowed. Bad news. The village in the woods behind us had been lost once again during the late-night hours in fierce close combat against a numerically superior foe. That meant the supply route was temporarily cut off, our village an island. A rifle company had just been committed to an immediate counterattack; the grenadiers of *Großdeutschland"* were fighting their way up from the south through the woods. They would have to first take the lane in the woods and the village before they could come to reinforce and relieve us.

An alert was not necessary. Every man in the *Kampfgruppe* was already committed and at his post. Two more patrols of riflemen and engineers got ready immediately and snuck off into the woods. The expectation caused nerves to tense up, as always, whenever you had to wait for an attack. On the outside, however, everyone gave the appearance of firm composure. Our situation was not a rosy one at the moment. Not even the strongest man could say that. Everyone could see what was up, whether commander or simple rifleman, but just as firm was the conviction that our village would be held.

The combat patrol conducted by the antitank elements returned back over the edge of the depression and rolled back into its old positions along the ice-covered road. Two hours had passed; a thousand meters away, the haystack was engulfed in bright flames. Yes, there's another measurement of time in warfare as opposed to maneuvers! The *Leutnant* rendered a short report, almost like a telegram, as was the norm. Our initial distrust had been justified. When the tank destroyers crawled up the closest fold in the ground, the patrol leader saw a barrel jutting out of the straw through his binoculars. The first round burst apart in the mountain of straw, which immediately caught fire. The second and third rounds hit right under the gun tube. Probably a Soviet tank. The *Leutnant* observed the fighting vehicle lurch back, but then everything turned into a blazing torch. Along the wood line, the patrol had slugged it out with Bolshevik antitank guns. The results could not be determined. A light snowfall had started and continuously reduced visibility.

The field mess ladled out a hot barley soup. At least the stomach would be a little bit warm. In that heartbreakingly cold weather, even pearl barley was a distinct pleasure. Unfortunately, it was only a short one. After a couple of spoonfuls, it was over. The neighboring battalion was calling!

"Enemy tanks approaching your village!"

The regiment also alerted us. It was two o'clock.

"I'll give you a bottle, if you knock one out," the regimental commander said.

"We'll try to earn us one," the commander replied.

Nothing could shake him. The antitank elements were there to hunt tanks, after all. A couple of short orders. The company commander rattled off with his tank destroyers. A gun from the howitzer battery covered the way into the village. We searched the area around us from the edge of the depression. Nothing could be identified. Even in the nearby village with its burning houses, the haze from the snow and the whirling flakes only allowed shadowy silhouettes to be seen.

THE BOLSHEVIKS ATTACK

All of a sudden, just like the first loud thunderclap of a storm, the sound of fighting from the neighboring village jumped into our ears. The Bolsheviks attacked under the cover of the snowstorm. Their tanks were supposed to support them from the flanks. New fire commands to the battery. They fired as fast as they could. Where were the rounds impacting? In the western portion of the village . . . over there . . . where the church raised its silhouette into the milky skies. That meant the Soviets had penetrated into the village. At such close range, the fires had to be exact. In the middle of a house . . . then another . . . new fires climbed high to join the old ones. The machine guns sang their song of the Grim Reaper uninterruptedly.

"Smoke!" the battery officer ordered.

The cannoneers scooted over to the ammunition vehicles. Go, go! But the path there had been turned into a sledding path for some time. One of them actually slid the entire way with both of the round baskets, with the result that the rounds proper rolled by themselves to the loader. Fifty meters back and forth, that'll get you warm. And a round is fired much too quickly.

Distance? 1,400! The two Soviet tanks, apparently heavily armored twenty-six-tonners, had pushed themselves dangerously close into the flank. But then the smoke rose like fog in a fall night out of the depression. It was whiter than snow and in balled clouds. The tanks had been deprived of all visibility. The pulled back as quickly as possible to the road on the far side of the neighboring village. Their rounds sailed over us.

HORRIFIC COLD

In the afternoon, night hovered high above the woods. It seemed to have gotten colder! The tears under the eyes—and under the nose—freeze solid in no time at all. The wind whipped through us thoroughly and remorselessly. For hours on end, the outposts and the guards perched in the holes they had dug out with great effort. The latest attack by the

Bolsheviks had collapsed in the concentrated fires of the German defenses. A platoon of infantry guns rolled into the village. It went into position on the side facing the neighboring village. That meant the regiment was expecting an attack on our village in the depression as well! The antitank elements came back. They did not have any hunting trophies. In war, nothing can be forced. The guns had been able to approach to within 1,500 meters. In the next depression, they would have been like targets on a gunnery range. The company commander had crawled forward on his stomach and observed everything. The tanks were positioned in the bend in the road in front of the neighboring village. It was not possible to close to within firing range in that terrain.

The young *Leutnant* led his platoon back from the "brush woods" in a column with five-meter intervals. Enemy patrols had attempted to approach several times. But the riflemen were on the ball. A couple of bursts of fire kept the Bolsheviks at a respectable distance. The engineer patrol had advanced as far as the Bolshevik battery positions, which was at the tip of the woods that jutted out towards the road like a linden leaf.

"I saw the muzzle flashes of three guns. Here . . ." He pointed to the spot on the commander's map. They were marked and the report was passed on to the regiment.

"See anything else of the enemy?"

"*Jawohl,* on the way back, we were bypassed by an enemy patrol and engaged."

"Casualties?"

"No. We were able to pull back under cover of our machine guns."

The commander had to pull practically every word out of him. He was the essence of a dependable engineer noncommissioned officer. Discovered the position of the Bolshevik battery—the piddling little fire afterwards, who wanted to make a big deal out of it?

"Go warm yourself up a bit and have a sip of hot tea. It's not going to be very quiet tonight and the outpost lines need to be reinforced!"

THE NIGHT BEFORE THE RELIEF

Once again, it had turned both evening and night in a quick death of the day. The noise of the fighting that had abated sounded like the rushing of the sea, but it never quit entirely for a single minute. The rounds sounded menacing gurgling above the village. It was a German battery that was placing harassing fires on the Soviet positions from a more distant village. A nice, calming sound from the heavens. The field telephone jangled once more on the table in the hole, where we would spend another night on guard. If only it didn't stink so badly! It took your breath away. But it was warm. The family had once again grouped itself next to and on the oven around the moaning old man.

The leader of "pest" was calling for the leader of "lamp." The village in the cut in the woods was once again in German hands after several self-sacrificing assaults. Casualties had been taken. The riflemen had assaulted with dogged determination. In exemplary fashion, disregarding the dangers, the company commander had died at the forefront of his men. The difficult struggle had lasted hours. The surprise assault of the "*Großdeutschland*" grenadiers had tipped the scales. The Bolsheviks were completely wiped out. Whoever was not left behind dead or captured saved his skin by disappearing into the underbrush of the dense woods. It was possible that they had been pushed back in the direction of our village. Over in the village along the road, the second company commander, *Leutnant* P., had been killed.

"Well, they also got *Leutnant* P. now . . . ," the commander said, more to himself than anyone else. He had been irrepressible in his humor and his pluck. Where had we seen each other the last time? It was in the muck along the Suscha, which he stormed a few days later with his company. That was when we saw him again, quite by accident, as is often the case in a division. He had picked up a *panje* cart and was headed slowly up to the front in it.

"My one-horsepower vehicle!" he said to us, laughing. Yes, *Leutnant* P. was always resourceful. Everyone liked him because of his pleasant spirit. Now he was resting in a small, unknown and hotly contested village, like so many of his comrades, who had given their lives for the freedom of the homeland.

"That's the way it is," someone said. "Always be prepared for everything—to the very end."

DUGOUTS ARE CREATED

The obligations of those living remained the same; the shoulders did not bend under the burden! The supply route was clear again. The prime movers were sent off to pick up the essential ammunition during the night. Muffled detonations were heard from the southern edge of the village. Engineers were blowing dugouts out of the frost-hardened earth. The routes to the neighboring village and the woods were mined. The rifle outposts also got mines ready. The grenadiers from *"Großdeutschland,"* who were held up by the fighting in the woods, would not be able to relieve us until later. The brigade commander had had it announced. We walked the positions one more time with the commander; a friendly word from the *Major* was like a warm gulp of tea for the soldiers in those miserable, roughed up positions.

"Don't fall asleep . . . relieve the observation posts after an hour, at the latest!" the commander drilled it in.

During the night, the temperature in the open areas, where the storm continued to rage unabated and in full fury, sank to -37 [-34.6 Fahrenheit].

The other rifle regiment attacked that night to relieve the villages on the southern edge of the woods. Despite ice, snow and a polar cold, it assaulted the villages. During that night, the grenadiers from *Infanterie-Regiment "Großdeutschland:* fought their way through the woods to the north. What did all of that mean? The fingers, stiff and half frozen, were barely able to pull the bolt back or pull the trigger or feed a new belt of machine-gun ammunition. The feet were dead weight on the body; the eyes burned from being so cold—but the heart was warm! The heart forced everything. That is the wonderful heroism of the German soldier. On a lonely peak in the world!

THE VILLAGE IS EVACUATED

During the night, it became clear that the village along the road could no longer be held. It no longer existed. We looked across to it through the cross depression running through the valley. The entire locality was a single mass of flame. A gruesome view of destruction as the tongues of flames, spitting their fireworks, turned the snow on the earth and the clouds into a Bengal red. But our senses weren't contemplating the Romantic period. The regiment telephoned that the battalion was evacuating the locality. Only one company would remain behind until the morning to screen. It was clear. It would have made no sense for the battalion to continue to hold out in the sea of flames and rubble. At that point, however, our village in the depression stuck out like an index finger into the Bolshevik front. If the neighboring village were evacuated, then the next attack would be directed against our village in the depression. That meant that the perpendicular defile had to be secured at all costs. Two antitank vehicles rolled to the outskirts of the village. The infantry guns had to occupy a position from which they could fire to two sides.

The rounds continued to howl above us. The battery behind us placed continuous harassment fire on the road in front of the burning village. The Bolshevik artillery continued to fire into the blazing ruins. Then we heard the familiar whirlwind of numerous reports. We held up.

"Rocket launchers!"

There was a rushing sound and howling . . . there was a crashing and a shaking on the opposite slope, just like the previous night. That had been intended for us.

"We'll have some nice artillery fire here in the morning!" the commander said. Tomorrow . . . reinforcements were supposed to arrive tomorrow . . . the grenadiers from *"Großdeutschland"* were supposed to relieve us tomorrow . . . tomorrow . . . and night was just starting . . . it was going to be a long one!

THE COLDEST NIGHT SO FAR

We went to our quarters hole. The brigade commander had called. The neighboring division had made good progress. The adjutant had already marked the reported positions on the map. That was, after all, the reason behind our holding out in these villages. The storm wind was shaking the fragile door on its hinges with wild fury. Another bitterly cold night, the coldest one so far in the campaign. Despite that, it did not keep us in the house. The skies behind the house were a flaming red, brighter than the red of mornings during those December days. That had to be the village in the woods; farther to the right, the riflemen of the sister regiment were attacking. It was like a beacon for us…

The eyes of German soldiers were staring towards the enemy that night . . . from the White Sea to the Black Sea.

The army in the East was doing its duty: for the homeland, for Germany, for Europe.

We listened attentively into the night. We waited . . .

The hours of a winter's night at the front are long!

We looked over silently towards the burning locality. The storm wind swept the flames like tattered flags from the houses.

We listened attentively into the night and waited.

Defend—that meant to be ready at any second and to be able to wait. To wait for the second that matters with stoic determination.

We didn't care for the cross route below the crest of the hill that was used for supply. We observed it with the instinctive distrust of the frontline soldier. If the village across from us were to be evacuated in the morning, then we would have the Bolsheviks right in our flank. Correspondingly, two heavy mortars were to set up during the night behind the outbuildings of the first few houses. The howitzer battery bumped and rattled its way out of the village. It had been directed to take up a firing position further to the rear. After all, the front lines would be here in the morning. Only the work gun[4] remained behind for protection against tanks. The forward observer reported in with his section. The commander briefed him, saying: "Pay particular attention to this depression!"

A messenger came sliding in along the ice rink of a road. "The sounds of engines in the depression, *Herr Major*!" We had already heard it. Whenever the storm took pause to catch its breath for a new round, the deep roar of tanks could clearly be heard in the vicinity of the village that was going down in garish red flames along the road. Sound traveled far during those winter nights.

"That's would be something for you," the commander said to the company commander of the antitank company. For the time being, there was nothing more to be said. We had raised our head warmers up above our eyes like the visor on a knight's helmet. The vapor trails of our breath immediately froze into little pearl droplets. The cold was barbaric. The *Oberleutnant* droned something into the upturned collar of his overcoat. It was probably something to the effect of "I'll have to take a look." A few minutes later, we saw him disappear with two men on the far side of the ridgeline in front of the "brush woods."

At that point, a German machine gun barked for a short while somewhere off to our rear. That had to have been at the location of the engineers, on the far side of the fork in the road, where a forlorn row of houses crawled down to the bottomland. Afterwards, it was quiet. Maybe someone was only warming up his barrel. It was also possible in that blurry

---

4. A work gun was generally a gun from the battery that set up in a displaced position in order to hide the location of the actual battery when registration or other missions (e.g., harassment fire) were being conducted.

light that terrain was distorted into strangely odd silhouettes. And it was a full-moon night! But the balloon of light remained behind the milky veil of a thick layer of clouds and only allowed the snow covering to gleam wanly and without shadows. It was better to have your finger on the trigger too early than to late—that was our rule of thumb.

We took the lay of the land one more time in front of the door to our quarters. Yes, the noise generated by a Soviet tank could still be heard. Then the Four Horsemen of the Apocalypse thundered across our quiet valley one more time and shook anew the tortured opposite slope with a salvo of Bolshevik rockets.

"Two hours until the next set . . ."

We patted off the dust on our overcoats that had sifted down on us. The concussion shook the fragile log cabin to its foundation each time, inasmuch as you could talk about a foundation in those shacks.

It was midnight. We sat around the table, silent and dozing off. Until someone pulled out a package of Christmas cards from a bag. The map section of the division had thought of it. There are a lot of talents in a division. A draftsman in a field-gray tunic had created a whole series of them. With military symbols, of course. Our mascot, the "Berlin Bear," as a piece of *Lebkuchen* dangling on a pine branch, with "Merry Christmas" on its stomach . . . a steel helmet full of Christmas alms packets—hopefully, the field post would hold up its end of the bargain . . . a fighting vehicle in the midst of a starry "Silent Night" . . . and the crowning achievement: a *Landser* at a guard post in a thick overcoat. What was he thinking of? He was thinking of "her," of course: an alluring vision popping up out of his head like Pallas Athena, with a short skirt and shapely legs and "everything else." "Merry Christmas and Happy New Year!" was also on one of the cards. Of course, that was the most sought after one. Yes, Christmas and New Year's would be here in a few days. At one time, we hoped for home leave and looked forward to it. But then we knew for certain that we would have to spend quiet holidays in the circle of our comrades. Perhaps in one of those terrible quarters . . . for many it was to be in a hole in the ground . . . behind a gun . . . on guard . . . in an outpost. In any event, in enemy territory far from the homeland.

War doesn't worry too much about the way humans organize their celebrations. It continues in the winter with grim harshness and demands superhuman strength from the warrior in enduring hardships. It would be a wartime Christmas that followed six months of extremely hard fighting. We knew that in our later years it sound a fine, painful note in our souls. We quickly wrote out some greetings and thought of those at home in Germany. Our messages would find some way out of that god-forsaken burg and back home. It was immaterial whether they arrived on time—the front and the homeland would celebrate a German Christmas and enter the New Year of the war with the same earnestness.

An hour later, the *Oberleutnant* crashed into our "living room" like the Ice Saints, bringing us back into the present situation. He didn't say a lot; at the moment, the oven was more important to him. His patrol had crawled out to within 500 meters of the enemy. A T-34, a heavily armed twenty-six-ton tank, had apparently gotten stuck on the roadside embankment on the far side of the burning village. It occasionally tried to rock itself free. That's when its angry buzz made its way over to us. The company commander showed the spot on the map. It was the bend in the road, where the Bolsheviks had blown up the bridge prior to their withdrawal. Two other tanks had taken up its outpost. That's why it could not be approached over the open terrain. Moreover, there were some infantry barricaded 100 meters in front of it.

"Nothing to be done!" the company commander concluded, pulling his boots off to warm his feet at the oven. If that's what he concluded, then that's the way it was.

"Perhaps the beasts will be at our door in the morning," a soldier said matter-of-factly. "Let's have some grog, or at least a gulp!"

"I'm making a wish!" That was a favorite soldier's game. You could fill a book with those wishes. The antitank soldiers would have loved to have received the bottle promised by the regimental commander by knocking out an additional tank. Every tree stand doesn't guarantee a stag, let alone an elephant. We could shove a few more pieces of kindling into the insatiable oven, that was all. Too bad! We would have liked to have had a reason to hold a small celebration that day.

If there's someone who needs to celebrate the holidays as they come, then it is the frontline soldier. *Oberleutnant* L., the company commander of the antitank elements, had been named as a brave man by the commander in chief in the Army Honor Roll. The commander had discovered that that morning. That meant something; it was akin to a small Knight's Cross among the soldiers. *Oberleutnant* T., the company commander of the rifle company attached to us, also received the same honor. But he was unable to appear. He was lying in his hole with a stiff back and throat. He was cursing like a mad man about his fall and was hoping to be able to smoke again by morning. The commander's sharp features turned into a smile, a smile that we knew well. He then pulled out his "emergency reserve," a small travel flask, and placed it on the table. Like a caring father, he had put away the quarter liter of *Schnapps*, which we thought had long since gone the way of all flesh. It was like Christmas! Soldiers are and remain easygoing large children. And that's a good thing. Life means a lot! It's everything they can offer. Things are at stake—throw them on the scales. Tomorrow is another day!

What do soldiers talk about, when they are not thinking about the homeland. What are the sources of their strength? About the inexhaustible subject of war. About the fighting behind them.

"Do you remember . . . what was the name of that hole?"

That's how all of the stories started. The Soviet Union was large and the road was long—hardly any of them registered the small events of their duty discharge of duty. It was only the peaks of bravery that glowed, peals that few climbed. Even getting into the Honor Roll took its own time.

In this case, it was back in the fall, when the final few kilometers around Kiev were being closed into a pocket. It was important to take the important bridges at Lochwiza in a *coup de main*, so as to allow the advance to link up with *Heeresgruppe Süd* to proceed rapidly. In the process, the *Oberleutnant* ran into a completely surprised engineer battalion, which had bivouacked on both sides of the road. Disregarding the fire coming from all sides, he exploited the surprise that came from overrunning them. Moving at full speed, he and his small armored vehicle ran through the enemy. Inspired by his example, the others followed and reached the far bank before the onset of darkness. The enemy was no longer able to reach his improved positions along the river. Four bridges were taken intact, one of them ninety meters long. It was back then, in September. The fall sun radiated warmth; we celebrated our "pocket fest" in the open a day later under a shady deciduous tree. The commander in chief of the field army and the division commander came and congratulated the leader of the plucky advance guard. And the *Major* bestowed his last bottle of sparkling wine to celebrate the historical day. Yes, it was back then, in the fall. "Do you remember?" Today, it had been many degrees below zero, and there had barely been a day since then that had not been without fighting!

2,000 METERS OF FIELD CABLE

If only the storm would not rage so crazily! It powerfully shoved the young *Unteroffizier* of the signals section into the room. He wanted to tear down the line to the neighboring village; the battalion command post had already moved. He wanted to know whether it was still possible. Hard to say or guess. The line was in a bad spot; it was only a few hundred meters in front of the Bolshevik positions. It would be a lot safer just abandoning the wire. The *Unteroffizier* did not want to do that under any circumstances. He had put down 2,000 meters; he wanted to get back as much as possible. He was willing to work his way forward all by himself. Determination was written all over his mummified face; his eyes looked straight into the commander's. He was told where the mine obstacles were. He was given a thimble of corn *Schnapps* in departing. "Take care, comrade!"

He did not come back until the morning. While he was in the process of spooling the wire, he explained, a Soviet tank approached him. It moved forward, turned off its engine, and observed. It then jerked forward again to repeat the same game. It had been an exciting hour—at least that's what we heard between the lines of his sober report—since the *Unteroffizier* in his snow shirt had to hide himself on the ground like a small mound of snow for that long. He did that until the tank finally moved back, and he was able to crawl back, meter-by-meter, with his precious roll.

"How much cable did you recover?"

"1,500 meters."

One noted his visible regret in not getting the other 500 meters.

"No frostbite?"

An hour in that weather could cost more than all of the cable was worth. He didn't think so. Well then, go get warmed up! He didn't want to hear of it. His section needed to lay more wire. He reported out with a sharp salute.

THEY DO THEIR DUTY SILENTLY!

A German noncommissioned officer! One of the many unknown and nameless soldiers, who does nothing but his duty silently and without words. The enormous amount of many small heroic deeds forms the firm foundation for the great victory. In the end, even in this world war, it is the performance of the tried-and-true noncommissioned officers and the reliable senior corporals that matters, the men who lead their sections, their machine-gun squads and their rifle sections and who lay day and night under the blazing heat of June as well as in the Dante-like ice hell of a winter in the east in December! Whenever we talk about front-line soldiers, then the men who stand in front of our eyes are the ones with the hard, narrow faces under the helmets.

When the new day torn apart the veil of twilight and the terrain started to sharply differentiate itself through its contours, the strength of the storm abated. But the miserable cold remained; the thermometer did not climb above -28 [-20.2 Fahrenheit]. The locality along the road had been burned down to glowing, smoldering ash. The rearguard disengaged from the enemy. The regiment told us when it would do so. In squads and in columns, the riflemen moved back to the individual farmsteads off to our right. For the time being, they were to be held. The grenadiers from *"Großdeutschland,"* who were combing the woods along the broad cut, were said to be arriving every hour to relieve us. There still wasn't any firing, however. But that could only be the calm before the storm. We were in suspense as to whether the *"Großdeutschland"* grenadiers would arrive before the Bolshevik attack.

The day started with the individual *rat-tat-a-tat* of a German machine gun, which hammered into the morning with a few long bursts. An antitank gun barked three times in between. Was that the beginning of the attack? No. After the echo faded out, silence once again descended over the valley. What was going on? A short while later, a Bolshevik prisoner was brought to us. He had a fresh dressing applied to his head. A Soviet horse-mounted patrol had appeared across from the combat-outpost line of the riflemen. Freezing, they had expected that all night. Gunner One blew his fingers warm and waited until it got closer. But the Bolsheviks remained under cover. So he fired a burst into the woods and shot three of the small horses; the others were able to escape.

The prisoner was a large Siberian from Vladivostok. A round had gone through both cheeks. He thought he was going to be shot immediately and couldn't quite fathom why his wounds were being dressed so carefully. The regiments that had just been freshly committed to battle from the Far East were still under the spell and rabble-rousing of their commissars. For that reason, their interrogations took place just like those at the beginning of the campaign. When the fear of death yielded to the feeling that they had saved their lives, the prisoners started explaining more in their slow and roundabout ways than we need to know in our hurry.

The Bolshevik belonged to one of the new Siberian rifle regiments, some of which had been wiped out in the difficult fighting of November. Around 200 men saved themselves by fleeing into the woods, including some 30 officers and 5 commissars. Those were the kinds of ratios we were finding ever more frequently. There were "commanders" without troops everywhere; they had usually abandoned their troops initially, only to establish tough bands of resistance elsewhere. For them, it was the last opportunity to escape a revenging bullet to the head. They still had two 12.2-centimeter guns and approximately ten machine guns at their disposal. There had been a lot of talk about surrendering or deserting. But the fear of being executed was too great, since there were also worries about the fate of families, who would then be exposed to a horrific terror. The *Politruks* had left no doubt about that. Just yesterday, six soldiers had been shot, after they had attempted to slip away during the night. The officers also talked about new reinforcements, especially in the form of tanks. Yes, he had seen them himself, he said. There were still eight of them behind the woods, including four of the larger ones. It was said that an attack would take place at this location today. That's all that had been said to him.

That was nothing new. Three nearby impacts made the paper-covered windowpanes shake so much that the dry plaster came crumbling out.

"This old shack won't be able to take much more," one said.

"Looks like it's starting up!"

A lot of words weren't needed. The riflemen were already back in the "brush woods," screening to the front and towards the road. Two tank destroyer platoons had already been sent out as patrols. The usual game: The distant report of firing; the sharp howling and hissing as precursors to the close-by detonations; the crashing of the rounds like exploding gigantic whips. The mushrooms of earth and the clouds of snow sprayed high like steaming geysers on the forward slope and the high ground behind it. The crest, with our supply route, was especially hard hit by heavy fire; they were like the fountains of underground springs with a tireless playing of water. The Bolsheviks were right to assume our positions were on the earthen hunchback, visible from afar. But our forces were insufficient to also occupy that line. Occupying the depression in front of it also did the trick.

THEY'RE COMING!

The wild hunt raced above the village. The droning, gurgling and roaring made the air tremble. But the depression was a large foxhole. The heavy rounds swept right above the roofs and into the opposite slope, which had already been plowed up by the rocket barrages. Only two rounds landed too short. They exploded at the outskirts of the village at the point where the work gun was in position. The *Oberarzt* was summoned. Three soldiers had been hit by shrapnel; in the case of one of them, his help came too late.

What was that, all of a sudden? We involuntarily tucked in our heads. A terrible hissing and howling, as if a thousand gigantic cats were right above our heads. A horrific sound from hell! "Tank rounds!" That was the professional determination. That meant the Bolsheviks were employing their tanks as artillery again. Sometimes it sounded like the rounds had lost their rifling and were simply tumbling through the air. *Rumms*—that went clean through two house walls. That means the tanks were firing indiscriminately with both antitank and high-explosive rounds. A dangerous weapon. In the neighboring village, the riflemen had lost their company commander to one of those antitank rounds, which slammed into the middle of a house. It was a damned discordant concert!

We continued to wait. For the Bolsheviks. We were certain their attack would take place before we were relieved. It turned noon. The grenadiers had to be through the woods pretty soon. Then the machine guns started hammering in a rapid cycle across the depression.

"They're coming!"

Individual groups sprang from out of the last houses of the village of ruins. You could only see them when they worked their way forward, since the Bolsheviks in this area all wore snowsuits. The lead elements were already at the road that ran perpendicular to our depression. There . . . all the way over to the right! A machine gun or mortar that wanted to go into position. The artillery observer had already identified the target. The radio section requested fire. A combination fuse jumped into the white heavens as a black *Flak* cloud. The direction and distance were good. Yes, our artillery was firing at that point. The first few impacts were too short. A hundred hearts were helping to direct the fire at that point. The next salvo landed in the middle of the target. They were running back! The mortars then fired away into the fleeing white coats. The fiery flowers then hissed from the infantry guns. The higher-pitch sounds of the antitank guns also mixed into the chorus that we preferred to listen to.

The shrubs that grew magically out of the snow as white clouds 500 meters in front of us had been sown by angels of death. The rounds followed the fleeing men and raced unrelentingly ahead of them as a steel-spraying obstacle. The riflemen manning the mortars were firing with uncontained glee.

"Another six!" their *Unteroffizier* called out. "We've got 'em!"

That was always the case. Whenever the tension of the fighting was relieved by the sound of your own weapons, then the soldier just looked at the enemy, who had to be destroyed, in a cold-blooded and remorseless manner. Only a few white-clad figures reached the edge of the village. The rounds of a second battery then started to crash into them. They growled powerfully over our village on the way there.

" *'Großdeutschland'* is coming out of the woods behind us on a wide front!" The adjutant reported.

That was in the nick of time, since more attacks would follow the first one. None of us envied the grenadiers and their mission. We had managed the estate well, but—honest to God—we were happy that we were getting out of that shit hole that evening. The Bolshevik rounds continued to sweep over the village.

GETTING RELIEVED IN THE MIDDLE OF THE FIGHT

"Things look pretty hot here!" *Major* K., the battalion commander said, as he took off his heavy fur cap. We knew the officer, who was well known for his pluck, from the campaign in the West. "As always, when *'Großdeutschland'* is being employed." Yes, the regiment had a lot of heavy fighting behind it; its grenadiers almost always had to fight at the hot spots. They were brave and glorious, well aware of the young but proud tradition. After all, wherever they were was also Greater Germany! Before they walked the line, the two *Majore* chatted a bit about common experiences, acquaintances and comrades, who were no longer with us— as was the case whenever old soldiers got together.

In the meantime, the patrol that the antitank elements had sent out returned. They had eliminated two antitank guns at the edge of the woods. The Soviet tanks had pushed their way further forward into the creek bed. The distance was too great for the antitank elements. One gun received a grazing wound on its superstructure, probably from a heavy 7.62-centimeter antitank-gun round. But it was just a deep cut; the round did not explode until it hit the ground further to the rear. Things had turned out well one more time.

"Well, this evening our assault guns will be here…"

It was always tough when a relief had to take place in a contested locality. Soldiers didn't like that.

"Where is the constant chugging of the Soviet machine guns coming from?"

We already knew that. They had to be behind the first few walls over there. The were engaging the road on the high ground that led to our village, from where the motorcycle messenger was coming at the time. Our antitank elements and mortars had been looking for the machine-gun nests for some time. There was a lot to be discussed in such situations and some experience to be passed on. The battalion commanders went forward with the company commanders. The grenadiers waited for the quarters to become available. They had assaulted the village in the clearing in the woods and had fought their way through the woods in the bitter cold. They would only be able to warm themselves up for a short while before they had to crawl back into the holes in the ground to fight anew.

TAKE CARE, COMRADE!

"Take cover!"

Damn it! Too late once again! The Bolsheviks were firing with mortars for the first time. In the middle of the road in front of the dilapidated hut that housed our command post. The grenadiers had scattered and were lying flat on the road. It was only the motorcycle messenger, who had not heard the impacts due to the noise of his own motor. He braked and slid. Get off that thing! Quick! Another impact. My God! He tumbled off the machine. After a couple of steps he collapsed and remained motionless. The comrades jumped over to him quickly; we pulled him into the room. The physician came. His overcoat and waterproof jacket came off quickly. Open up the field jacket. The physician could no longer help him.

Without a word, he pointed to the small hole above his heart that a single piece of shrapnel had ripped open. Badly shaken, his comrades took their leave. "He had done Poland and France," a *Feldwebel* said softly. "Now he has to lose his life here." Fate was wanton and incomprehensible for humans. For the rest of the day, not a single round impacted at that spot.

The Bolshevik machine guns fell silent. The last few rounds must have been direct hits. The vehicles slowly rolled up the steep slopes leading out of the village. Those were the engineers. The riflemen had already marched out. The powerful assault guns then appeared over the crest. Careful! No amount of driving artistry could help. The heavy fighting vehicles slid the last few meters into the valley like giant bobsleds before they righted themselves again. But everything went well. The approaches were a miserable grind in that type of ice!

THE COUNTERATTACK

The antitank elements brought up the rear. Enough time to talk about the fighting in the woods. The Bolsheviks had committed the remnants of a Siberian division to an immediate counterattack. The division order had been taken from the fallen commander of a separate engineer battalion. The thrust was to be continued into our rear with other formations and the positions in our villages cut off. A Siberian rifle regiment, a battalion from a second one, an engineer battalion, infantry guns and mountain howitzers attacked the numerically weak outposts in the village in the woods after a thirty-minute artillery preparation. It was no disgrace that the defenders had to yield to that superior force. The start of the attack was stated as 0430 hours in the order; the location of the division command post was also given. The grenadiers had quickly smashed the "pincers" and taken back the village in the woods in an aggressive counterattack.

Fighting in woods in that type of cold and ice—where the assaulting soldier has to perform gymnastics and balance himself with every step, in order not to fall flat on his face, where he can barely hold his weapon in his cold-stiffened hands, where he can barely move his fingers, where frostbite yields blisters as big as when you are scalded, where wounds weigh three to four times as much in the painful frost—that demanded a kind of heroism from every individual that the homeland cannot even begin to conceive, despite the best of intentions. It is Immense what is demanded and what is done. They are the best soldiers. And the command post of the Bolshevik division? We saw the location that the order gave flame up the previous night above the woods. The other rifle regiment of our division had assaulted it in a night attack. During the night, as previously mentioned, where the storm had dropped the temperature to 37 below [-34.6 Fahrenheit]. The route to the rear was open again.

The skies were steel blue and clear with the moon and the stars above the small village and the depression. We wished the men well, who would continue to watch and wait, until the old call alerted heart and weapon: They're coming! The Bolsheviks would find the grenadiers ready. On the high ground, we stopped for a moment and looked back. In the bright light of the moon, the snow-covered roofs looked quaint. "Pile of crap!" the commander murmured. He didn't say it quite so politely, actually, but he was talking to us from his heart. The antitank elements rolled through the sleeping woods in the night, woods that had experienced such bitter fighting. We didn't say anything while we moved. Everyone was lost in thought, and the thoughts circled around the village in the depression.

The Soviets attacked with strong forces the next day, as expected. We discovered that by means of new orders from the division. They were attempting to surround the village from three sides and assault it. But they encountered the iron defensive wall of the *"Großdeutschland"* grenadiers. Four of the Bolshevik tanks were knocked out. The attacks collapsed with heavy casualties in the fires of the artillery, the assault guns, the mortars and the machine guns.

MARCHING AND FIGHTING

We had long since marched to another village. Where our orders had taken us. Some sort of a new "Whatchamacallit" with —ka, —wa, —ki at the end. We didn't even write it into our daily logs. It was 1000 hours.

"Let's listen to the Armed Forces Report!"

A few minutes connected to the homeland via the ether so as to have a view of the world beyond "our" village. A military commercial radio was a holy relic within the company. We cared for the battery as if it were the apple of our eyes. Even when our fingers were itching sometimes to turn on music, so as to hum along to *Lili Marleen*. The commander told us to find something for ourselves to sing. Love was distant, like our homeland.

New Year's. We wanted to turn on some music.

"If we have time for it!" someone said drily. We would think of Germany, just as the homeland was thinking of us.

There was a thaw until midnight; then it dropped to 17 below again [1.4 Fahrenheit]. All routes were a sheet of ice; no hardship was spared for the army in the East.

The march continues. Until victory. That is both a belief and a promise for all.

Somewhat quiet on New Year's Day—and mail from home. That would be something! That would be something to look forward to!

Until then: march, march, and fight. Despite the ice and snow.

"Get ready!"

It goes on. Into the new war year!

We will continue to march and fight!

THE DIVISIONAL HISTORY

Since the narrative of this chapter is intended more as a "mood piece," it is difficult to determine exactly what villages are being discussed, although the general thread can be found in the divisional history as follows:[5]

The German leadership thereupon decided to concentrate all of its forces one more time to bring about a change in the fighting. The *2. Panzer-Armee* was directed to cut off Tula from the east and the west and, by doing so, clear the direct route between Moscow and Tula. The strongly fortified "strongpoint" of Tula would then be cut off from its rearward lines of communications and the *2. Panzer-Armee* freed up to attack, since the city could be encircled by infantry forces. The *2. Panzer-Armee* had ceased to be an armored field army for some time. It had the following numbers of tanks operational on 30 November: *Panzer-Regiment 6* = 28; *Panzer-Regiment 35* = 34; and *Panzer-Regiment 39* = 10.

The thirtieth of November was the first Advent Sunday of that eventful year. The forces prepared for the reorganization and had no time for a quietly contemplative celebration. During that time, the *3. Panzer-Division* announced its achievements since 22 June to 22 November 1941: 52,289 prisoners taken; 485 tanks, 71 armored cars, 905 artillery pieces, 203 antiaircraft guns, 567 antitank guns, 366 mortars, 1,540 machine guns,

---

5. *Traditionsverband*, 216–20.

3,130 trucks, 100 staff cars, 19 motorcycles, and 157 tractors captured or destroyed; 89 destroyed, 119 shot-down, and 63 captured aircraft. The fighting forces were 1,300 kilometers from the western borders of Russia and had covered 4,500 kilometers. The ammunition columns had covered 17,000 kilometers; the fuel columns, 20,000!

The *3. Panzer-Division* occupied its assembly areas for the attack. *Oberst* Kleemann commanded the righthand *Kampfgruppe*, which consisted of *Schützen-Regiment 3*, the *3./Panzerjäger-Abteilung 543*, the *2./Pionier-Bataillon 39*, the *6./Flak-Regiment 59*, and the *2./Artillerie-Regiment 75*. To secure the assembly area, the *I./Schützen-regiment 3* pushed forward on 1 December and took the localities of Djukowa and Grezewo. The lefthand *Kampfgruppe* of *Oberstleutnant* Zimmermann consisted of the *I./Schützen-Regiment 394*, the *1./Pionier-Bataillon 39*, a battery from *Artillerie-Regiment 75*, the *1./Panzerjäger-Abteilung 543*, and a tank platoon under *Leutnant* von Arnim. *Kradschützen-Bataillon 3* (*Major* Pape) relieved the screening group of the *II./Schützen-Regiment 394*. The motorcycle infantry were reinforced by a platoon of antitank elements. The third *Kampfgruppe* was led by *Major* Frank. Attached to him were *Panzerjäger-Abteilung 521*, the *3./Panzer-Regiment 6* and the *3./Pionier-Bataillon 39*. That *Kampfgruppe* staged in the Nowosselsjskije–Wasselki–Kornitschi–Arssenjewo area on 1 December and prepared to advance west, reconnoitering routes in the direction of Makejewa–Dubki. *Kampfgruppe Oberstleutnant Audörsch* was relieved by *Pionier-Bataillon 45* (a separate engineer battalion), with only the *5./Artillerie-Regiment 75* remaining in its old positions. The *I./ Infanterie-Regiment "Großdeutschland"* (*Hauptmann* Hagen) was attached to the division and prepared for operations outside of Karniki. *Oberstleutnant* Dr. Weißenbruch was directed to bring the remaining battalions of the divisional artillery—1st Battalion under *Hauptmann* Haas, 2nd Battalion under *Hauptmann* Nebel, and 3rd Battalion under *Hauptmann* Kersten— into position in such a manner that they could place harassing fires on Leshla and Iwrowka. The elements of *Major* Petsch's *Pionier-Bataillon 39* that were not attached to *Kampfgruppen* screened the crossings over the Schat at Petrowka and positioned all of its bridging vehicles there for immediate employment. Bridging Column 1 provided a platoon each of sixteen-ton assets to the 1st and 2nd Companies of the battalion, with the 3rd Platoon remaining the battalion's reserve. *Aufklärungs-Abteilung 1* was located in Karniki.

The night of 1–2 December was clear and illuminated by the moon. The wind had died down. As a result, it had turned colder and the thermometers showed -20 and lower [-4 Fahrenheit]. It was still dark over the snow-covered terrain, when the batteries of the *3.* and *4. Panzer-Division* opened fire on the Russian positions. *Artillerie-Regiment 75* concentrated its fires along the flanks of the attacking *Kampfgruppen*, in an effort to eliminate threats from that direction.

Shortly after 0400 hours, the riflemen of the two divisions moved out to attack west. *Schützen-Regiment 3* initially advanced with its 1st Battalion (*Major* Wellmann) to the southwest in the direction of Dubki. The 1st Company moved ahead in its *SPW's* and reported the locality as occupied by the enemy. The 2nd Company closed rapidly, while the 3rd Company worked its way towards the village through a depression from the north. The Russians occupying the strongpoint were surprised. Although they defended desperately, the fight was short. Dubki was taken and cleared. *Major* Wellmann immediately reorganized his companies for the continued advance. *Hauptmann* Peschke's 2nd Battalion followed closely behind the 1st Battalion with engineers and antitank elements. They moved on a route further south. The battalion took Posslowa and pressed past Dubki to the west.

Schützen-Regiment 394 likewise broke into the first Russian position. Its 1st battalion worked its way towards Romanowa. The Soviets were prepared for that attack and placed considerable artillery and mortar fire on the battalion. In addition, the reservoir in front of the village had been blown up. The ice had sunk, so there was only one crossing point over the defile. The battalion then had to toil across it. The *1./Pionier-Bataillon 39* constructed a ford across the Sosha for the riflemen. The company commandeer, *Hauptmann* Kalkbrenner, was wounded in the process, along with fifteen enlisted personnel. *Leutnant* Harzer assumed acting command of the engineer company. The 2nd Battalion of *Oberstleutnant* Dr. Müller—whom the soldiers referred to as *Angriffsmüller*[6]—attacking to the left, put down tough resistance outside of Bronikowo, before it was able to penetrate into the locality. The battalion's casualties were high. In the first few hours alone, fourteen vehicles were lost, unfortunately also including the fully loaded battalion ambulance. The regiment lost forty-

---

6. "Attack Müller."

seven men dead and wounded in the attack; the regiment's 2nd Battalion alone accounted for thirty-five, with the 8th Company suffering nineteen!

Schützen-Regiment 3 had reached the large forest that stretched from the southwest to the northeast. The 1st Company, moving as the point element, was able to cross the woods through a well-maintained cut. It reached the village of Kolodesnaja, which was in a clearing. The riflemen were offered a tragicomedy there. The Russian soldiers appeared to have no idea the Germans were attacking; they were busily engaged with target practice. The company's machine guns soon scattered the Soviets, who escaped into the nearby woods, abandoning all weapons and equipment. The company took sixty prisoners.

The battalion pivoted to the northwest, combed the closest woods and took the village of Dorofejewka after eliminating an enemy battery. The electricity was still functioning there! But there was little time to celebrate. The battalion continued its advance and reached Torchowo after 1300 hours. That meant the day's objective had been crossed! The Tula–Wenew road had been blocked! The 1st Battalion had achieved that success without taking any casualties.

The 2nd Battalion moved out behind the 1st Battalion again, but moved directly west from Dorofejewka, occupying Barybinka and Krjukowa. The enemy fled at those locations in undisciplined flight into the woods to the north and the west. The *I./Artillerie-Regiment 75* had to change positions in order to be able to have the range to fire. As a result of the rapid overcoming of the initial Russian resistance, it was easy for the armored group of *Major* Frank to follow the riflemen.

The groups from *Schützen-Regiment 394* and *Infanterie-Regiment "Großdeutschland"* that were employed on the left encountered strong enemy forces and were still involved in heavy fighting by the onset of darkness to the southwest of Dubki and Tretschtschewa. The last locality was finally taken by the *"Großdeutschland"* grenadiers, while the riflemen of *Schützen-Regiment 394* attempted to clear the large expanse of woods at Teminewa-Gamowo.

By evening, the Soviets appeared to have rapidly recovered from the shock of the initial successes of the *3. Panzer-Division.* While the *Kampfgruppen* set up their security for the night, the Soviets placed heavy fires—especially from "Stalin organs"—on the localities that had been occupied by the Germans, inflicting considerable casualties. The artillery fire disrupted all of the wire lines and, since the radios were not working either, the division headquarters had no contact with the lead elements in the evening. *Generalmajor* Breith therefore ordered his command post moved forward the following morning.

Shortly after 0600 hours on 3 December, *Schützen-Regiment 3* conducted a reconnaissance-in-force around the occupied villages with its *SPW* company, since it was determined that the enemy was still to the rear of the regiment. The 1st Company encountered the enemy at Olenina, to the south of its parent battalion. The enemy had even occupied the village of Kolodesnaja in the clearing in the woods the previous night. Among other things, it took the regiment's vehicle that stored the personal demand items. The 1st Battalion committed its 3rd Company and *Leutnant* Braun's platoon (*SPW's* from the 1st Company) against the village. The riflemen were able to make good progress back through the woods, but they received considerable fire once outside the village. The acting company commander, *Leutnant* Oesten, was felled by Russian bullets. It was impossible to advance through the fire and enter the locality again. The company was pulled back to Dorofejewka, where it screened.

Hauptmann Peschke's *II./Schützen-Regiment 3* started turning back strong Russian armor attacks on Krjukowa at first light. The battalion did not enjoy a single quiet hour; it also suffered terribly under the enemy fire and the cold. The division ordered the battalion to pull back to Torchowo, where the companies screened the road between that village and Wolynzewo. It was there that the lead company of the motorcycle battalion, the 2nd Company, arrived and provided welcome support. The motorcycle battalion proper occupied Iwrowka and the high ground to the west. The *I./Infanterie-Regiment "Großdeutschland"* closed the gap between the two regiments northwest of Dubki and was able to enter the village.

Schützen-Regiment 394 advanced to the west that day in the face of heavy enemy fire. The combat vehicles were not sent forward and left east of the river. The Russians defended the village of Gamowo especially hard, using artillery and heavy mortars. Since a frontal attack promised little success, *Major* Frank attempted to bypass the village with his tank battalion. It was not possible for the tanks and the riflemen of *Schützen-Regiment 394* to take Teminewa until 1900 hours. After 2200 hours, *Leutnant* Lange led an engineer assault detachment to the west, where it entered the woods outside of Nowossjolki.

The advance of the *3. Panzer-Division* on 4 December never stood under a lucky star. From the very beginning, it was questionable whether the forces available were sufficient to accomplish the mission. The enemy grew in strength by the hour; the winter mobility and the simple needs of his Siberian forces also came to his aid. Enemy formations that had been bypassed or pushed back held out in the deeply snowed-in woods in the rear of the division.

Infanterie-Regiment "Großdeutschland" took the hotly contested Kolodenaja for the second time that day and relieved elements of *Schützen-Regiment 3* from their previous limit of advance. The Russians, who had transitioned to the attack, were able to take back Krjukowo in the afternoon and even felt their way forward with patrols, even though all of them were turned back. The southern *Kampfgruppe* of *Schützen-Regiment 394* met with more success. In the morning, the regiment pressed to the northwest and took Demidowka and Nowossjolki. The success was all the more significant, inasmuch as the Tula–Wenew was finally blocked, once and for all. Tanks and mounted riflemen continued reconnoitering further to the south and southwest so as to block the path of any enemy forces possibly attempting to break out of Tula.

Generalmajor Breith, who temporarily established his command post at Krjukowa, ordered *Schützen-Regiment 3* and the attached *2./Artillerie-Regiment 75*, which had been pulled out of the line, were to be prepared to launch an attack towards the high ground west of Meschtscherskoje, fifteen kilometers southeast of Tula. The ongoing movements could only be partially executed, since the vehicles were not cooperating. The oil and the fuel were freezing at temperatures of -27 [-16.6 Fahrenheit], which even went down to -31 [-23.8 Fahrenheit] at night. Even the battle staff of the *3. Panzer-Division* no longer had any operational motorized vehicles!

It turned even colder during the night of 4–5 December. The thermometer showed -37 [-34.6 Fahrenheit]! Technology capitulated. The engines would no longer start; the machine guns would not fire; the tank turrets would not traverse. German forces were immobilized on that morning and exposed to the onset of Russian attacks! The *4. Panzer-Division*, which was already blocking the Tula–Moscow road, had to pull back to the east, leaving behind all of its vehicles, since new Siberian regiments had inserted themselves between it and the *17. Panzer-Division*.

The *3. Panzer-Division*, which was positioned in the villages west of the Tula–Wenew road, had to defend against constant Soviet attacks, which took place all along its front. The enemy tried especially hard at Nowossjolki and Krjukowo to shatter the lines of the *3. Panzer-Division*. In the process, the Siberians advanced through the thick woods south of the road and reached Kolodesnaja late in the afternoon. They attacked the village and the men there by surprise, entering the locality and butchering everything that got in their way. The commander of the *IV./ Infanterie-Regiment "Großdeutschland"* was shot down with his headquarters and elements of the 17th Company. Only a few infantry were able to escape the slaughter, clothed only in their shirts and trousers. The German casualties were high. In addition to the dead officers and men of *"Großdeutschland,"* forty motorcycles, several trucks, one fuel vehicle, one assault gun, one heavy infantry gun, and numerous small arms were lost. The Soviets set up for the third time in Kolodesnaja. The division no longer had the strength to eliminate that "boil" in its front. The field army ordered the *XXIV. Panzer-Korps* to attack one more time via Krjukowo so as to establish contact with the *296. Infanterie-Division*, which had reached the Upa. *General* Geyr von Schweppenburg, who had intended to allow the *3. Panzer-Division* to rest that day, acquiesced to the order and had a *Kampfgruppe* formed to execute the mission under the command of *Oberst* Kleemann. To that end, the *I./Schützen-Regiment 3*, an artillery battalion, a motorcycle infantry company and the rest of *Panzer-Regiment 6* were pulled out of the front lines.

That afternoon, however, the commanding general radioed the field army headquarters in Jassnaja-Poljana. His impression of the development of the situation had changed: "Situation fundamentally changed, since the enemy has also broken into the gap between the *17.* and *4. Panzer-Division*; strong enemy forces along the Sserpuchowo–Tula rail line and road. No relief is expected from the *XXXXIII. Armee-Korps* any more. Own tanks not operational!"

The fifth of December 1941 saw a change in the fortunes of the war in the East! The daily logs of the headquarters of the *2. Panzer-Armee* recorded that day: "Combat power of the brave forces is at an end after incredible exertions! It is imperative to preserve the force! The field army will move back to the Don–Schat–Upa position incrementally."

Afterword

The new war year began just like the old one ended: with difficult fighting. There was an alert on the second day of Christmas! It was imperative to interdict a penetration of the Bolsheviks in an area that required close to 150 kilometers round trip to the location we were committed. On New Year's Day, the division moved out to attack. The Bolsheviks employed heavy tanks. An icy storm raged; it was 42 below [-43.6 Fahrenheit]. Large snowdrifts and, in some cases, unchartered routes demanded the most of every individual man. On the second day, the area of penetration was sealed off, the enemy ejected and the winter position retaken!

During that January, the division was committed two different places at hot spots of a field army. The gap in the front had to be won back in a tough contest, piece-by-piece. The fighting was hard and fierce; it was fought to the very limits with every once of commitment. The German soldier vanquished the Bolsheviks in proven heroism, wherever he faced them. He did not bend to the gruesome winter and its hurricane-like snowstorms. He remained the victor.

The thirty-first of January 1942 was a proud day in the military history of the Berlin-Brandenburg armored division. On that day, the Armed Forces Report from the *Führer* Headquarters announced:

> In the area northeast of Kursk, a counterattack conducted by German infantry and armor forces under the command of *Generalmajor* Breith led to a complete success after several days of fighting. An enemy force of several divisions and armor formations that had broken into the German lines was defeated and thrown back to the east, all the while suffering heavy casualties.

The *Führer* awarded the division commander, *Generalmajor* Breith, the Oakleaves to the Knight's Cross of the Iron Cross with the following telegram:

> I am awarding you, as the 69th member of the German armed forces, the Oak Leaves to the Knight's Cross in appreciation for your heroic actions in the successful counterattacks against superior enemy forces.
>
> /signed/ Adolf Hitler

At the same time, it was a sign of thanks from the Supreme Commander to every warrior of the division.

They had done their duty!

Through a ford. Even though this body of water can be crossed, such crossings were fraught with difficulties, with steep banks making entry or exit difficult, especially after preceding vehicular traffic had eroded the bottom ground.

The mud is knee deep as it transitions to winter. The motorcycle infantry look as though they have been pulled out of the morass. Although the motorcyclists were issued a special rubberized coat to help combat the elements and keep them dry, even it had its limitations under constant conditions such as this.

It has become a hard winter. The machine gunner is aiming an *MG-34*, the standard medium German machine gun of the time.

Unending fields of white.

This armored car has camouflaged itself in white. The *Sd.Kfz. 222* was a light armored car outfitted with a 2-cm automatic cannon and a coaxial machine gun. It was a mainstay of the divisional reconnaissance battalion.

In the wintertime, the *panje* sled is the best means of transportation.

Positions are dug in the rock-hard earth by means of pick and spade. Contemporaneous accounts mention that hand grenades often had to be used to assist for this purpose.

A machine-gun outpost—with an *MG-34* on a heavy tripod—stands guard in a dugout.

A staff car of the *12. Panzer-Division* gets an assist in negotiating snow and ice. The Russian winter would prove to be a major nemesis of the German Army.

War trophy! A knocked-out Soviet T-35 has piqued the curiosity of these soldiers. Although formidable looking, the early Soviet heavy tanks were knocked out relatively easily due to design flaws.

The bleak Soviet winter landscape. Vehicles attempt to negotiate poor roads under terrible weather conditions. The supply chain of the German Army—never the best to begin with—was stretched to the breaking point in the advance on Moscow.

GRÄBER IM OSTEN

Dort, wo die Stämme der Birken im fahlen Lichte sich baden,
silbern im Grau, von fallender Feuchte genetzt,
stehen die Kreuze, von trauernden Händen gesetzt
— liegen die Gräber der Kameraden.

Drüber wandern die Wolken, aus ruhlosen Winden geboren,
Gleichnis des Lebens: so wird und verweht die Gestalt!
Kinder der Stürme auch ihr, die des Krieges Gewalt
aufrief zum Kampf an der Zukunft flammenden Toren!

Stärker als Leiden am Tod ist die Liebe zum Lande der Väter,
stärker als Liebe zum Leben die Liebe zur Tat:
ruhe im Glauben der Treue, du toter Soldat —
ewig waltet dein Ruhm. Und später, ja später,

wenn deine Kinder und Enkel den Frieden genießen,
den zu erstreiten dein heiliger Atem verging,
werden die Gräber der Helden für immer den Ring
um die blühenden Felder der Freiheit schließen!

Graves in the East
There, where the trunks of birches are bathed in pale light,
silvery gray, netted with falling dew,
are the crosses, placed by mourning hands
—are the graves of our comrades.
The clouds wander over there, borne by restless winds,
An allegory of life: The figure forms and blows away!
You are also children of the storms; the power of war
Called you to the fight at the flaming gates of the future!
Stronger than the suffering at death is the love for the land of one's fathers,
Stronger than the love of life is the love of accomplishment:
Rest in the belief of faithfulness, you, dead soldier—
Your glory exists in perpetuity. And later, yes later,
When your children and grandchildren enjoy the peace,
Which you fought to obtain with your holy dying breath,
The graves of the heroes will always close
The ring around the blooming fields of freedom!

Witnesses in blood to our victories: our fallen comrades will remain unforgotten. It was common German practice early in the war to place the headgear of the fallen soldier on the cross at his gravesite.

On watch in the East.

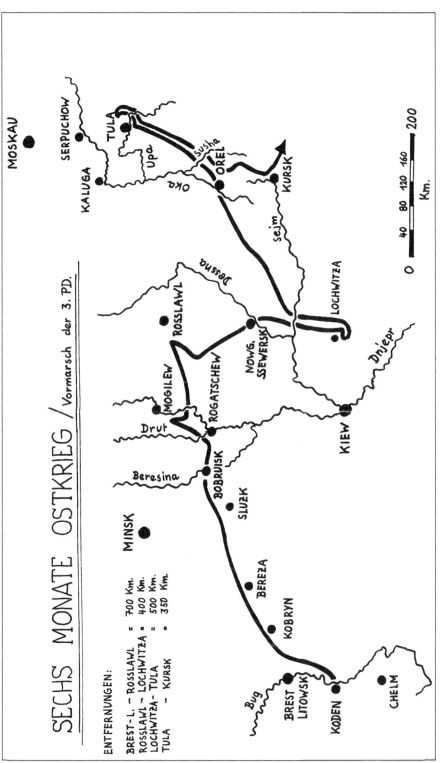

Six months of war in the east: Route of the 3. *Panzer-Division*. Legend: *Entfernungen* = Distances.

APPENDIX A

German Military Rank Table (Army and Waffen-SS)

ENLISTED			
U.S. Army	*German Army*	*Waffen-SS*	**English Equivalent**
Private	*Schütze*	*SS-Schütze[1]*	Private
Private First Class	*Oberschütze*	*SS-Oberschütze[2]*	Private 1st Class
Corporal	*Gefreiter*	*SS-Sturmmann*	Acting Corporal
(Senior Corporal)	*Obergefreiter*	*SS-Rottenführer*	Corporal
(Staff Corporal)	*Stabsgefreiter*	*SS-Stabsrottenführer[3]*	

NONCOMMISSIONED OFFICERS			
U.S. Army	*German Army*	*Waffen-SS*	**English Equivalent**
Sergeant	*Unteroffizier*	*SS-Unterscharführer*	Sergeant
(None)	*Unterfeldwebel*	*SS-Scharführer*	Staff Sergeant
Staff Sergeant	*Feldwebel*	*SS-Oberscharführer*	Technical Sergeant
Sergeant First Class	*Oberfeldwebel*	*SS-Hauptscharführer*	Master Sergeant
Master Sergeant	*Hauptfeldwebel*	*SS-Sturmscharführer*	Sergeant Major
Sergeant Major	*Stabsfeldwebel*		

1. *SS-Mann* used as the rank designation prior to 1942.
2. Rank not used prior to 1942.
3. This rank did not exist officially, but it has been seen in written records.

OFFICERS			
U.S. Army	*German Army*	*Waffen-SS*	**English Equivalent**
Second Lieutenant	*Leutnant*	*SS-Untersturmführer*	2nd Lieutenant
First Lieutenant	*Oberleutnant*	*SS-Obersturmführer*	1st Lieutenant
Captain	*Hauptmann*	*SS-Hauptsturmführer*	Captain
Major	*Major*	*SS-Sturmbannführer*	Major
Lieutenant Colonel	*Oberstleutnant*	*SS-Obersturmbannführer*	Lt. Colonel
Colonel	*Oberst*	*SS-Standartenführer*	Colonel
(None)	(None)	*SS-Oberführer*	(None)
Brigadier General	*Generalmajor*	*SS-Brigadeführer*	Brigadier General
Major General	*Generalleutnant*	*SS-Gruppenführer*	Major General
Lieutenant General	*General der Panzertruppen etc.*	*SS-Obergruppenführer*	Lt. General
General	*Generaloberst*	*SS-Oberstgruppenführer*	General
General of the Army	*Feldmarschall*	*Reichsführer-SS*	Field Marshal

Order of Battle:
3. Panzer-Division

Activation: The *3. Panzer-Division* was activated on 15 October 1935, with its headquarters in Wünsdorf (near Berlin). The division was mobilized and put on a wartime footing on 1 August 1939.

Commanders:[1]

15 October 1935: *Generalleutnant* Ernst Fessmann

? June 1937: Friedrich Kühn[2]

12 October 1937: *Generalleutnant* Leo *Freiherr von Schweppenburg*[3]

7 October 1939: *Generalleutnant* Horst Stumpff[4]

31 October 1939: *Generalleutnant* Leo *Freiherr von Schweppenburg*

? September 1940: *Generalleutnant* Friedrich Kühn[5]

4 October 1940: *Generalleutnant* Horst Stumpff[6]

13 November 1940: *Generalleutnant* Walter Model

---

1. This list of commanders is taken from *Lexikon der Wehrmacht* (http://www. lexikon-der-wehrmacht.de/Gliederungen/Panzerdivisionen/Gliederung.htm) in its entry concerning the *3. Panzer-Division* (accessed 20 February 2012) and Peter Schmitz, Klaus-Jürgen Thies, Günter Wegmann, and Christian Zweng, *Die deutschen Divisionen, Band 1, Die Divisionen 1–5*, Osnabrück: Biblio Verlag, 1993. The *Lexikon* does not list the prewar commanders.
2. There is no mention of Kühn in the divisional history *Traditionsverband der 3. Panzer-Division, Geschichte der 3. Panzer-Division* (Berlin: Verlag der Buchhandlung Günter Richter, 1967), 488. Kühn's tenure in this position was, therefore, most likely as an acting commander.
3. The *Traditionsverband* lists the assumption of command for Schweppenburg as 1 October 1937.
4. The *Traditionsverband* makes no mention of Stumpff for this short period.
5. Schmitz, 216, lists the assumption of command for Kühn as 15 February 1940. The *Traditionsverband* makes no mention of Kühn.
6. Schmitz, 216, lists the assumption of command for Stumpff as sometime in February 1940. The *Traditionsverband* specifically lists Stumpff's assumption of command as 15 February 1940.

2 October 1941: *Generalleutnant* Hermann Breith[7]
1 October 1942: *Generalleutnant* Franz Westhoven[8]
25 October 1943: *Generalleutnant* Fritz Bayerlein[9]
5 January 1944: *Oberst* Rudolf Lang[10]
25 May 1944: *Generalleutnant* Wilhelm Phillips
1 January 1945: *Generalmajor* Wilhelm Söth[11]
19 April 1945: *Oberst* Volkmar Schöne[12]

Organization for Battle
Motorized/Mechanized Infantry
• *3. Schützen-Brigade.* Formed on 15 October 1935, with a peacetime
garrison location of Eberswalde. It was redesignated as the *3.*
Panzergrenadier-Brigade on 5 July 1942 and disbanded the following
November.

> • *Schützen-Regiment 3:* Formed on 15 October 1935, with a
> peacetime garrison of Eberswalde. On 5 July 1942, redesignated as
> *Panzergrenadier-Regiment 3.* Reconstituted in December 1944.
> • *Schützen-Regiment 394:* Formed on 1 August 1940. On 5 July 1942,
> redesignated as *Panzergrenadier-Regiment 394.* Reconstituted in
> December 1944.

Armor
• *3. Panzer-Brigade.* Formed on 15 October 1935, with a peacetime
garrison in Berlin. On 15 January 1941, it was reorganized and
redesignated as the Headquarters of the *5. leichte Division.*

---

7. Schmitz, 216, lists the assumption of command for Breith as 22 October 1941. It
   further lists Kurt *Freiherr* von Liebenstein assuming command of the division on
   1 September 1942. The *Traditionsverband* gives Breith's assumption of command
   date as 1 October 1941
8. Schmitz, 216, lists the assumption of command for Westhoven as 25 October
   1943.
9. Schmitz, 216, lists the assumption of command for Bayerlein for 20 October
   1943. The *Traditionsverband* lists Bayerlein's assumption of command date as 15
   October 1943.
10. The *Traditionsverband* lists Lang's assumption of acting command on 10 Janu-
    ary 1944.
11. Schmitz, 216, lists the assumption of command for Söth as 20 January 1945.
    This is also the date given by the *Traditionsverband.*
12. Schmitz, 216, lists the assumption of command for Schöne as 1 May 1945. This
    is also the date listed by the *Traditionsverband.*

• *5. Panzer-Brigade*. Formed on 10 November1938, with a peacetime garrison in Bamberg. On 27 January 1941, it was reassigned to the *3. Panzer-Division*. On 21 February 1942, it was disbanded.

> • *Panzer-Regiment 5*: Formed on 15 October 1935, with a peacetime garrison in Wünsdorf. Reassigned to the 5. leichte Division on 12 February 1942. Surrendered in Tunis in May 1943 and never reconstituted.

> • Pa*nzer-Regiment 6*: Formed on 15 October 1935, with a peacetime garrison in Neuruppin

Reconnaissance

• *Aufklärungs-Abteilung (mot) 1*: Formed under the code name of *Kraftfahrt-Abteilung Königsberg*. Redesignated as *Aufklärungs-Abteilung 1* on 15 October 1935, with a peacetime garrison in Königsberg (present-day Kaliningrad). Redesignated as *Panzer-Aufklärungs-Abteilung 1* on 24 April 1941. On 25 April 1942, consolidated with *Kradschützen-Bataillon 3* (see below), with the latter formation retaining the designation.

• *Kradschützen-Bataillon 3*: Formed on 15 October 1935, with a peacetime garrison in Freenwalde. Consolidated with *Aufklärungs-Abteilung (mot) 1* (see above) on 25 April 1942. Redesignated and reorganized as *Panzer-Aufklärungs-Abteilung 3* on 28 April 1943. Reconstituted in December 1944.

• *Aufklärungs-Abteilung (mot) 3*: Formed under the code name of *Kraftfahrt-Abteilung Wünsdorf*. Redesignated as *Aufklärungs-Abteilung 3* on 15 October 1935, with a peacetime garrison in Stahnsdorf. Reassigned to the *5. leichte Division* on 15 January 1941.

• *Panzer-Aufklärungs-Abteilung 88*: Formed on 15 October 1940 from *Aufklärungs-Abteilung Werder*.

Artillery

• *Artillerie-Regiment 75*: Formed on 15 October 1935 (headquarters not until 6 October 1936). Peacetime garrison in Neuruppin (with the 2nd Battalion in Eberswalde). The regiment was redesignated as *Panzer-Artillerie-Regiment 75* on 18 October 1942. Reconstituted in December 1944.

• *II./Artillerie-Regiment 49*: Formed on 11 November 1938, with a peacetime garrison in Magdeburg. A heavy artillery battalion that was assigned in direct support of the divisional artillery. On 1 August 1940, it was redesignated and assigned to the divisional artillery as the *III./ Artillerie-Regiment 75*.

Air Defense Artillery
• *Heeres-Flak-Artillerie-Abteilung (mot) 314*: Formed on 10 March 1942. On 4 June 1942, consolidated with the divisional artillery as the *IV./Artillerie-Regiment 75*. On 24 April 1943, it regained its separate status.

Antitank
• *Panzerabwehr-Abteilung 39*: Formed on 15 October 1935, with a peacetime garrison in Wünsdorf. Redesignated as *Panzerjäger-Abteilung 39* on 1 April 1940. Reassigned to the *5. leichte Division* in January 1941 and surrendered in Tunis in May 1943, never being reconstituted.
• *Panzerabwehr-Abteilung 543*: Formed on 26 August 1939. Redesignated as *Panzerjäger-Abteilung 543* on 1 April 1940. Reassigned to the *3. Panzer-Division* on 21 January 1941 to replace *Panzerjäger-Abteilung 39*.

Combat Engineers
• *Pionier-Bataillon 39*: Formed on 6 October 1936, with a peacetime garrison in Rathenow. Redesignated as *Panzer-Pionier-Bataillon 39* on 1 May 1940. Reconstituted in December 1944.

Divisional Troops
• *Panzer-Divisions-Nachrichten-Abteilung 39*: Formed on 15 October 1935, with a peacetime garrison in Stahnsdorf. Reconstituted in November 1944.
• *Feld-Ersatz-Bataillon 83*: Formed for the division on 31 March 1941. Redesignated as *Feldersatz-Bataillon 75* on 9 September 1943. Reconstituted in November 1944.
• *Division-Nachschubführer 83*: The division support command. Divisional support elements not designated otherwise were given the numerical designator of 83.

Personalities Associated with the *3. Panzer-Division* (Operation Barbarossa)

OSKAR AUDÖRSCH

Oberstleutnant Audörsch was born on 27 February 1898 in Colbiehnen (East Prussia). He entered army service in 1916 and was commissioned a *Leutnant* in November 1917, serving in a variety of infantry assignments. After the war, he served in *Freikorps Hasse* and was later retained by the *Reichswehr*. He served in a variety of assignments in the inter-war years, including military sports and ski academies. From 26 August 1940 to 14 January 1942, he was the commander of *Schützen-Regiment 394*. He then received staff assignments in Berlin, followed by acting and then formal command of the *25. Panzer-Division* (August 1944-May 1945). He received the German Cross in Gold in April 1943. He survived the war and passed away in Ulm on 5 June 1991.

HERMANN BREITH

Generalmajor Breith was born in Pirmasens on 7 May 1892. He became an officer candidate in the Imperial Army in 1910. He was an infantry officer, who was retained by the *Reichswehr* after the end of the Great War. He started serving in motorized battalion in 1925; in the early 1930's he was transferred to Berlin, where he served in the motorization directorate. Promoted to *Major* at the end of 1934, he was transferred to the *Kraftfahr-Lehr-Kommando Zossen* in 1934, where he became the commander of what evolved into *Panzer-Regiment 5*. In April 1936, he was promoted to *Oberstleutnant*, shortly thereafter commanding *Panzer-Regiment 36* (*4. Panzer-Division*). He led that regiment in the campaign in Poland, where he earned both classes of the Iron Cross (repeat awards, since he also received them in World War I). He was then entrusted with command of the *5. Panzer-Brigade* (*4. Panzer-Division*: headquarters for *Panzer-Regiment 35* and *Panzer-Regiment 36*). He led the brigade during the campaign in the West, where he distinguished himself and was awarded the Knight's Cross. He then rotated through several assignments at the Army High Command, before being given command of the *3. Panzer-Division* on 22 October 1941. He gave up command in October 1942 and eventually became the commanding general of the *III. Panzer-Korps*, after being promoted to *General der Panzertruppen* in March 1943. He held corps command until the end of the war.

In addition to being one of the few recipients of the Swords to the Oak Leaves to the Knight's Cross of the Iron Cross, he was also mentioned by name four times in the Armed Forces Daily Report. He survived the war, was released from captivity in 1947, and died in Pech/Bad Godesberg on 3 September 1964.

ULRICH KLEEMANN

Oberst Kleemann was born on 23 March 1892 and entered military service in a Dragoon regiment in 1913. He was commissioned a *Leutnant* in 1913, where he held both cavalry and infantry assignments. He was retained in the postwar *Reichswehr*, continuing to serve in a variety of cavalry assignments. In October 1935, he started his association with mechanized forces by being assigned as the commander of *Kradschützen-Bataillon 1*. By January 1938, he was an *Oberstleutnant* and commander of *Schützen-Regiment 3*. By December 1939, he assumed command of *Schützen-Brigade 3* as an *Oberst*. He was promoted to *Generalmajor* in November 1941 and transferred to the army officer manpower pool, pending assignment to command the *90. leichte Afrika-Division* in April 1942. That was followed by additional division and corps commands, including *Panzer-Korps "Feldherrnhalle"* near the end of the war, and eventual acting field army command. He ended the war as a *General der Panzertruppen* and the recipient of the Oak Leaves of the Knight's Cross to the Iron Cross. He died in an accident in Oberursel on 1 January 1963.

GÜNTHER VON MANTEUFFEL

Oberstleutnant von Manteuffel was born into the famous Manteuffel officer family in Weimar on 4 October 1891. He entered military service as an officer candidate on 1 December 1911 and was commissioned a *Leutnant* on 18 August 1913. Details concerning his World War I service are sketchy, but he was awarded both classes of the Iron Cross, as well as Knight's Cross of the House Order of Hohenzollern. He was not originally retained by the *Reichswehr*, but he succeeded in reentering service in 1922 as a *Leutnant*. In the prewar years, he served with *Reiter-Regiment 4* almost exclusively, until being posted as the commander of *Kradschützen-Bataillon 3* in October 1935. While serving in that capacity, he was promoted to *Oberstleutnant*. He led that battalion during the campaign in Poland. In December of that year, he was named commander of *Schützen-Regiment 3*, which he then led in the campaign in the West. Promoted to *Oberst* in November 1940, he remained the regimental commander until October 1941, when he was transferred to the army officer manpower pool. He then held a variety of commands, eventually becoming the commander of the *1. Ski-Jäger-Brigade*. From the beginning of 1944 until April 1944, he was the acting commander of the *16. Panzer-Grenadier-Division*. He ended the war in command of quiet sectors of various military commands in Denmark and northern Germany. He passed away in 1962.

OTTO MORITZ WALTER MODEL

Model commanded the *3. Panzer-Division* during most of the actions described in this book. Born in Genthin (Saxony) on 24 January 1891, he came from a non-military family. He was commissioned an officer in 1910, starting a lifelong career in the military. He distinguished himself in World War I, receiving a recommendation to be posted to the General Staff, despite his outspoken nature, which often got him in trouble with superiors.

He remained in the postwar German Army, serving in various command and staff positions and rose to the rank of *Generalmajor* prior to the outbreak of World War II. As a General Staff officer, he served as a corps chief of staff during the campaign in Poland and then as a field army chief of staff in the Battle for France. He was an ardent proponent of modernization and one of the innovators in the formation of the concept of *Kampfgruppen*. He was given command of the *3. Panzer-Division* in November 1940, a command he held until November 1941.

He later went on to corps, field army, field-army group, and theater command. His fame grew in the later war years, and he was known as one of the best defensive tacticians and planners. His ambiguous role at the Battle of Kursk does not remain without controversy, however, since his offensive efforts in the northern arm of the pincers were seen to be somewhat half-hearted and not well planned. In 1945, when *Heeresgruppe B* was surrounded in what became known as Ruhr Pocket, Model committed suicide (21 April 1945) rather than face captivity and potential war crimes charges from the Soviet Union.

He had the distinction of being the youngest *Generalfeldmarschall* in German Army history. In addition, he was one of only twenty-seven recipients of the Swords and Diamonds to the Oak Leaves of the Knight's Cross to the Iron Cross.

OSKAR MUNZEL

Oberstleutnant Munzel was born on 13 March 1899 in Grimmen (Pomerania). He entered military service in 1917 in an Ulan regiment. He was commissioned a *Leutnant* in Russia in 1918. He was retained in the postwar *Reichswehr*, and became involved in motorization and mechanization issues early on. Promoted to *Rittmeister* in 1933, he received General Staff officer training, before being assigned to *Panzer-Regiment 6*, as the commander of its 5th Company. From 1937 to 1941, he was assigned to the General Staff and responsible for officer development in the *Panzerwaffe*, taking two months out to command *Panzer-Regiment 5*, in preparation for *Unternehmen "Seelöwe,"* the proposed invasion of the British Isles. On 1 June 1941, he returned to *Panzer-Regiment 6*, where he was given command of the 2nd Battalion. He assumed command of the regiment in December of that year and was promoted to *Oberst* in January 1942. He left the division at the beginning of 1943, whereupon he commanded the armor school and then assumed acting command of the *14. Panzer-Division* (September 1944). He went on to be promoted to *Generalmajor* (December 1944), command of a corps group, and formal command of the *2. Panzer-Division*.

He spent several years in Allied captivity, being released in 1947. In 1951, he became a military advisor to Egypt, returning to Germany in 1956 to join the fledgling *Bundeswehr*, where he eventually simultaneously became a *General der Kampftruppen* and inspector general of the *Panzertruppe*. He retired from the military in 1962, wrote numerous books and articles concerning the *Panzerwaffe*, and died in Bonn on 1 January 1992.

ERNST WELLMANN

Oberstleutnant Wellmann was born on 14 January 1904 in Samter (West Prussia). He entered the *Reichswehr* from the police in 1924. By 1928, he was a *Leutnant*. By the end of 1935, he was transferred into *Schützen-Regiment 3*, where he assumed command of the 6th Company in January 1936 as a *Hauptmann*. He remained in that position through the campaigns in Poland and France. In August 1940, he assumed command of the 1st Battalion. He received the German Cross in Gold on 8 June 1942 and became the commander of *Panzergrenadier-Regiment 126* (*23. Panzer-Division*) two months later. That September, he received the Knight's Cross. He returned to the *3. Panzer-Division* on 1 April 1943, where he assumed command of his old regiment, the re-designated *Panzergrenadier-Regiment 3*. Promoted to *Oberst* on 1 September 1943, he received the Oak Leaves to the Knight's Cross to the Iron Cross at the end of November 1943. I May 1944, he joined the staff of the inspector general for the *Panzertruppe*, where he was responsible for the mechanized infantry section. In March 1945, he was given acting command of *Panzer-Division Holstein*, a nominal armored division. He survived the war and passed away in Karlsruhe on 17 July 1970.

Stackpole Military History Series

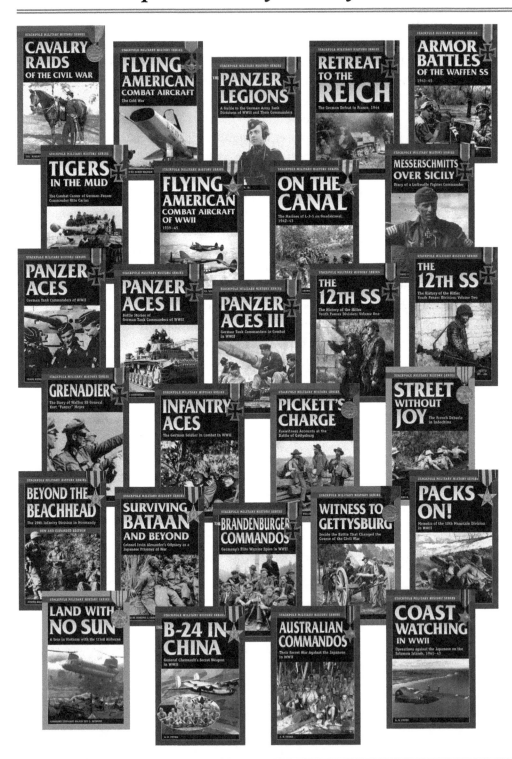

Real battles. Real soldiers. Real stories.

Stackpole Military History Series

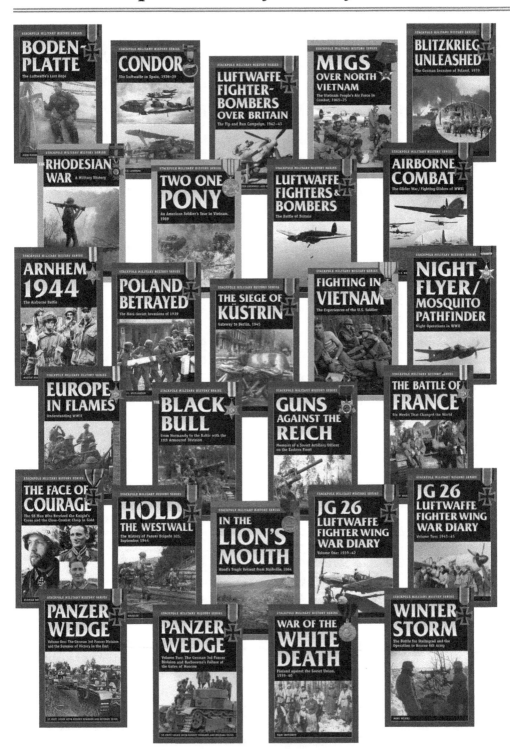

Real battles. Real soldiers. Real stories.

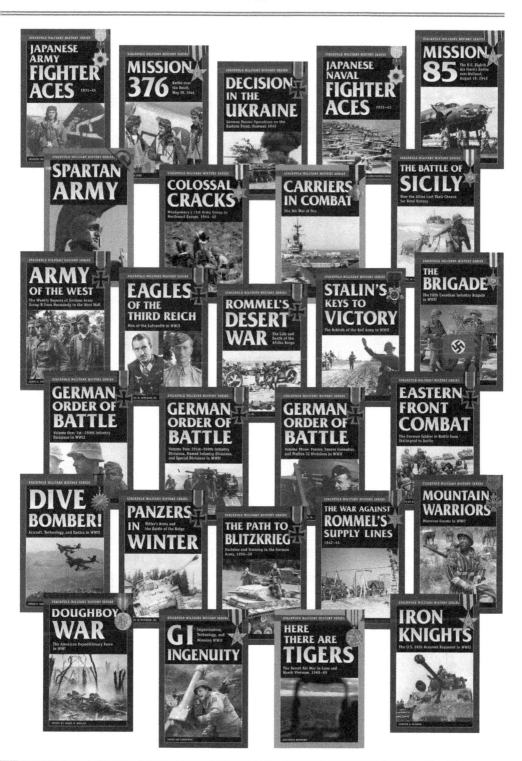

Stackpole Military History Series

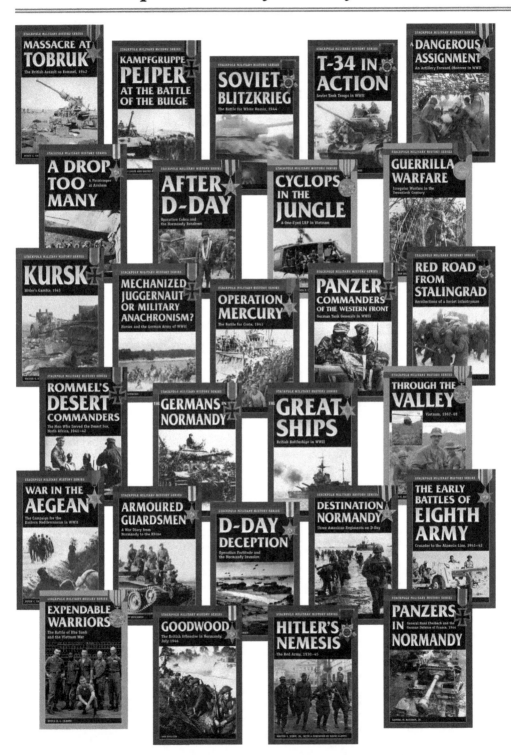

Real battles. Real soldiers. Real stories.

Stackpole Military History Series

PANZERGRENADIER ACES
GERMAN MECHANIZED INFANTRYMEN
IN WORLD WAR II
Franz Kurowski

The panzergrenadiers were the footsoldiers who went into action alongside the Third Reich's legendary armored fighting vehicles. Whether in the Wehrmacht or Waffen-SS, these troops endured all the horrors of infantry combat— from the mud and snow in the East to the hedgerows in the West—but they did so next to thundering giants like the Panther and Tiger. Master storyteller Franz Kurowski brings to life the exploits of some of the very best of these mechanized infantrymen—winners of the Knight's Cross, heroes of the homeland, aces of the battlefield.

Paperback • 6 x 9 • 400 pages • 43 photos

WWW.STACKPOLEBOOKS.COM
1-800-732-3669

Stackpole Military History Series

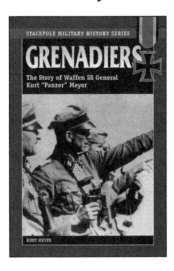

GRENADIERS

THE STORY OF WAFFEN SS GENERAL
KURT "PANZER" MEYER

Kurt Meyer

Known for his bold and aggressive leadership, Kurt
Meyer was one of the most highly decorated German
soldiers of World War II. As commander of various
units, from a motorcycle company to the Hitler Youth
Panzer Division, he saw intense combat across Europe,
from the invasion of Poland in 1939 to the 1944
campaign for Normandy, where he fell into Allied
hands and was charged with war crimes.

Paperback • 6 x 9 • 448 pages • 93 b/w photos

WWW.STACKPOLEBOOKS.COM
1-800-732-3669

Stackpole Military History Series

ARMOR BATTLES
OF THE WAFFEN-SS
1943–45

Will Fey, translated by Henri Henschler

The Waffen-SS were considered the elite of the
German armed forces in the Second World War and
were involved in almost continuous combat. From
the sweeping tank battle of Kursk on the Russian
front to the bitter fighting among the hedgerows
of Normandy and the offensive in the Ardennes,
these men and their tanks made history.

Paperback • 6 x 9 • 384 pages
32 photos • 15 drawings • 4 maps

WWW.STACKPOLEBOOKS.COM
1-800-732-3669

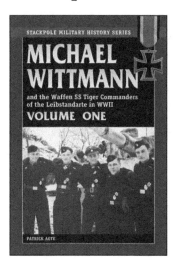
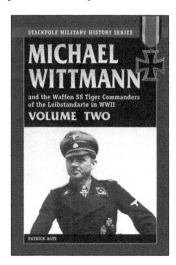

Stackpole Military History Series

BLITZKRIEG UNLEASHED

THE GERMAN INVASION OF POLAND, 1939

Richard Hargreaves

At dawn on September 1, 1939, the Germans launched
their land, air, and sea assault on Poland, sparking the great
conflagration of World War II and shocking the world with
the speed and ferocity of their blitzkrieg. With thundering
panzers and screaming dive-bombers, forces of the Third
Reich ruthlessly crushed the port of Danzig into submission,
drove the Polish Air Force from the skies, and took Warsaw
amid great bloodshed. After six weeks of gallant resistance,
the Poles surrendered, no match for the Nazi war machine.

Paperback • 6 x 9 • 368 pages • 37 photos, 13 maps

WWW.STACKPOLEBOOKS.COM
1-800-732-3669

Stackpole Military History Series

THE PATH TO BLITZKRIEG
DOCTRINE AND TRAINING IN THE GERMAN ARMY, 1920–39

Robert M. Citino

In the wake of World War I, the German Army lay in ruins—defeated in the war, sundered by domestic upheaval, and punished by the Treaty of Versailles. A mere twenty years later, Germany possessed one of the finest military machines in the world, capable of launching a stunning blitzkrieg attack that shredded its opponents in 1939–40. Distinguished military historian Robert M. Citino shows how Germany accomplished this astonishing reversal and developed the doctrine, tactics, and technologies that its army would use to devastating effect in World War II.

Paperback • 6 x 9 • 320 pages • 10 photos

WWW.STACKPOLEBOOKS.COM
1-800-732-3669

Stackpole Military History Series

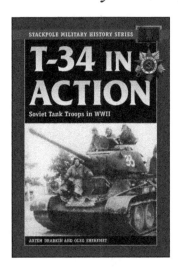

T-34 IN ACTION
SOVIET TANK TROOPS IN WORLD WAR II
Artem Drabkin and Oleg Sheremet

Regarded by many as the best tank of World War II, the Soviet T-34 was fast, well-armored, and heavily gunned—more than a match for the German panzers. From Moscow to Kiev, Leningrad to Stalingrad, Kursk to Berlin, T-34s rumbled through the dust, mud, and snow of the Eastern Front and propelled the Red Army to victory. These firsthand accounts from Soviet tankmen evoke the harrowing conditions they faced: the dirt and grime of battlefield life, the claustrophobia inside a tank, the thick smoke and deafening blasts of combat, and the bloody aftermath.

Paperback • 6 x 9 • 208 pages • 40 photos, 5 maps

WWW.STACKPOLEBOOKS.COM
1-800-732-3669

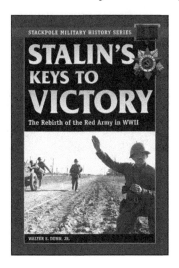

Stackpole Military History Series

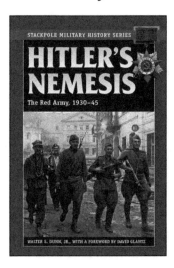

HITLER'S NEMESIS
THE RED ARMY, 1930–45
Walter S. Dunn, Jr.

Hitler's Nemesis "fills a major gap in our understanding
of the Red Army at war. . . . By adding flesh and sinew
to what had formerly seemed a gaunt skeleton, he has
placed recognizable faces on that great gray mass of
men whom the German Army fought against. . . .
Here, laid out in detail for the reader, are the infantry,
armor, artillery, and cavalry formations which enabled
the Red Army to survive and emerge victorious after
four years of struggle." —from the foreword
by David Glantz

Paperback • 6 x 9 • 288 pages • 23 b/w photos

WWW.STACKPOLEBOOKS.COM
1-800-732-3669

Stackpole Military History Series

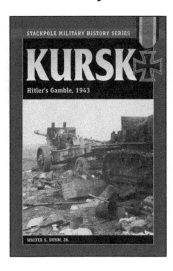

KURSK
HITLER'S GAMBLE
Walter S. Dunn, Jr.

During the summer of 1943, Germany unleashed its last
major offensive on the Eastern Front and sparked the epic
battle of Kursk, which included the largest tank engagement
in history. Marked by fiery clashes between German Tigers
and Soviet T-34s in the mud and dust of western Russia, the
campaign began well enough for the Germans, but the
Soviets counterattacked and eventually forced Hitler to end
the operation. When it was over, thousands lay dead or
wounded on both sides, but the victorious Red Army had
turned the tide of World War II in the East.

Paperback • 6 x 9 • 240 pages • 9 photos, 1 map

WWW.STACKPOLEBOOKS.COM
1-800-732-3669

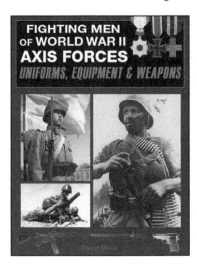
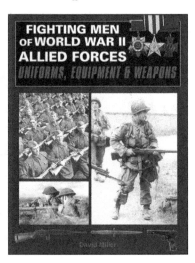